POSTMODERN
SOPHISTICATIONS

POSTMODERN SOPHISTICATIONS

PHILOSOPHY, ARCHITECTURE, AND TRADITION

DAVID KOLB

THE
UNIVERSITY OF CHICAGO PRESS

CHICAGO & LONDON

THE UNIVERSITY OF CHICAGO PRESS, CHICAGO 60637
THE UNIVERSITY OF CHICAGO PRESS, LTD., LONDON
© 1990 by The University of Chicago
All rights reserved. Published 1990
Paperback edition 1992
Printed in the United States of America
99 98 97 96 95 94 93 92   5 4 3 2

Library of Congress Cataloging-in-Publication Data

Kolb, David.
    Postmodern sophistications : philosophy, architecture, and
tradition / David Kolb.
        p.   cm.
    Includes bibliographical references (p.   ).
    ISBN 0-226-45027-9 (cloth)
    ISBN 0-226-45028-7 (pbk.)
    1. Aesthetics. 2. Postmodernism. 3. Aesthetics, Modern—20th
century. 4. Architecture. 5. Architecture, Postmodern. I. Title.
BH301.P69K64 1990
111´.85—dc20
                                                                89-38915
                                                                    CIP

To my parents, Harry and Mary Kolb,
with gratitude for their love and support

CONTENTS

A group of photographs follows p. 86.

ACKNOWLEDGMENTS

An earlier version of the first chapter of this book was published in the journal *Spring* and a version of the eleventh in the *Annals of Scholarship*. Several chapters were given as lectures at the University of Chicago, the University of Kansas, Clemson University, and the University of South Carolina. I appreciate the perceptive responses my ideas received from those audiences. I would like to thank the many people with whom I have talked about these matters, especially Paul Ricoeur, Stephen Moore, Edward Casey, David Brent, Jerry Walker, Durham Crout, John McCumber, Allan Megill, and fellow members of the Postmodern Architecture panel at the International Association for Philosophy and Literature conference in 1987. I owe a debt to Mark Okrent for many conversations, to Kenneth Shapiro, Stephen Moore, Yasutomo Morigiwa, and Philip Isaacson for having had the patience to read and comment on earlier versions, and to anonymous readers from the University of Chicago Press for many helpful suggestions. And I thank my wife, Anne Niemiec, for showing me new possibilities. This book is dedicated to my parents, Harry and Mary Kolb, from whom I first learned about concern and compassion.

INTRODUCTION

Looking through an architectural publication on the "new regionalism" several years ago, I came upon the following paragraph:

> In America—and especially in more recently developed portions of America—regionalism has not only to do with extending the valid character of a place but also with the creation of places. Can we, out of our varied and particular landscapes, climates, economic forces, political perspectives, and social customs, create a collection of rich and vital architectural expressions comparable to those we so admire in other parts of the world? Can we make traditions as well as extend and expand them? Can we capture what is real and poignant about ourselves and our surroundings and express it in built form both for ourselves and for future generations? What is an appropriate role for regionalism in America in the latter part of the 20th century?[1]

What leapt out at me were the phrase "the creation of places" and the question "can we make traditions as well as extend and expand them?" I had been thinking for some time about what it means to live in our peculiarly multiple world. In an earlier book I had compared several philosophical treatments of the process of modernization. Now I was trying to think out those issues more concretely, for a less specialized audience.[2]

Working through these ideas, I found myself taking advantage of a long-standing interest in architecture. I grew up surrounded by New York's wonderful medley and was an avid teenage reader of Frank Lloyd Wright; I was converted to a belief in progress and pure form by the beauty of Mies van der Rohe's Seagram building. In the late sixties I was stirred from my dogmatic slumbers by Robert Venturi and by a summer's work for Baltimore's city planning department. In the seventies I became excited by the way architecture and planning were moving away from the purity and system celebrated by the great modern architects and were returning to historical styles in a new spirit. Living in Chicago brought home how diverse modern architecture could be, and living in Maine showed how a regional tradition could be continually renewed, but also how it could be made into a simulacrum of itself. Stays in Japan showed me a different interweaving of

2   modern and traditional spaces. Architecture helped me pursue my questions about our relation to history.

Do we stand sufficiently above traditions that we can manipulate and make them from some detached point of view, as if they were tools for our purposes? My work on Hegel and Heidegger inclined me to a description of modernity as having attempted to establish such a distance from history. I wanted to say that we are more historically located than that, but still give fair weight to our abilities to change and weave and adapt.

In the paragraph quoted above, the question whether we can "make" traditions suggests that we lack tradition and have to produce it. But the next sentence asks about "capturing" what is "real and poignant" about us. Here we are treated as already involved in something that needs to be expressed and shaped, not made. It is that tension between the "already" and the "to be made" that I want to explore. It seems obvious that neither can be privileged over the other, but how do we deal with their relation? As technology knits the world together and separates us from one another, as the old unities of nation and local tradition seem no longer to bind us yet cause us more trouble, as the world seems out of control yet all too controlled, we are in danger of envisaging our situation with concepts that no longer hold, or that perhaps never held as we thought they did.

Are we finding a new relation to history and tradition? I have tried to discuss this with attention to the involved builder rather than the canny observer. The builder lives, as we all live, amid factual necessities. Some of these are due to shortages, others to methods that must be used because no one has thought of a better way. Some, the more important, are goals and projects already under way that shape our identity. These have no ultimate grounds, but neither can they be simply escaped, though they may change over time. And they are plural. A self exists at the intersections of such projects, not above them.

So architecture makes a good companion. Architects have grappled in detail with problems of rootedness and continuity. The surrounding environment cannot be wished away; the ways people live cannot be arbitrarily changed; all this must be taken into account, which is not to say it must be passively accepted. We can learn from the discipline and facticity of architecture not to be taken in by extreme positions that claim for us a freedom either wider or more narrow than the freedom we have. The difficulties of creating good architecture can illuminate our tasks in building cultures and worlds together amid the products of our past.

MODERN AND POSTMODERN

In this book you will not find a total discussion of modernism and postmodernism; I select instead those issues that help with my question about our making traditions and places for ourselves. I deal with debates in philosophy and social theory about how we criticize ourselves and our society, and I deal with historical reference and innovation in postmodern architecture. Modernism was especially well defined in architecture and especially hostile to tradition and history. Watching that hostility change toward a renewal of the vernacular and to ironic acceptance and deconstruction provides a good study of contemporary ways of dealing with our past.[3]

The word *postmodern* now slips easily off the tongue, along with post-industrial, postcolonial, postpatriarchal, and the like. While it may become too vague, there are important issues to be considered in its vicinity. So much of our thinking about ourselves revolves around the division between traditional and modern: the old secure life versus the new rootless life where traditional values are attacked (or traditional restrictions finally broken). The basic modern institutions of the free market and constitutional democracy offer new liberties within an overall framework that seems to impose very little content and very few values of its own. Joined to those institutions is the enterprise of science. We have told ourselves this story many times. Now we are adding a new story about how the modern age has grown old. From the postmodern perspective, modernity appears as an historical era that stays within its own unrecognized limits.[4]

Both the modern and the postmodern define themselves in opposition to the imagined fixity of traditional modes of life. We constantly appeal to this division when we debate cultural changes, international relations, or economic development. A great deal of social commentary worries about the survival of premodern attitudes and movements that are said to lack modern critical distance and rationality. I will discuss later a typical example of this claim, Habermas's account of how modern society arises from breaking down restrictive tradition. In this story, cultures modernize as they differentiate natural relations from social ones, introducing reflective distance and rational control.

The words *modern* and *postmodern*—and their relatives (post)modernism, (post)modernist, (post)modernity—have a wide variety of uses.[5] I am interested in the sense of *modern* that refers to a specific kind of society, thought, and art. We know the modern social tally sheet: a secular society, the free market, constitutional democracy, civil

4   rights, nationalism, bureaucratic administration, industrialization, capitalism, science and technology, progress. The words come easily but the institutions took generations to build. There are also the more abstract descriptions: rationalization, integration, self-assertion, individualism, and a strange combination of differentiation and homogeneity. There are many different pictures of modernity, depending on which of these elements are taken as explaining the others.

The kind of thinking we call modern emphasizes the individual and the search for systematic, scientific certitudes. It begins around the fifteenth or sixteenth century, which is also the beginning of the kind of society we call modern. The kinds of art and literature we call modern are not easily characterized, but most break away from the traditional genres, and they encourage abstraction and the independence of the work of art. Such art only appears toward the end of the nineteenth century. Why is it so late? In many ways it seems less a part of social modernization than a reaction to it. Modern art and literature often attack the rationalization and efficient unity thought to be the mark of social modernity. The art protests against modernization's belief in progress and the self-assurance of the modern subject, who is revealed in so much modern literature as hollow and unsure.[6] Postmodern literature can then be seen as a continuation of aesthetic modernism's fight to destabilize established unities.[7]

Modern architecture, however, was less in opposition. While the great modern architects shared the attempt to discard traditional restrictions and genres, they also affirmed their belief in the very values and processes being attacked by their literary and artistic counterparts: rationality, progress, the promise of a uniform technological society. Architectural modernism is more allied with social modernization than are the other arts. And when our century's architects resisted social modernization they usually did so by reasserting traditional styles; in architecture the rational modernists were the avant-garde. It is not until recent deconstructive experiments that architecture attempts moves as radical as those made in postmodern literature.[8] I will leave my discussion of the various meanings of the phrase *postmodern architecture* to chapter 8.

Arnold Toynbee, in 1946, seems to have been the first to use the word *postmodern* in anything like its current sense. He so named the time since the last decades of the nineteenth century, when the great modern syntheses began to break down. The word was picked up around the same time by poets (Randall Jarrell, in particular) and a bit later by literary and then architectural critics.[9] In each case it named a breakdown of older unities and the transgression of prohibitions that had been set up by modernism. The word has come to philosophers just when the artists and architects are getting pretty tired of it. Announcements of the imminent death of postmodernism began in 1979 and have continued ever since.

Analyses of postmodernism as involving all of society usually speak as if the modern attempt to make everything present and available has succeeded all too well. In the paranoid media analyses of Jean Baudrillard everything is reduced to a play of surfaces and simulacra that escapes and imposes control. Modernity has pushed itself over the limit into a new world. Sometimes this kaleidoscope world is seen as something new that has resulted from technological or economic changes. Often, though, it is understood as our bringing into the foreground an underlying human condition (usually concerned with the nature of language or representation) that was hidden from previous societies by their illusions about permanence and fixed identity. This latter interpretation makes postmodern society something special and complete because of its very lack of integrity.

A postmodern sensibility can be found in some rock videos, in the novels of Italo Calvino, or in the buildings of Charles Moore. The unity of representation has been shattered, and the great modern projects seem to have exhausted their possibilities and to have continued as caricatures of their old earnestness. This sensibility delights in the transgression of the boundaries that separate styles and genres. It plays with complex self-reference in parodies that try to deflate unity or closure or totality. It refuses the distinction between high and low culture. It plays with history while refusing progress, and it seeks incompatibilities and differences that refuse to be reconciled into a rational or emotional harmony. It can mourn the loss of stable reality, or it can be intoxicated by the shifts and dislocations of images in our networks of stimulation.

In philosophy and critical theory the term *postmodern* has been appropriated by some to label deconstruction and related Nietzschean tendencies that attack goals and distinctions basic to the Western tradition since long before modern times (cf. Silverman and Welton 1988). The attack on modernity is part of doubts about metaphysics, presence, logocentrism, and the hold of established dualisms, and it is deeply worried about "the institution of will into reason" (Lyotard 1986, 216). This kind of thinking is not exactly philosophy or literary criticism or social theory; it is "a discipline that threatens to escape disciplinary confines . . . whether as sober analysis or as euphoric

6   programme, marking at long last the end to the illusion of self-transparency in thought" (Donougho 1987; cf. Vattimo 1988).

Others, however, would distinguish that general category of postmodern thought into two types. The first proclaims that modernity is over, that a new age has begun. The new age makes use of the past, and of modern achievements, but it has its own new freedoms and its own self-definition. The second type of thought is deconstructive, and works to undermine the unities and closures found in modernity, without escaping from them into some new age.[10]

I will follow this latter scheme in distinguishing between postmodern and deconstructive thought. This in turn will help me to distinguish between a postmodern architecture, which includes various modes of ironic historicism (Moore, Bofill, Portoghesi, and others), and a deconstructive architecture, which includes various experiments toward questioning representation, the unity of form, and the standard definitions of the architectural task (Eisenman, Tschumi, Fujii, and others). This is not an absolute division either for thinkers or for architects, but it will prove useful as a way of talking about various ways of questioning modernity.

In this book, I am interested in modernity as the attempt to institutionalize an individual or social subject free from traditional restrictions. The modern individual or community is supposed to be able to make its life and places as it chooses them to be; in the strictest sense it would have no traditions or places, since nothing would locate it except facts laid out for judgment and manipulation.[11] What comes "after" or "against" the modern will be what breaks modern unities and compromises modern purity, and so questions the promise of transparency and control. This is done both in the ironic manipulation of history and in the deconstructive experiments. For the most part this book deals with the former trend, which is much more common; the latter receives less continual attention, but shapes the discussion at crucial points.

The division between premodern, modern, and postmodern is not merely a result of academic fads or media hype. The first two terms are deeply ingrained in our self-image: we are the people who are no longer bound by restrictive premodern traditions. The third term is emerging in a replay of that modern move to freedom, only now the modern itself is seen as restrictive.

The three terms are seductive, but to use them in sequence is to tell a modern story about progress. Although I will use the terms freely, I mean to question any such story. For one thing, any facile periodization tends to reify itself and block our vision of what is going on. However, taken as marking a site for examination, rather than a definitive solution, *postmodern* may be helpful.

I also want to show that underlying the contrasts among premodern, modern, and postmodern is a questionable distinction between simple inhabitation of the world and distanced freedom. Once we challenge that presupposition, we find that there is no unified postmodern age, that the modern totality could never succeed, and that our situation is not so different from the premodern as the modern (and many postmodern) stories would have us believe.

As will be evident, my own sympathies are divided. I join in the critique of modernist illusions while remaining skeptical of many postmodern proposals. I relish the return to history in architecture, but I find that a steady diet of ironic historicism soon grows boring. I think that deconstruction has crucial insights that we cannot do without, but that it must remain marginal in order to preserve its own nonidentity. To build places for ourselves we cannot merely undermine totalities and worry that any positive construction will repeat metaphysics and modernism. We have to place lines and bricks and institutions, so we need to come to terms with history and tradition.

The link between formalism and arbitrariness is the Achilles' heel of modernism, in art and in society. Ironic postmodernism does not escape this weakness; only a more finitely historical thought can do so. We should distrust claims about simple identities in the past and pure processes in the present. If power and project and process only exist as articulated, and that articulation is never a neat, centered imposition of form, then most of the standard tools for defining our situation need to be rethought.[12]

THE COURSE OF THE BOOK

The first few chapters of the book deal with our ability to criticize, looking at the Greeks and moderns, then at the moderns and postmoderns. Later chapters deal with questions about criticism and building. It would be wrong, however, to expect that the first chapters work out a theory which is then applied to architectural questions. While the later chapters are more focused on specific issues in architecture and planning, the ideas developed there about language and building together provide fuller answers to the questions asked in the earlier chapters.

I begin by looking at the Greeks. There we find Plato's project of building a rationally guaranteed way of life opposed to the Sophistic

8   manipulation of tradition for arbitrary ends. The first chapter examines the figure of Socrates and his way of inquiry. His quest defined a process of criticism which contained its own internal goals. For Plato, the only other option was the manipulative relativism of the Sophists. If we suspect this choice, and its ideal of self-transparent reflection, how do we manage discernment and self-criticism?[13]

The next several chapters consider rhetoric, in its ancient robes as the opponent of philosophy, then in its trendy clothes as the replacement for philosophy and everything else. In the second chapter I look at Plato and Aristotle and see how their systematic constructions are embedded in another, shifting discourse. The third chapter challenges Plato's metaphysical distinction between philosophy and rhetoric, and discounts Plato's fear of the Sophist's power. In the fourth chapter, I turn to the contemporary debate between rational programs for self-criticism (Jürgen Habermas) and rhetorical modes of criticism (Jean-François Lyotard). I compare their dispute with that of Plato and the Sophists. Taken together, these chapters reveal that the old dispute between Plato and the Sophists is not the best lens for viewing contemporary problems.

In the fifth chapter I turn to the question of individual and social self-discernment, and I argue for something more than arbitrariness and less than Habermas's full rational disclosure. The sixth chapter disputes Habermas's story of modern self-criticism, and finds that in their relation to history Habermas's rational critics are surprisingly close to Lyotard's avant-garde creators of new language games, and that neither does full justice to the way we are set in motion by language and tradition.

In the seventh chapter, I look back at our premodern ancestors. The premodern has been created to be the Other to modern (and postmodern) self-definition. We distort our ancestors to fit our own myths that oversimplify what it means to inhabit a human world.

The eighth chapter argues for the modernity of much postmodern architectural theory, defining modernity in terms taken from Weber, Hegel, and Heidegger. I follow up this theme in the ninth chapter, where I ask what it means for an architect to be located in history. Though argued in terms of architectural language, the implications touch anyone seeking to construct or criticize. The discussion of limits is continued in the tenth chapter, which looks into one way we change and extend our languages. I take up a series of issues concerning what I call "metaphor," and related questions about intention and the unity of form. That metaphorical extension of language is not the same as ironic play with traditional elements. In the eleventh chapter I examine irony directly and argue that too often we mistake the kind of double reference appropriate to our situation.

The last three chapters bring the issues together by examining the difficulties of making places for ourselves. Neither a Platonic nor a Sophistic solution will help us build together in a finite world. Habermas's analysis of system and lifeworld, Heidegger's notion of place, and the problems of pluralism and consumer culture come in for their share of discussion. The twelfth chapter looks at some of the theories offered to explain our inability to create vital places today. In the thirteenth chapter I examine possible guides that might help us discover who we are. In this and the fourteenth chapter I discuss regionalism and examine the problems of creating places together and caring for the whole without agreeing on a unified total vision.[14]

The illustrations accompanying the text show several of the buildings discussed, as well as a range of others that go beyond the commercialized postmodernism that has recently become so familiar.

] 1 [
SOCRATES AND THE
STORY OF INQUIRY

We start where it all starts, with Socrates and Plato. It had started earlier, of course, but Plato, that master rhetorician, persuaded us that the crucial issue was the confrontation between Socrates and the Sophists. In this and the following chapters I hope to blunt the force of that confrontation without giving in to either side.

Socrates made men think about the basis of their beliefs and values; after trying him for corrupting the youth and upsetting the order of life, they condemned him to die. In prison, he talked with his disciples about life after death, then drank the hemlock and was silent. So the story goes. It is historical; we take it literally.

There was indeed a man Socrates, son of Sophroniscos of Athens. He was born around 469 B.C. and died in 399 B.C. after being condemned during the tumultuous times after the Peloponnesian War. He was married, had children, perhaps worked as a stonecutter. He was short and ugly but brave and incredibly hardy, a heroic solder when heroism was demanded. He had aristocratic friends and spent much of his time in conversation in public places or at his friends' homes. He asked questions and talked about virtue, love, and justice. When he was younger he may have studied the new physical theories of the day; when he was older he had little to do with such topics. He did not approve of democratic government. Some of his students went on to become famous philosophers and virtuous men; others became notorious tyrants and traitors. When brought to court he defended himself but refused to engage in easy rhetoric or to accept exile. He died nobly.

This Socrates seems an interesting person, but not quite the shining figure we know. That figure exists in the words of Plato. A more strident, less captivating Socrates exists in the words of Xenophon. Because Socrates really did die for his convictions, his life obtains added cachet, though we are not sure precisely what those convictions were that he died for. But a quest for the historical Socrates is not enough. It is the story Plato tells that influences us, whether or not it is literally true.

In a letter that is perhaps authentic Plato is reported to have said, "there is not now and never will be a written work of Plato's; what are now called Plato's are those of a Socrates become young and beautiful" 11

12 (*Second Letter* 314e). *This* Socrates fascinates us with his irony and his seriousness, his detachment and his erotic dedication to truth and to his hearers, his ability to weave words and thoughts while eyeing the goal and judging his own ignorance. "I tell you that to let no day pass without discussing goodness and all the other subjects about which you hear me talking and examining myself and others is really the very best thing that a man can do, and that life without this examination is not worth living" (*Apology* 38a).

To foster this examination of life Socrates questions, argues, goads, teases, laughs, accuses, anything that will move his hearers. Beyond what he says shines the beauty of the quest and the beauty of the good embodied in him. "What Socrates reminds me of is one of those little statues of Silenus you see for sale, an ugly little man holding a flute in his hands, but when you open the figure up there are images of the gods inside" (*Symposium* 215b). We are attracted to this wise old man who is a playful erotic child. This rich significant Socrates enfolds the historical facts. He presents the figure of the Inquirer, and offers to tell us the story of our lives as a journey begun in ignorance and confusion—in search of ever wider knowledge and ever deeper grounds—until we come into the luminous presence of full reality. Plato's Socrates does argue for particular theories in ethics and metaphysics, but his significance transcends his theories. His quest opens the conversation that makes room for such theories.

In pursuing his inquiries Socrates does the things we have come to expect of philosophers. He analyzes concepts, seeks precise definitions and principles, tests methods, attacks views by pointing out inconsistencies and providing counterexamples, and so on. In the game of *logos* he knows all the moves. But at times he announces that he is leaving the *logos* and entering the *mythos*. Then he tells stories. They range from little anecdotes to grand and glorious visions of the fate of the soul.

In the *Phaedo* we hear of the immense earth in one of whose murky hollows we live, while above on the true surface live men who see the stars as they really are. Our souls will be carried about and purified by the great interior rivers of the world until the time for their rebirth. In the *Phaedrus* we see the great procession of gods and souls above the world, and the fall of a soul that loses its wings and descends to our confused realm, to find its wings again through love. In the *Republic* we are told of judgment after death and how souls must choose lots for their next lives. And there are many more stories.

These myths puzzle us. Socrates insists on the need for conceptually clear principles; he attacks Homer and Greek religion for telling lies;

he announces that he is continuing an ancient quarrel between poetry and philosophy. Then he tells myths. Why? They have been interpreted as persuasive rhetoric substituting for argument, or as metaphysics for the masses, or as mystical intimations.

I will not try to settle this question. The myths have many different functions; I want to single out one without claiming it is the whole. Socrates's myths, especially the larger ones, are placed strategically to influence our present life rather than to give us news about a future life. They tell us how to live here and now by creating plots for our lives.

> Now perhaps all this seems to you like an old wife's tale and you despise it, and there would be nothing strange in despising it if our searches could discover anywhere a better and truer account, but as it is you see that you . . . cannot demonstrate that we should live any other life than this, which is plainly of benefit also in the other world. (*Gorgias* 527a)

> Now, Glaucon, the tale was saved, as the saying is, and was not lost. And it will save us, if we believe it. . . . We shall hold ever to the upward way and pursue righteousness with wisdom always and ever. (*Republic* 621c)

The myths do provide conjectures about a future life that can be taken into account in some calculation of costs and benefits. But there is a more basic influence. The myths give a scope to the movement of life. They turn moral theories into life plans. They encourage us to emphasize and link together feelings and episodes we may not have noticed or may have considered marginal: feelings of emptiness and insecurity, and a desire for more purity and clarity than the senses can provide.

The stories provide plots that outline stages of moral growth. These stages have internal contrasts among themselves, contrasts that may be present in our everyday life even if the otherworldly goal is left aside or taken metaphorically. The description of the stages turns our life into a progress. Our life can become a unified journey when the stories give it a direction.

Plato's moral myths can remain in force even if his literal metaphysics is denied. The moral progress has its own logic that can survive denial of the ultimate goal. The myths are not the metaphysics in rhetorical fancy dress. In some ways the reverse is true: the myths ground the metaphysics. Imagine that everything in Plato's metaphysics is true: the forms, the half-real world of the senses, the afterlife, and so on. Is it self-evident how such a world would be lived? Perhaps it would cause terror, or boredom, or be as remote from everyday experience as quan-

14 tum mechanics seems to be now. We give the metaphysics impact by finding ourselves within stories that weave its structure into stages for our lives. And the metaphysics does not have to be literally true for the internal development of those stories to shape us.

Yet we find Plato's stories strange; they have seldom survived as living forces except where they have been incorporated into Christian stories. Perhaps they could still work on us as can the tales of Achilles or Oedipus. But now as in Plato's time they are only a few among many. For us all those old stories—the hero Heracles, the resourceful Odysseus, the dutiful Marcus Aurelius, the Christian saint—have been further supplemented by newer stories—the hero of science, the revolutionary, the Nietzschean man of power. We are tolerant of this multiplicity. We are not inclined to demand one exclusive story about the development of our lives, and Plato's myths may give way to other, perhaps richer tales. We accept this.

Why then are we not surprised by the continuing dominance of the story of Socrates? For this story, too, is a myth. I do not mean that when Socrates argues about the nature of mathematics or the analysis of some ethical concept he is telling a myth. His arguments have to be judged on their own terms according to their subject matter. When Socrates argues he is not telling a myth, but he is *enacting* one. Socrates and his interlocutors argue about metaphysics and the good life. Later thinkers argue against Socrates, but in rejecting his conclusions they still play his game. They do not wish to say what he said, but they willingly do what he did. They reject his arguments and the moral path proposed in the myths of the soul, but they have accepted his story of the path of inquiry.

This path stretches from ignorance to total knowledge. We are to take nothing for granted, seeking foundations and basic principles until we come into the presence of the Truth. Values can be founded on contact with the forms that are the ground for all beings. Plato believed that the world was structured so as to make such a goal possible.

Later thinkers may refute the forms, deny that values can be based in metaphysics, restrict knowledge to the physical sciences which Plato considered unworthy of the name "knowledge," and despite these basic changes, still describe their own journey of inquiry in Socratic terms.

It would seem that Plato's intellectual story is even more independent of the rest of his theory than are his moral myths. Socrates embodies a story of our inquiries holding ever to the upward way. The Socratic journey encourages us to emphasize and link together feel-

ings and episodes that we may not have noticed or may have considered
marginal: wonder about just what defines things, longing for a solid
ground, desire for a knowledge beyond our opinions and history. In
the light of this tale we can see our thought as having a direction. We
can distinguish stages and see progress toward a goal of completely
grounded knowing. This creates unity in our intellectual life; it makes
into a connected story what might otherwise have been only scattered
curiosity. Our cognitive life becomes a whole when the story gives it
direction.

The path of inquiry contains internal contrasts among its stages,
contrasts that can continue to structure our life when the specifics of
Plato's theories are denied, or even when the final goal is declared impossible to realize. Socrates has shown us an intellectual ethics for
behaving well on the journey: erotic attraction to the good, communal
dialogue, impartial questioning, openness, and refusal to insist on
one's own opinions. This ethics of the journey and the internal stages
of the path take precedence over its end. Whether the journey has an
end and what kind it might be become matters to be adjudicated according to the method and ethics of the journey itself. Socrates's story
defines a self-critical process that forms its own goals independently of
any historical or cultural setting. We will see this again in Habermas,
and later I will explore a more situated self-criticism.

The Socratic path gives unity and coherence to our cognitive struggles. It is a specific journey with its own qualities. Apollo at Delphi
declared Socrates the wisest of men. After his condemnation Socrates's execution was delayed while Athens sent a ship to Delos to
commemorate the victory of Theseus over the Minotaur, the ancient
day when the crafty Athenian hero freed men from the need to sacrifice
to the half-beast. Socrates's path seeks victory over the beast in us, over
our passions and our selfishness. The light at the summit of the path is
both moral and cognitive. Socrates brings the goals of spirit: unity,
simplicity, transparency, clarity, and necessity. Our shifting polysemous
soul will become uniform, and the images in the cave will be left behind
for clear vision where what exists stays fixed in pure identity and presence. Socrates makes us live the story of the transcendence of all stories
into clear vision.

Plato's practice may belie this, but such is the tale he tells. In Plato's
eyes there was little choice. The only alternatives were the blind confusion in the old stories or the willful chaos lurking behind the fashionable skepticism of the Sophists.

Is it strange that after so long we still agree so much with Plato's de-

16 scription of our cognitive situation? While there are many stories of our moral development, the cognitive quest remains much as Socrates defined it. Those who reject Plato's doctrines still tend, when they describe their intellectual life, to journey on Socrates's path. Other cognitive routes have been suggested from time to time, such as skeptical contentment, or paths leading to mysticism or to placing poetry above principles, but these stories have remained without wide influence. Socrates's story gives professional identity to groups; it has become the official self-portrait of philosophy and science. Could a university or a laboratory describe itself without the Socratic story of ever firmer grounds and ever more total vision?

How is it that Socrates has triumphed? Has he really defined the only way minds can inquire, their final relation to the past and to the world?

The times are changing. David Hume preached contentment with ungrounded custom; Nietzsche taught everlasting conflicts of interpretation; Heidegger talked of an inquiry that listens without seeking any overall goal, partial illumination that is not part of a full vision to come. There are semiotic, pragmatic, deconstructive stories, and others from the East.

We are not sure how to judge and evaluate these stories. Or rather we are not sure whether we should judge and evaluate them, since that is an activity performed in the Socratic way. The new stories have not yet changed our institutional or personal identity as inquirers, but they are present more actively than ever before.[1]

The great modern systems of philosophy and science have kept to the Socratic way, while some postmodern thinkers have enlisted under the banner of his enemies, the Sophists. But it is no longer only a choice between Socrates and Sophism. Whether the Socratic myth will be successfully challenged we do not know; what path of inquiry might take its place we cannot tell; that no single story reigns supreme we can only begin to imagine. Yet it has never been self-evident that our inquiring must be unified in only one story. Will the day come when we will see as many stories structuring our cognitive curiosity and inquiry as we hear tales of the stages of moral, emotional, and spiritual life? No story tells us what will happen next.

THE LAST WORD IN GREEK PHILOSOPHY

To replace the interminable old myths but avoid the premature closure offered by the Sophists, Plato sought a method which would find the guaranteed last word. What does it mean to have the last word, to settle a debate? In the modern view debates are settled by experts. Debates can be *ended* by force or by influence; a rhetorician, or a charismatic leader, or a soldier can stop people from talking, for a while. But it takes an expert to *settle* a debate, to pin it down so it cannot float any more. The scientist is our model expert who has the facts and the proofs. The experts join together to produce the total last word, Unified Science. All the facts, and all the laws for each region of facts, and all expressible in one basic language: it is with this that Descartes suggests we can become "the masters and possessors of the earth." This word will deflate illusions, settle debates, and give a basis for our actions and plans. If we want to rebuild our city (an image both Plato and Descartes favor) we are told we would do well to put our decisions on such a firm foundation.

This picture of the last word has been under scrutiny lately. We are not so confident of it as we used to be. In this chapter I want to look back at the Greeks who are supposed to have inflicted this metaphysical notion of the last word upon us. I will argue that the practice of the Greek philosophers was more flexible than the reports of their theories would have us believe. Maybe our own practice is or could be more flexible as well.

Aristotle

I turn first to Aristotle. The way he describes the last word can make it appear similar to our own. He speaks of sciences that concern different kinds of beings, coordinated by a basic metaphysical system into something like a total map of reality. But this resemblance to modern ideals is not as close as it seems. First, Aristotle's sciences do not give all the facts. Most facts are what he would call "accidental": the color of your hair, the weight of this book. Aristotle believes there can be no science of the accidental fact; science studies the essences of things to find principles that are necessary and unchanging. Aristotle is not in-

18 terested in the color of your hair except insofar as it might indicate something about being human, or color, or hair in general. So Aristotle's "map of reality" leaves out much that would interest us.

Also, his map works differently than ours. The various sciences he sponsors do not connect directly. When we draw a map we expect regions to be contiguous, but for Aristotle the regions are not even on the same plane. The principles of one Aristotelian science are not derivable from those of another. Two of his sciences might discuss the same being, as the cow in the field can be studied as an animal in biology or as a changing being in what Aristotle calls physics, the general science of changeable things. But these two ways of studying the cow do not reduce to one basic treatment. There is no one language that will tell us all we need to know about the cow; Aristotle is not a reductionist. The principles of physics need to be amplified and specified in order to tell us about the cow as an animal. On the other hand, biology does not tell us how to find the more general principles of physics. Moderns presuppose that the last word will be delivered in one unified language. Aristotle's sciences speak a bundle of languages with analogies between them. There is no one vocabulary for writing a report on all the facts.

Aristotle does have metaphysics. That highest science does talk about all that exists using the same principles concerning matter and form, actuality and potentiality, substance and the four causes. A cow, a poem, a man can all be discussed using this vocabulary. But on this level Aristotle has left aside what makes them different. Metaphysics is not a summary but an abstraction; a poem and a cow are not potential and actual in the same way. Nor does Aristotle provide us with a basic set of entities and relations that are to underlie everything. At most he gives us the prime examples of what it means to be, but to be a prime example is not to be basic in the way that electrons and photons are basic for us.

We want to understand things by reducing them to a realm of basic entities described in a basic language. Aristotle has a different project. We try to understand by discerning identical formal structure in a variety of instances. Aristotle does not do that, either, though his teacher Plato did. Aristotle finds analogous structures that are not purely formal and are not true of everything in precisely the same way.

The modern complete last word would contain a continuous report in a univocal language that told us all the truth. A real being would be one that showed up in that final report. Aristotle takes whatever beings come to presence naturally and finds ways to talk about them in relation to first principles that operate analogously (that is, both identically and differently) in each region. He tells us how a poem embodies these principles and how a cow does. He is not so much writing a systematic report on everything true as he is bringing each kind of thing into the nearness of those first principles.

When he is explaining his methods Aristotle tells us that knowledge should be expressed in chains of syllogistic arguments. But his most important works have quite another form. They contain arguments, but the arguments are found within a shifting discourse that clarifies the concepts and leads us to the first principles. This is not just an expository convenience; we need this shifting discourse, itself without a firm structure of first principles. The shifting discourse locates the science amid its alternatives, gives it a bearing on our life, justifies our acceptance of its principles. The shifting discourse provides a medium in which we can come near to the first principles.

Aristotle does not see his scientific last word, such as it is, as settling our practical debates. For that we go to the man of practical wisdom who is good at making prudential decisions. The man of practical wisdom does not possess a special scientific knowledge. He cannot work from a special science because for Aristotle all sciences concern the necessary and essential features of things, about which no one deliberates or makes choices.

This separation of science from practical decision may sound familiar to us. Our standard modern picture has science setting forth an acknowledged public set of facts that provide a framework within which private interests and chosen values battle for policy influence. But Aristotle's separation is almost exactly the reverse of ours. What is private, for him, is scientific knowledge, which is possessed by an elite who have the leisure to study. What forms the public space for discussion is not scientific reporting but shared deliberation and concern for the common good.

PLATO

Turning from Aristotle to Plato may seem to bring us closer to the modern view. I claimed above that the analogous unity of Aristotle's sciences made his last word different from the standard modern one-level picture. Aristotle criticizes Plato for lacking a sense of analogy and trying to meld everything into one science with a mathematical basis. It sounds as if Plato better fits our standard picture. When we consider the ferocious education Plato suggests for his philosopher kings we may think Plato has put it all together in the modern mold: scientific politicians using the last word in knowledge to rule wisely.

20   This picture is half mistaken. The philosopher kings' education is not all that encyclopedic. Their studies emphasize skills, not factual content (*Republic* 521d). Plato tells us (503e) that they must learn to abstract and contemplate, to move from becoming to being. They are taught to discern the necessary laws about the natures of things. Astronomy is useful for the calendar, but mostly it is a vehicle for higher mathematics beyond what has practical value in commerce and military matters. Nor do the apprentice rulers study much theory about society beyond knowing its essential structures and divisions. They do not have a descriptive social science. What they do learn, in long years of apprentice administration, is how to apply general principles to particular cases. They learn, that is, to exercise prudence and practical wisdom.

Once they are trained they spend their time not in endless Socratic discussion but in administration. They make decisions about the size of the grain crop, the military situation, and who should marry whom. Their education helps them to decide not because they have some modern report on all the facts but because they have learned to see in each situation the matters that need measure. And they understand how to approach the forms that are the sources of harmonious measure.

If the work of the philosopher kings were merely to define the virtues and set up a general constitution, one Platonic solon would suffice. If the forms were not relevant to daily decisions then at most a guiding group of philosophers would be needed to keep an eye on the general trend of events. In Plato's *Laws* the Nocturnal Council functions just that way, for in the city of the *Laws* philosophy is not involved in everyday decisions. But in the city of the *Republic* the philosopher kings attend to details. They do so not by consulting some cosmic encyclopedia but by taking the matters at hand into the nearness of the first principles, the forms that measure all things. This is the last word for Plato. While there is a systematic interrelation in the realm of the forms, the use of this science is more occasional than systematic. Commentators who have wondered whether Platonic practical science would be a deductive ethics have missed the point. There was to be no finished dialectic. There was to be no book that said it all. We cannot underestimate this difference from our own standard ideals. Platonic practical science was not frozen and presented all at once; it was the perpetual activity of relating changing things to ever better understood first principles.

None of Plato's proposed cities were real, but his Academy was. Imagine the Academy at work: groups would be investigating regions

of being, say geometry and biology, seeking their necessary principles. 21
There would also be general conversation about the highest forms and
common characteristics of all things (being, unity, goodness, same-
ness, difference, and so on). Members would try to relate the regions
they were studying to those core principles. But this sounds suspiciously like Aristotle's picture of the sciences. Where the Platonic
enterprise differs is in a greater emphasis on methods of conceptual division and on the goal of deriving the principles of the various regions
from the core forms by some quasi-mathematical process. This goal
might have led to a rationalist total science, but it remained only a background hope.

So the general Academic activity was not the development of a modern system of the world but a movement from particular regions to the
core principles and then back to a purified version of the region under
study. There seems to have been little attempt to devise one language
for reporting a total picture. Indeed the one work of Plato's that most
closely approaches *our* ideal of a total picture, the *Timaeus,* is expressly
denied the status of scientific knowledge.

THE SOPHISTS

Plato's unified science was to show forth the necessary connections
among the forms that defined the essence of reality. Matters at hand
would have been brought near the explored forms for illumination and
measurement. Decisions could then be made on how to achieve a moving harmony that imaged the unity of the forms. Aristotle objected to
the tight unity of Plato's central knowledge, and he denied the practical
efficacy of approaching the forms to seek measures. Exploring the essences of things afforded for Aristotle the highest intellectual satisfaction, but little practical guidance.

Understanding the reasons why Plato and Aristotle differed on the
practical impact of the speculative last word takes us into Greek
culture. There are philosophical reasons, to be sure, having to do with
different conceptions of causality and of the relation of the universal to
the particular. But I want to emphasize a social reason for the disagreement between Plato and Aristotle, because it brings to light a problem
about last words.

I deliberately described the Platonic scientist in a way which makes
him or her sound like someone consulting an oracle. Take your problem into the nearness of the highest, and emerge bearing an answer.
Behind the Platonic scientist lie Empedocles, the poem of Parmenides,

22   and a line of seers approaching the archaic origins. In our world we worry about the tension between the politician and the scientist. Before that came the tension between the king and the prophet, the tribal leader and the shaman, Oedipus and Tiresias. Tiresias, near to the origins, possesses dark wisdom and pronounces last words. Oedipus, the man of deeds, is qualified by past experience to deal with present problems.

The uneasy interaction between these two breaks down about the time of Socrates. We might see this as a collapse of traditional modes of legitimizing both oracles and leaders. New sources of power are discovered in trade and the economy, and in the new instrument of rhetoric. Plato describes "a little bald-headed tinker who has made money and just been freed from bonds and had a bath and is wearing a new garment and has got himself up like a bridegroom and is about to marry his master's daughter who has fallen into poverty and abandonment" (*Republic* 465e). The nouveaux riches are pushing out the old clansmen; the old sources of power are being undermined.

With the advent of money and Sophistry anyone could have power, anyone could have the last word. No longer could one be sure the leader was near to the gods. Plato grew up amid this change. He sought for a new legitimation, a guaranteed last word that could not be bought. This word would not be guaranteed in the old way, from its source in some special person. It would be guaranteed because it was anonymous, because it came from no one in particular and was available to anyone willing to undertake the discipline of approaching the forms that were the true origins of things. The philosopher king was not to speak from personal charisma or persuasive skill, but from a source independent of his or anyone's particular desires. That word would be spoken and received out of a desire deeper than our idiosyncratic loves, from a level where we are and seek the same.

To make this possible Plato had to beat out the Sophists. But he also had to remove Tiresias; there can be no unique person whose mystic anointing brings him near to the dark heart of reality. One move will banish both the Sophists and Tiresias. To put it mythically: in Homer, Zeus has the last word; he ends disputes among the gods. But behind him are the Fates, shadowy presences who spin and weave and cut— but they do not speak. Theirs is the last move, but they have no word. An opaqueness clouds the origins of things. Compare this with the tenth book of Plato's *Laws,* which decrees harsh opposition to Democritus and others who would affirm ultimate opacity. Plato makes the archaic origins available for speaking. It may be difficult, he says, but it is possible to see and to say. This provides a last word that is neither yours nor mine. Thus there is no room for the Sophists, since the sayable forms will banish relativism and scheming. Nor is there any room for Tiresias; if there is mysticism in Plato it is not of the dark.

Plato's philosopher kings were to bring this word to bear as a measure for life. Aristotle agrees that the origins of things can be seen and spoken, but he does not claim that they can define our practice. His man of practical wisdom does not have a word but a skill, a virtue, almost the knack that Plato feared in the Sophists.

Why does Aristotle not fear the Sophists? Plato saw in them symptoms of our deep weakness: our ability to put a false image in place of the truth and hide from ourselves even the need for a question. Aristotle seems to find the Sophists faintly amusing specimens to be examined for mistakes and tricks in argument. Is it only that Aristotle, being younger and not an Athenian, had not experienced the tragedies that unbridled rhetoric brought on Athens during the Peloponnesian War? Or was it that society had changed in the intervening years and the Sophists were no longer serious professional rivals to the philosophers?

Perhaps both of these are true, but I think there is a deeper reason that points to a flaw in the Platonic program for scientific politics. Plato's hope for an effective last word demands that people be converted. Socrates gave his life trying to make people stop and think and talk. If they could be brought to see that their own words lacked foundation they might find that their desire for wholeness drove them to join the search for the origins of things. Since "it is impossible that a multitude be philosophical" (*Republic* 494a), people must be pulled out of the multitude's shared certainty. But Socrates cannot talk to every person one by one to dissolve the multitude and reconstitute it as a community joined in the Socratic quest. This impossibility reduced Plato to the dream of catching the multitude before it formed, banishing adults and raising the children in philosophy.

The last word remains politically impotent. Plato's adventures in Syracuse show that the philosopher's group can only appear as one more cabal. Plato wrote the *Laws* for this real world where wisdom can be at most the goal of a small elite and the ruler's main qualification must be prudence, not philosophy. What we know of the political activities carried on by the Academy fits this pattern.

This leaves Plato's project turning in the shifting discourse that seeks origins, with elite groups pursuing various incomplete sciences that relate only partially to one another, and with practical decisions

24 left to prudence and a purified rhetoric. This leaves Plato, in short, with Aristotle.

Perhaps not quite. In Plato what I have called the shifting discourse stands out more strongly than in Aristotle. Though his ideals for scientific achievement are more grandiose, Plato's text is less sure than Aristotle's. I do not mean the textual descriptions of the ideal, but the actual wandering dialogues, a discourse without fixed starting points or first principles. While the dialogues announce beginnings and origins, they themselves do not stand firm. Any fixed position must be arrived at through the shifting discourse; we start nowhere special except where we are. That discourse has its own drive. It pushes people around; yet it obeys no fixed rules, refusing to be methodical or literal in its pursuit of literal method. It is not a partial science, yet it surrounds and renders accessible the hope of science. In its own way it has the last word.

Perhaps it still does. Modernity seeks the total uniform system; the Greeks did otherwise, even though they are our ancestors. Modernity wants universal theory to illuminate private choices; Aristotle wanted shared choices to culminate in a life of private theory. But modern total science is not *our* last word any more, if it ever really was. We, perhaps postmodern, are caught in the shifting discourse, building without firm starting points and with no sure direction in which to seek the origins that slip away from us. Perhaps everyone has always been in the shifting discourse, whatever else they have said.

] 3 [
THE POWER OF THE SOPHIST

To attack Plato, turn to his ancient enemies for advice. Those who want to undermine Plato's quest for grounded systematic unity and certainty must get along without the firm criteria sought in the traditional philosophical discussions of knowledge, ethics, and politics. So thinkers such as Lyotard give a sympathetic portrayal of the Sophists as useful for understanding our own situation.

As in Plato's time so today the role assigned the Sophists is more symbolic than historically accurate. They are cast as the Other even when they are evaluated positively. This is not to deny that historical research has dealt with the Sophists on their own and not exclusively as a foil for Socrates; such discussions start as early as Hegel's lectures on the history of philosophy, and recent scholarship has made them appear as thinkers grappling with problems of knowledge and truth, inventing ways to talk about language, and starting the kinds of ethical discussions that Plato and Socrates continued in new ways (cf. Kerford 1981 and Feyerabend 1987). To some extent this forces the Sophists into current debates in analytic philosophy, but it does allow us to see them somewhat outside Plato's shadow.

My concern will not be with this search for the historical Sophists but with how they are invoked as the Other. Whatever the dimensions of their role in Greek intellectual life, it has passed, and their role in the wider Western tradition has been through portraits painted by other thinkers for their own purposes.

PLATO'S SOPHISTS

Plato painted the minor Sophists as fools and charlatans, the major Sophists as earnest teachers, but all of them as devoted to a pernicious anti-philosophy that endangered individual and social health. The Sophists offered a new education to fit men for their role in the new democratic and commercial world. They acquainted their students with current developments and gave them a knack for rhetorical persuasion. When they spoke about knowledge and reality they produced ideas drawn from Parmenides and Heraclitus that licensed a facile relativism.

If Plato were speaking in today's terms he would call the Sophists

26 radical conventionalists about truth and morality, thinkers who insofar as they talk about it at all measure truth in terms of individual or group perception. They teach a grab bag of persuasive methods without subjecting them to any tests. Plato does not present Gorgias as cynically offering arguments he knows are bad, but as someone who cannot understand the difference between a good and a bad argument. In the end Gorgias does not care about such a difference; what matters is the immediate persuasive effect of his words.

The Sophists traveled about Greece offering education to upwardly mobile urban youth. Sophistic education stood in contrast with the traditional education based on the great myths and aristocratic military values. The Sophists as presented by Plato and Aristophanes tested the old ways by the standards of their own desires. They delighted in pointing out inconsistencies in the old stories, and they replaced them with a new story about personal and social power: truths depend on personal perception, norms depend on who is in power, rhetorical training can put power in your hands.

Plato agreed with the Sophists that the traditional education was no longer useful. Those old stories no longer helped people find their way in the confusion of Athenian life, nor could they stand up to Socrates's demands for grounded integrity of vision. But Plato feared Sophistic education, which he saw leading to opportunistic manipulation. At best the Sophists produced a skilled speaker bent on shallow self-indulgence; at worst they created dangerous leaders and a docile public; always they destroyed faith in reason and moral virtue.

The reduction of Gorgias's cultivated tone to Callicles's frank will to power set the mode for subsequent evaluations of the Sophists. In Plato's Socratic story, discussions of value and truth cannot be polarized by any desire short of the overwhelming desire for complete wholeness and integrity. The search for truth and justice cannot be guided by a desire for success in business, political influence, or prosecution of the war against Sparta. Such goals would limit any discussion that might put the chosen purpose in question. The Sophists dispense their teachings for pay; they make wisdom something you can buy and use for your own purposes. Socrates takes no pay and he stands ready to question your purposes.

Neither the tradition nor the Sophists tested their standards of belief and conduct by the rigors of Socratic self-questioning. What was needed was a commitment to the search for a guaranteed knowledge based on standards that could put in question all our presuppositions and desires save the desire for wholeness and truth. One must inquire until it becomes luminously clear what the basic structures of the world are, and how these shape the proper human way to live. Plato's theory of the forms filled in the ontological details, but the quest for unity and grounded truth need not be tied to that particular theory. As philosophy went on, other theories played the foundational role, but the Socratic quest continued. That quest contained its own internal goals.

Both Plato and the Sophists agreed that the values and beliefs of the past were not reliable guides for action. Both insisted on a reflectively critical attitude toward tradition. For Plato this meant testing tradition against the necessities revealed in the Socratic quest for knowledge. For the Sophists this meant using tradition where it helped attain one's goals. Although Plato was in the end more respectful of traditional values, neither he nor the Sophists let students remain unquestioningly within the traditional ways. Athenian conservatives were correct in classing Socrates with the Sophists insofar as the effect of their teachings on tradition was corrosive in both cases.

KNOWLEDGE, OPINION, AND METAPHYSICS

The goal of grounded knowledge and guaranteed norms defined for Plato the quest that came to be called philosophy. Lately the term *metaphysics* has been used to describe the central activity of philosophy in Plato's sense. Heidegger first made this use of the term popular in his discussions of the "overcoming" of metaphysics and the "end of philosophy" (Heidegger 1947, 1977a). Since then, other thinkers have used the term more freely than Heidegger but in the spirit of his discussions, which are themselves now branded as too metaphysical.

In this context *metaphysics* denotes the attempt to base our lives on the availability of true reality to ground our knowledge. It allows us to survey the necessary structure of the world unified into a systematic whole that we can represent to ourselves in a clear language. Plato had a particular theory to offer, but rival theories that dispute his conclusions still keep the goal and methods of metaphysics. The dogmatic materialist is in this sense as metaphysical as Plato. Even the logical positivists who were bent on rooting out what they called metaphysical views can be classified as metaphysical thinkers in this other sense of the word because of their belief in a sure ground that can be made present through psychology and logic.

The Sophists stand opposed to Plato's search for true knowledge and so, it would seem, to metaphysics. It is their refusal of reason and their reliance on opinion in matters of ethics and politics that interest

28   postmoderns. I might note in passing that the historical Sophists should be judged metaphysical by those who like to apply that label. It is possible to be a relativist or a conventionalist and still be metaphysical in Heidegger's sense, if one believes that there is some central ground for our lives that is or can be purely present to us, and on which the relativity of knowledge turns. For the Sophists who invoke the distinction between nature and convention (*physis* and *nomos*) that ground is nature as a field of contesting desires for satisfaction and power. Opinions and norms are determined by the strength of the desires and the skillful power of individuals who manipulate one another. One can know one's desires and can know the power available. There is among the Sophists nothing comparable to the subtle discussion of the elusive nature of desire that is found in Plato's *Philebus,* to say nothing of contemporary treatments of desire that have learned from Freud that desire can never be encountered as full and unambiguously present.

The realm of opinion is described by Plato as the opposite of the realm of knowledge. Opinion is fallible, changeable, ungrounded, linked to the shifting sands of perception, and formed by persuasion. Knowledge is infallible, fixed, grounded in the presence of its unvarying objects, and formed by rational argument. Recent philosophy, however, tends to define knowledge as justified true belief. The difference between opinion and knowledge is to be found in how they are supported. This is a non-Platonic way of supporting Plato's distinction since it dispenses with a separate realm of secure entities as the objects of knowledge. But this view is still metaphysical in Heidegger's sense, since it seeks unified certainty based on the presence of the justifications that turn opinion into knowledge.

REASON AND PERSUASION

As Plato pictures them, the Sophists are not so much anti-rational as pre-rational; they have not made the proper distinctions. They teach how to achieve power by changing the ideas of one's fellow citizens. Manipulation and argument are the same. If one lives in the realm of opinion, why should it matter how opinions are changed, especially if people are happier and more harmonious afterward? Even Plato resorts to the noble lie, and he has Protagoras give a noble defense of persuasion as healing people and improving their adjustment to the city. It is not necessary that they agree with the process; they will come to agree.

In fear of manipulation, Plato insists on a strong distinction between acts of Sophistic persuasion, with their hidden violence against the nature of reason, and acts that lead to rationally motivated agreement among participants in argumentation. Sophists influence our beliefs; Socrates seeks mutual understanding based on shared reasons.

Plato claims that these two kinds of communication should be mixed only in a "true rhetoric" that would be firmly based on rational argument. In his dialogues, though, Plato is more flexible than his sharp division might seem to allow. The Socrates he portrays is in his way a supreme Sophist; he tells myths and uses many tactics of persuasion. Plato the author is even more protean and difficult to hold to the standards he enunciates. But his official doctrine emphasizes the search for unities, foundations, and system in the constant presence of true reality.

Those who uphold Plato's distinction today usually appeal to method, but there is no agreement on what methods are acceptable. The first step in distinguishing between forceful persuasion and rational agreement has often been to cite deductive logic. If we look at a pattern of sentences we can measure them against the logically valid patterns. Rational argument must follow these patterns while persuasion need not do so. This is a necessary but not a sufficient condition, since logical arguments could be employed with false premises for persuasive effect. The next step is to require logical arguments to guarantee the premises, but as both Plato and Aristotle point out this strategy fails since it would be impossibly circular to justify deductively all statements.

These problems are compounded in the real world where we want to judge not patterns of sentences so much as speech acts. A perfectly logical pattern of sentences can be used in an irrational way, by emphasis on its complications, by speed of delivery, by using it as a badge of expert status, and so on. It would be good if we could distinguish Sophistic persuasion from rational argument by their purposes, but this begs the question. Each is trying to bring the other person to agree; it is the way the purpose is specified which differs, and it is just that difference that is being questioned.

Since Plato, mathematics has served as the best example of purely rational argument. It seems to need no other discursive modality. Mathematics can be such a clear discourse as long as there is no disagreement about its basic definitions and premises. But this should not be the model for philosophical or practical discourse where the problem is to arrive at acceptable definitions and principles and classifications, not to start with them.[1] In discussions where principles are in question, we have to switch to another more flexible mode of discourse that speaks about the basic premises and criteria being used.

30   As I said in the previous chapter, much of what Plato and Aristotle wrote falls into this other type of discourse, which Plato calls the upward way *to* principles and Aristotle calls dialectic, a mode of discourse about basic principles and concepts that is not yet explicitly structured by those principles.[2] In this mode it is more difficult to distinguish rational agreement from persuasion because there are fewer shared rules to rely upon.

A promising way to talk about different kinds of discourse is to look at the different intellectual virtues required. Plato and Aristotle cite virtues whose practice makes this discourse good in its kind. So we have the portrait of Socrates contrasted with the portrait of the Sophists, and Aristotle's discussion of intellectual virtue in book VI of his *Ethics*. Socrates and the Sophists both share the ability to see possibilities, to size up their audience, to put words together well. But Socrates's willingness to question everything and to be proven wrong, his tolerance for indefinitely postponed conclusions, coupled with his dedication to the search for grounds and principles, make a picture quite different from the Sophist in a hurry to persuade. On the other hand, in real-life situations when conclusions must be reached without the infinitely extendable time frame of the Platonic dialogues the picture of Socrates begins to blur.

Judgments about whether a given act embodies a given virtue are notoriously difficult to agree upon. And can we be sure that the intellectual virtues are unchanging? The end of metaphysics is accompanied by the promotion of new intellectual virtues. Nietzsche offers his counterimages to Socrates. Derrida, Lyotard, and others try to persuade us of new intellectual virtues. Aristotle's *phronesis* is now joined by irony, playfulness, a spirit of transgression, and sensitivity to occasions for the creation of new language games. These cannot simply be added to the older lists, nor are the new promoted by the sort of communication and texts that are in accord with the old. If there are such new virtues, the problem of delimiting acceptable means of persuasion becomes even more difficult.

METAPHYSICAL FEAR

At the beginning of the modern age when Descartes started his examination of method, he made explicit his fear that he had been persuaded by custom, education, and social pressure to believe what a true method would find to be false. A proper method would let him start over and avoid the persuaders. But method for Descartes is more than logic;

it is an attempt to replace the Platonic and Aristotelian discussion of first principles with a disciplined intuition of self-evident clear and distinct ideas. A distinction between the logically valid and the psychologically persuasive was not enough for him; it had to be supplemented by the appeal to intuition. Since his time debate over proposed methods that will render unnecessary a discourse about first principles has often replaced that discourse, without conclusive effect.

Today we have techniques of manipulation on a scale that would have done Callicles proud. They are not playful transgressions; we do well to fear the link between such power and what passes for knowledge. If there is only persuasion, Plato warns us, there is no discourse except the confrontation of power and propaganda. If we cannot draw the line, he says, all means of persuasion will be acceptable. Violence may be done to us in crude or subtle ways, and we will not be able to stop it. Even worse, we may not be aware of it.

We fear violence: on the global scale, nuclear war, on the national scale, the violence of social disintegration, the war of all against all. We fear as well the calm created by power making us behave. We fear especially the insidious violence of a false consciousness that would make us believe. We fear we will behave not because we have reached a consensus, nor because we have calculated threats and rewards, but because we have had our opinions changed. The government, the capitalists, the church, our own unconscious needs may play the Evil Genius, and we may live a lie without being aware that we have been (re)programmed. But if there is only opinion and our opinions are the result of persuasion, what's the difference between being programmed by our upbringing and being reprogrammed by Protagoras's clients?

For all that Plato's metaphysical quest is out of fashion, do we still share his fears enough to need his remedy? Must we keep a distinction in kind between Sophistic persuasion and acts of rational convincing? Postmoderns say no, and I want to make a preliminary argument that will have the effect of weakening the need for such a distinction.[3]

In what follows I take for granted the end of metaphysics in the traditional Platonic sense of a search for secure foundations in a constantly present basic reality. There is more to be said about that "end" but I want to limit these remarks to how it involves the Sophists and the fears they symbolize. My point will be that if we reject Plato's description of the realm of knowledge we should also balk at his description of the realm of opinion. If we take for granted that Plato's quest is flawed, then Plato's fears of Sophistic persuasion should be weakened as well. It is not enough to challenge his metaphysical cure; we need to examine

32 how he has described the disease. In doing so we can perhaps soften the current debate about rationality, which is fueled by Plato's hopes and fears. In a way I am reiterating the Nietzschean point that to deny one half of a conceptual dichotomy does not always leave us with the other half exactly as it had been described.

Plato is wrong on both sides of his dichotomy between philosophy and rhetoric. If philosophy is the search for an unshakable presence of true reality, the realm of rhetoric and opinion is described as if it were completely malleable: beware the Sophist who can persuade you of anything he wishes. Behind this description is another metaphysical presupposition of a pure power of persuasion capable of being applied at will against opinions that are passive and yielding. Like philosophy that soars above space and time, so Sophistry for Plato involves a power of persuasion that lies outside the limits of context and history.

If, however, our opinions are not passive effects but are themselves ways in which we are in motion, and if powers of persuasion derive not from some pure will but from those motions and projects we find ourselves among, then the fear of the Sophists may be cut down to human scale. The realm of opinion turns out to have considerably more resistance than is apparent in the descriptions we get from Plato (or in those from postmoderns who reproduce that power of persuasion, now as a free movement of transgression or ironic re-creation).

I call this power *pure* because it is by its nature unarticulated and so able to assume an indefinite number of forms. It has no limits that we can find, no defined strengths and weaknesses. It has no shape that can be gotten around, and by its subtlety it can get around behind us and influence us without our knowing. Any normal power of persuasion or force has a shape and limits that allow us to begin to deal with it, to confront it or to avoid it. But this power is outside history, able to use tradition or depart from it as seems most persuasive. It is the shadow of Plato's pure love of truth, which also can overreach any historical situation, but unlike Plato's love of truth, this power has no natural goal to give it a measure.

This power resembles some modern definitions of free subjectivity as self-moving towards arbitrary goals. Followers of Leo Strauss and others who want to use Plato's polemic against the Sophists to analyze the modern situation play up this parallel, seeing the cure to be a return to natural measures. Yet by taking steps against it they concede the possibility of a power without form or measure. I am arguing that no such power is possible, that all power, both the power of persuasion and our power of creation and choice, is found already in particular motion.

Our powers and projects are definite in a way that is not a limitation on some prior pure power. Our measures are historical but they are not easily escaped, because they hide no pure drive within them.

We are horrified by the fantasy of a subtle use of violence that could change us without our knowing it. This would be the ultimate weapon of offense or defense. But whether this pure power appears in its positive role as the Method for finding truth, or in its negative role as the Sophistic power of persuasion, the same mistake occurs.[4]

Fears of Sophistic persuasion in the public sphere resemble the fears of being deceived in private life that have played such a role in modern philosophy since Descartes worried about whether the material world was really there. We fear that we have been already persuaded, without a chance to compare, judge, and assent. Some power has twisted our world so that we live a lie that we cannot identify as such. Descartes's deceptive God or Evil Genius was a perfect persuader, since he operated outside any context.

In its original, epistemological form this fear has long come under attack in texts such as Hegel's introduction to the *Phenomenology of Spirit,* Nietzsche's "How the Real World Became a Myth," Pierce's writings on Cartesian doubt, various texts of Heidegger, Wittgenstein, Austin, Bousma, and, more recently, the attacks of Putnam, Davidson, and Rorty that question whether it is even meaningful to think of us as totally deceived. This is an impressive litany of names, and it testifies to widespread skepticism about the effectiveness of epistemological skepticism. It is not so easy to make that fear sound plausible today. The corrective has been to convert global to partial doubt, to look at situations piecemeal, and to ask what practical difference it would make if the skeptical story were accepted. In its theoretical form skeptical doubt can be reduced to a combination of the everyday doubts we ought to have about our opinions in detail and the overall attempt to improve our pictures of the world. When we give up the dream of being perfectly sure, we can give up the fear of being perfectly deceived.

Fear of a practical power of persuasion that we could never locate or resist is a version of epistemological skepticism. The fear of the Sophist should be reduced to a combination of our everyday detailed attempts to avoid being manipulated and the attempt to make our social arrangements more open. We should give up the fantasy of a totally manipulative, or a totally unmanipulative, society. As Plato would say, we are creatures of the middle, neither being nor nonbeing.

Those who oppose postmodernism claim that if we accepted the postmodern descriptions of our situation we would be opening the

34 gates to Sophistic persuasion and relativism. On the other hand, some of those promoting the various postmodern moves so praise our power of creating new language games, or of making free with historical materials, that they assign us some floating position apart from history. Both the fear and the praise assume pure power: Plato's erotic quest for certainty, modern context-free reason, Sophistic persuasion, and postmodern irony have all too much in common.

Crude power and attempts to manipulate us are always present; we learn to see them, to recognize new ploys, and to take steps. This is not easy, but it is not impossible. We know what to do, even if we do not always do it. It makes sense to be worried about the persuasive efforts of the capitalists or the military or the government or the media or the advertisers or our own unconscious desires. But we are neither a pure energy struggling to free itself from a prison of circumstance nor purely malleable clay waiting to be shaped by the forces about us.

We find ourselves in historical situations we did not create, with goals and values we did not choose. We work at revising and correcting as we build new places for ourselves. There are no impermeable walls keeping us in, just as there are no magic methods of escape. There is no pure power to know or create or persuade which is being resisted by inert opinion or society. Our powers come from the historical situation; they are already shaped.

We are at once in motion in different ways. Our world is multiple and conflicts give us plenty of occasions to examine or remake our values and opinions. No magic is needed, only some sensitivity that our daily life keeps alive by rubbing us raw all too often. And if modern society especially tries to blunt that sensitivity we must work against that pressure. But it is a pressure, not an irresistible force, or we could not discuss it. Our task is not to out-think or out-feel the Sophists. But it is to keep alive the questions and conflicts that we find ourselves among, and keep alert for new dimensions or pressure and opportunity.[5] The next several chapters discuss the place and limits of self-criticism, so that later we can investigate building together in history and context.

This deflationary, pragmatic approach to the Sophist's power takes the drama away but returns us to the world of real confrontations and struggles. The reality is more humdrum, which is not to say easy. Indeed it may be more difficult than it would be if Plato's positive or negative fantasy were realized. Crude power and persuasion we know how to deal with, but we have to be continually alert as these take new forms or we discover kinds we did not know were operative. The worries are less threatening, but they demand more continued effort. Self-reflection can help, and a whole frontier of ethical and political philosophy opens up when we resist the fantasies of totality. We return to the in-between, but, both science and skepticism aside, that is where we have always known that we were.

] 4 [

POSTMODERN
SOPHISTICATIONS

The fear of the Sophist is the fear that we may be so manipulated that we have no secure place to collect ourselves, and no time to stop and think. In the previous chapter I tried to diminish that fear by examining its presupposition. But many thinkers who would accept my conclusion would not accept the further, postmodern claim that we have no unified self to collect. Indeed that seems to open the way for the Sophists: without a secure center how could we think critically? In this and the next chapter I explore the issue of criticism without security; later the issue will recur in thinking about architectural decisions. Here I discuss Jörgen Habermas and Jean-François Lyotard, who are often taken as representative modernist and postmodernist. Each believes the other insufficiently critical.

Postmodern thinkers try to describe a realm of opinion that does not stand in opposition to a realm of knowledge. The attack on Plato's dream of founded knowledge and on metaphysical centering has become bound up with assaults on other suspected enemies such as logocentrism, patriarchy, and instrumental reasoning. By a curious reversal the quest that Plato envisioned as the guarantee of true human flourishing has for many postmodern thinkers become linked with repression and false consciousness. The Sophists and their realm of opinion then come as a liberation.

LYOTARD AND HABERMAS

In his dialogue *Au Juste* (translated as *Just Gaming*), Lyotard explains how he sees the Sophists as relevant to our life today. The Sophists affirm that there is no knowledge in matters of politics and ethics; there is only opinion. We too must reject the claims of such knowledge, for those claims lead to the continuing "rationalist terrorism" we experience from those with a pretended science of politics, be it capitalist or Marxist. Socrates's quest is no longer credible. Neither are the related stories told by the Enlightenment and the nineteenth century about progressive human liberation or the growing embodiment of the human spirit in the world. Instead of these Socratic and modern tales we are coming to understand the variety of language games and their irreducibility one to another. There is no foundation to reach and no unified story to tell.

Yet we still need a politics. Judgments must be made, and Lyotard admits that the conventionalism about values usually attributed to the Sophists would lead to the conclusion that whatever any group comes to agree on is by definition right for them. In such a situation there would be no possible politics, only consensus. "But we know what that means: the manufacture of a subject that is authorized to say 'we' " (Lyotard and Thébaud 1985, 81). In a world where consensus has become a commodity, in a world after the Nazis, we cannot accept conventionalism as the base of political ethics. It would allow injustices that we must reject even though we can give no firmly grounded reason for rejecting them. This is Lyotard's major disagreement with the Sophists. As usually portrayed they would seem to allow actions and regimes that should not be allowed. Lyotard also admits that the Sophists defend a realm of opinion that is too fixed on past practice and convention (and, he should have added, on an unproblematic notion of desire).

Lyotard does argue that at least some of the Sophists went beyond conventionalism. They teach that "there must be laws, but no laws are given." We find ourselves already addressed by prescriptions in our encounters with others. That we be so addressed and have norms placed upon us is a fact prior to any reflection, a fact that cannot be made to go away. Yet no particular norm or prescription can have its content guaranteed.[1]

For Lyotard, we are put in the position of obedient listener and we cannot neutralize the address made to us. Yet we cannot take as definitive any particular prescription. Some are unjust. We are addressed; we are called to respond; but we must judge how to respond in each particular case. In doing so we have no rules to follow. In his attempt to ground some particular content, Plato tries to reduce prescriptions to descriptions taken from a superior realm, but this does not certify the prescriptions; it only changes the game. Language games are to be accorded their own autonomy. Prescription should not be reduced to description.

Nor can we return to rational politics based on metaphysical assumptions and methods. By "rational politics" Lyotard refers mainly to conservative natural law theories and doctrinaire Marxist views that claim rational authority. There is not much in Lyotard about the rational politics discussed on the Anglo-American scene derived from the utilitarian and contractarian traditions. Perhaps he knows little

38   about them; perhaps they appear too systematic and metaphysical; perhaps he dismisses them, as would Nietzsche, because he sees them enforcing mediocrity and not allowing the true liberation of a creativity that goes beyond limits and refuses to base life on cost-benefit calculations.

Lyotard describes the problem he sets out to solve in his book *Le Différend*:

> Given (1) the impossibility of avoiding conflicts (the impossibility of indifference), (2) the absence of a genre of universal discourse for regulating conflicts [Platonic metaphysics and its descendants], or, if you wish, the necessity that the judge be partisan, find, if not a way of legitimating the judgment . . . at least how to save the honor of thinking. (1983, 10)

Thinking's honor will be saved if we can avoid "might makes right." Lyotard hopes to overcome conventionalism by joining themes from the Sophists with themes from Kant to create a politics of opinion.

We need to make our judgments in reference to an Idea, in Kant's sense of that word. For Lyotard an Idea is not a rationally constructed concept that gives us criteria for judgment. It is an extension of an existing concept into a description of an unrealized state, a goal that may be impossible to experience (or even contradictory were it to be realized) but can still guide our judgment by giving it a direction. The irreducible differences between the various kinds of language games can be so extended into an Idea. Lyotard proposes the Idea of a society where there is no majority, where all language games are allowed to flourish and new ones are constantly invented, and none are allowed to dominate the others. This Idea does not provide rules for deciding any particular dispute, but it gives a direction or horizon within which we can have room to *feel* our reactions to a particular case. This mirrors what Kant says about aesthetic, rather than moral, judgments.[2]

As ideal citizens of the realm of opinion, for Lyotard, we would constantly be inventing new moves and "master strokes" in the language games we find ourselves involved in. And we would be creating new games involving new rules. Despite their diversity, language games remain structures and forms that cannot capture that which is unrepresentable: desire, life. We must honor the uncapturable by constant innovative ferment. The postmodern person is always to be moving beyond the language of the tribe, acquiescing in nothing, always creating anew. Lyotard admits (1984, 79) that the postmodern

extends that part of the modern movement that aimed at always start-   39
ing over from new beginnings.[3]

Whatever the problem with this injunction, and elitist as it may be, it plays an important role. In transposing an aesthetic goal of originality to the broader realm of language games generally, Lyotard introduces constant criticism and innovation into the realm of opinion. In its way this plays the same role as Plato's *eros,* the search for fuller reality that keeps us dissatisfied with where we are. Like *eros* it is a manifestation of desire, but not a desire for totality and fulfillment. We do not search for ever deeper grounds but for ever newer moves and games, and there is no final goal to specify criteria for judging novelty or mastery. Yet there is criticism; if a new form of life catches on and spreads (as might, for example, a new way of painting, or a managerial system with a new hierarchy of values), the effect is a criticism of the old way of life for not embodying our desire. Such changes, however, do not follow any linear progress toward some perfect way of life.

Lyotard's critics do not find this adequate. There has been an acrimonious debate between Habermas and Lyotard concerning the role of rational agreement. For Habermas, Lyotard's fragmented vision provides no real place for a community to recollect itself and think critically about its goals and practices. While Habermas would agree in rejecting the isolated critical ego that withdraws to some secure point in order to picture the world, he would not accept Lyotard's fragmentation of language. Insofar as we are self-conscious about acting within a community that shares values, that is, insofar as we speak a language in anything like a modern mode, Habermas believes we are involved in one overarching process of coordinating our actions through seeking for truths based on rational argument.

Language is not simply a code for transmitting information between computing devices; language is part of the net of interpersonal relations that binds people together into a community. Those relations allow us to feel and act in common. Coordinating action is not simply a matter of arranging parallel responses to stimuli. In its fullest sense, such coordination demands that we all act, together, as rational agents. It is this conjunction of rationality and sociality that in various ways distinguishes Habermas from the Sophists, from Lyotard, and from Plato.

Habermas opposes Lyotard because the many language games are all involved in a larger structure. In order to coordinate action among rational speakers, people must implicitly offer each other assurances that

40   they are able to meet challenges about the truth of what they say, its appropriateness to the situation, and their sincerity in speaking. Often, established institutional criteria can be used for settling these issues of truth, appropriateness, and sincerity, but with speech acts that are not tightly bound to institutional procedures, real communication requires an implicit promise that those three dimensions of validity can be explicitly discussed and their claims satisfied. We have the power to step above our practices and question them for their validity. This means that even in the case of communication that is institutionally structured, the norms of the institution can be questioned for validity whenever the participants desire. And the procedures used to settle those questions can themselves be queried in the same manner. Any language game exists as a particular way of structuring this basic web of intersubjective promises and claims, which has as its guiding ideal a rationally motivated consensus about the world and our interpersonal connections.

While this sounds like the Socratic story as Plato tells it, for Habermas there is no individual enlightenment at the end of the dialogue, only mutual agreement. There is no demand that some absolute foundation be reached; Habermas is concerned that challenges to validity claims always be appropriate, but such rationality is procedural in nature, and its results are always provisional.

Although Habermas does not demand a Platonic substantive base for rationality, Lyotard and others portray him as a "dinosaur of the Enlightenment" (Lyotard 1985, 168) who continues Plato's hopeless quest for certitude and consensus. On the other hand, Habermas has insisted that the seemingly radical claims made by Lyotard and others, claims reminiscent of the Sophists, are crypto-conservative. He charges that proponents of the postmodern who see the Enlightenment as a failed or totalitarian project of rationalization provide no process by which existing institutions or culture can be challenged in any way that can command legitimate assent. They leave us open to persuasion and manipulation, and at most they recommend counter-persuasion. But if this is all that is available then there is no politics, only social engineering.

Lyotard too believes that there is more to language than information transfer. But rather than stressing interpersonal connections and the reform of institutional goals and criteria, he sees a need to violate established language games by making new statements that cannot be communicated in clear language. As he says, "the problem [is] not consensus (Habermas's *Diskurs*), but the unpresentable, the unexpected power of the Idea, the event as the presentation of an unknown and unacceptable phrase which then gains acceptance by force of experience" (1986b, 217; cf. 1984, 81–82).[4]

Lyotard's creative individual makes new masterstrokes and new rules that are unexpected by those who play the ordinary games. What is important now is "suppleness, speed, and the ability to metamorphose" (1986b, 219). So too the Sophists worked surprising moves. Lyotard emphasizes that they were *antilogikoi*, always finding two or more opinions, always questioning received ways, always refusing to let opinion stay settled down. In *The Postmodern Condition* Lyotard urges disputation and paralogism in order to stimulate conflict and novelty. But the Sophistic refusal to let opinions stay settled was a stage in the process of "making the weaker case appear the stronger." The multiplicity of opinions was involved in a strategy of persuasion that leads the listener to accept what the Sophist wants him to think. The Sophists were not interested in a multiplicity of opinions for its own sake.

The darker side of Sophistic persuasion is invoked by opponents of postmodernism. Instead of the Sophists as innovators, we have Callicles's lust for power. The *Protagoras* portrays the Sophist as teaching manipulation in the name of education. The historical Gorgias, in his *Defense of Helen*, is eloquent about the power that persuasion has over opinion: Helen is blameless because she has been manipulated through words. Is this any different from what Lyotard proposes?

I argued earlier that we should not share Plato's extreme fears about the Sophists, though we need to be alert and critical. But it is not very clear what kind of individual or community self-reflection helps the process of criticism. Habermas says: "Post-empiricist philosophy of science has provided good reasons for holding that the unsettled ground of rationally motivated agreement among participants in argumentation is our only foundation—in questions of physics no less than in those of morality" (Habermas 1982, 238). Lyotard would agree that we stand on unsteady ground, but not with the concept of "rationally motivated agreement among participants in argumentation." If by "rationally motivated" we were to mean "acceptable according to the rules of the game," Lyotard would agree, but he would claim that the rules of the game themselves can be changed and there is no rule or process for agreeing on new rules.

Habermas, on the contrary, claims that the process of communication as rational agents guarantees the possibility of bringing the area for discussion and consensus to a higher level where we can work at

42 agreeing on rules or changes in rules. Relying on the goals and criteria implicit in the structure of communicative action, we can fight against mystified and distorted agreement where relations of force or causality, rather than evidence and validity, determine our beliefs and practices. Lyotard, claims Habermas, has no way of distinguishing between legitimate and ideological agreement about the rules for forms of life. He leaves us no recourse against Sophistic persuasion.

A GERMAN PLATO AND A FRENCH SOPHIST?

Just how far can we pursue the parallels between Plato and Habermas, Lyotard and the Sophists? Is it significant that just those darker aspects of the Sophists that most bothered Plato tend to be downplayed in Lyotard's presentation of their views?

Plato's Sophists, insofar as they talk about truth at all, subordinate it to persuasion, and end by making all use of language instrumental. Plato proposes a new discourse, the metaphysical quest and its dialogical method, which escapes means-end calculations, though it serves the larger purpose of grounding the individual and society. Similarly, Habermas accuses the postmoderns of being unable to distinguish persuasion from argument, and he urges a liberating self-critical discourse.

Plato seems close to Habermas in many ways, but Habermas can be made to look more Platonic than he is. For one thing, Plato makes a sharp distinction between the unforced dialogue of philosophy and the force and violence of action in the world. The difficulty of returning the philosopher back into the cave, the willingness to use the noble lie, and the belief that the multitude can never philosophize all indicate that for Plato there was a difficult transition from the purified atmosphere of Socratic discourse to the realm of practical decisions. Habermas refuses the strict separation (found also in Hannah Arendt) of the idealized realm of discourse from the realm of strategic action. His ideal discourse is tied to the task of coordinating action, and so it is always potentially involved with power and violence.

Also, Plato seeks personal unity and fulfillment, and a grounded effective community life, by means of direct contact with substantive truth, which Habermas would deny we can achieve. Yet, Plato's practice is closer to Habermas than is Plato's doctrine. I argued earlier that as dialogue extended and practical results were not forthcoming, the end of the metaphysical quest was indefinitely postponed. As the search became longer and deeper, in the dialogues and in the Academy, the search itself, with its concomitant virtues and pleasures and its internally structured activity of criticism, became self-sufficient. The

metaphysical goal remained as a distant pole orienting the way of dis-   43
cussion. The resulting mixed discourse, seeking the final truth yet
finding its satisfaction in the incremental criticisms made during the
search, closely parallels Habermas's notion of the Idea of uncoerced
communication as a norm for everyday communicative action and
criticism.

If Habermas is not quite Plato, neither does Lyotard quite fit with
the Sophists. It is true that he locates himself on the side of rhetoric and
persuasion. Speaking of one of his previous books, Lyotard explains
that it was not meant to present an argument.

> Here is a book the writing of which . . . perpetrates a kind of vio-
> lence. . . . What is scandalous about it is that it is all rhetoric; it
> works entirely at the level of persuasion. . . . This is a book that
> aims to produce effects upon the reader, and its author does not ask
> that these effects be sent back to him in the form of questions. This
> kind of writing is generally taken to be that of the rhetorician and
> of the persuader, that is, of the maker of simulacra, of the sly one,
> the one who deceives. To me, it is the opposite.

Lyotard explains that in the Platonic dialogue each participant is really
trying for the power to control the effect of his words on the other.
This produces

> a discourse in which each of the participants is, in principle, trying
> to produce statements such that the effects of these statements can
> be sent back to their author so that he may say: this is true, this is
> not true, and so on. In other words, so that he can control, or con-
> tribute to the control of, these effects.

By contrast, the more rhetorical style of the book in question opened
up a space for the reader, who is not dominated by the author.

> I was trying . . . to limit myself to the delivery of a mass of state-
> ments barely controlled in themselves, and, insofar as the relation
> to the addressee is concerned, they were drawn up more in the spir-
> it of the bottle tossed into the ocean than in that of a return of the
> effects of the statements to their author. Without knowing it, I was
> experimenting also with a pragmatics that, for some Sophists, is a
> decisive aspect of the poetic. . . . These theses are advanced not in
> order to convince or to refute but to persuade—let us say, to take
> hold of or to let go. . . . These theses are not up for discussion. But
> actually they can be discussed. . . . It presupposes that the reader
> does not allow himself or herself to be intimidated, if I may say so.
> (Lyotard and Thébaud 1985, 4–5)

44   It is clear that Lyotard is not identifying his attempts with the manipulation traditionally attributed to the Sophists. Yet his talk about "effects" intentionally blurs the distinction between convincing by argument and convincing by force. How does something "take hold"? While he admits that the most rhetorical of texts can still be discussed and its theses analyzed, he does not allow that a second text can reexamine and test the truth of the first text, as Socrates would claim.

> It is not really a matter of arriving at the truth of the content of the theses of the book, but rather a question of coming to grips with the new effects produced by the new situation of a joint discussion. And there will be no attempt then . . . to tell the truth of . . . the other books; it will be rather an attempt to produce a new book. The effects that had been produced upon us will be constitutive elements of the new book . . . not the clarification, the correct version, of the previous ones, but one of their effects upon two addressees, you and me, who are in no way privileged. (Lyotard and Thébaud 1985, 6)

This notion of the effect of a text leaves many open questions. How does one bring it about that the reader is not intimidated? Whose responsibility is it to do so? Is it enough to presuppose that the reader will be alert and tough, and that it is up to the reader alone to judge what kinds of effects are appropriate, or should the writer exercise self-restraint? Are there kinds of effects that are never appropriate?[5]

Still, despite his vagueness, Lyotard's comments about not controlling the effect of his words show that for him rhetoric is not a matter of calculating means-end rationality. At its best it is neither pure self-expression nor pure calculation but a continual, often mutual creation of novelty. This distances his ideas from the Sophists, since for them rhetoric involves calculation of effects and mobilization of means to success.

Habermas, on the other hand, does hold that discourse should return to the author in the form of questions, so that the effect of the discourse can be mutually assented to. True mutual dialogue is not a form of control but a means to rationally motivated agreement. "The fundamental intuition connected with argumentation can best be characterized from the process perspective by the intention of convincing a universal audience and gaining general assent for an utterance" (1981b, 26). This distinguishes argumentation from rhetoric since rhetoric always works with an eye to the limited factual situation of its audience; knowing your audience provides the "handles" persuasion needs. An audience defined in completely formal, universal terms offers no definite points of contact for the rhetorician to use in calculating the means of persuasion.

The generality of the intended audience can also pose a difficulty for
Habermas, since the goal of gaining universal assent will only work if
the universal audience can be described in such a way as to allow the
intention of addressing it. The notion of shared coordination of action
allows Habermas to find some constraints on speaking, since speaker
and audience share goals that can be defined in a purely formal way.
Whether these universal goals do not cause Habermas other problems
will be an issue in a later chapter concerning the role of historical and
traditional content, a role that I think neither Lyotard nor Habermas
has described correctly.

One way of distinguishing Lyotard from Habermas is to say that for
Lyotard the only possible description of the universal audience would
be as "players of some language games," while Habermas wants to describe the audience in terms of the specific language game of communicative action, which involves a whole network of speech acts and their
requirements.[6]

For Lyotard the general picture is of a competition (an *agon*) where
innovations strive for an acceptance that comes not by rational rules
but by something close to an act of aesthetic judgment. Justice involves
not consensus but respect for boundaries and differences. Habermas
orients language toward consensus and insists on the primacy of communicative action. Even if it is not the only function of language,
communicative action overrides the others as the vehicle of a growing
social self-awareness.

Habermas thinks of human relations with an eye on Hegel's notion
of mutual recognition in an intersubjective network where the parties
agree because they have cooperated in creating (or at least validating)
their relationship in general and in detail. But this is not through a social contract between already fully formed individuals. In Hegel's
vision of society I attain my individuality and selfhood only in coopera-
tion with others, through actions and structures that recognize others
as full persons who are at the same time recognizing me as a full person.
History is the story of the gradual purification and rationalization of
the structures by which people come to recognize and constitute one
another as selves. Complete mutuality is attained when there are no
inequalities built into the structures by which persons attain their selfhood; then social structures and acts come about through the mutual
approval of each member. In such a state nothing is different from what
it appears to be: there is no hidden content or secret interest. The reasons for any structure or act are in principle accessible to all.

For Lyotard there can be no public sphere of discourse that is not
divided and agonistic. He speaks not of agreement but of moves and

46 countermoves, masterstrokes and changing the rules. A new language game may sweep us along or answer to desires that go beyond their present articulations, a new prescriptive address may call us to respond, but none of this happens in the transparent, mutually controlled intersubjective space that Habermas sees as ideal.

So, although Lyotard and Habermas both agree that language is not essentially a tool for calculated manipulation, the opposition between them can resemble that of the Sophists versus Plato, at least in terms of agonistic display versus cooperative inquiry.

Yet, as we have seen, it would be too simple to say that Habermas favors critical judgment and Lyotard opposes it. Lyotard sees constant innovation as a critical tool. Nor do the targets of his criticism differ much from those of Habermas. Despite Lyotard's talk about rhetoric and persuasion, he as much as Habermas fights the leveling effects of the mass media. Both of them worry about the increasing concentration of education on technical mastery to the exclusion of communicative and creative skills. Both of them are concerned that in our times impersonal systems that maximize efficiency are distorting human ways of interacting. Both examine the structure of our interaction with one another; both seek norms already implied in what we do, norms that when put into practice more explicitly will make room for the voiceless and the exploited to speak effectively. Both seek justice, and agree that in its name we must fight the totalizing forces of modern systems. Both agree that we must develop new social practices that let us take time out from the bombardment of information and pressure, time to think and create anew. In all this Habermas and Lyotard are on the same side, and it is the side Plato would approve.

Facing the media barrage and the distorted communications of the contemporary world, what Habermas urges seems more classical: that we take time to collect ourselves together, to think and demand arguments. He urges mutual recollection and concentration in order to clear the channels of communication. But this is not the same as Plato. Plato wants us to build our city through a dialogue based on the *logos* we all share, and that deep reason that makes our dialogue possible leads the individual to a vision of the forms definitive of reality. The cooperative group discussion works to facilitate individual enlightenment. Perfected individuals would then form an elite that could apply grounded knowledge in managing a properly ordered community. While Habermas too would have us work cooperatively to establish consensus based on reasoned agreement, this leads to no foundational knowledge nor to any Platonic social manipulation by experts.

Lyotard insists that Habermas would substitute one form of total

uniformity for another. But in practice both thinkers urge piecemeal 47
reform. Habermas is not demanding we institute global change all at
once, and Lyotard is not telling us to go off and play by ourselves.

For Lyotard, if our communications are distorted, we should invent
new ways to communicate. If society is dominated by a few kinds of
language games, we should devise more. Divergence and creativity are
the answer: secession, not consensus. This does not mean that we
should play new games by ourselves. Such isolation would only create
smaller domineering societies. What is needed is a plurality of language games and modes of life acknowledged as such. We think we
have that now, but the plurality is dominated by the rules of efficiency
and capital accumulation. There is one overriding game in our society:
exchange.

Although it is not a process of rational appraisal, the creation of
novel language games effects a critique of the world we know. Present
practices will be criticized not by discussing them but by creating new
practices that by the way they take hold show up the unspoken desires
frustrated by previous forms of life. This process does not converge;
there is no cumulative learning process such as Habermas describes.
New games will be in a public space not structured by any one language
game (such as capitalist accumulation) nor by any one set of goals (even
ones as refined as Habermas's consensual structures).

That public space will be open and tolerant; is Lyotard, for all his
radical panache, a liberal at heart? He denies the charge, "Does what I
say lead to an advocacy of neoliberalism? Not in the least. Neoliberalism is itself an illusion. The reality is concentration in industrial,
social, and financial empires served by the States and the political
classes" (Lyotard 1986b, 218). But this is not enough; neoliberals too
fight concentrations of power (cp. Rorty 1988, chapters 3 and 8).
What makes Lyotard in one sense *more* a liberal than Habermas is that
participants in Lyotard's different language games are never forced to
justify either the rationality or the appropriateness of the games they
play. In his concern to safeguard the different forms of life from external
domination Lyotard renders them immune to internal challenge, except through the creation of a competing game that may seduce away
their players. Because there is no mutuality demanded, judgments of
justice, about which Lyotard is very concerned, come only from outside.

MODERN AND POSTMODERN

While Habermas champions modernity, he opposes the contemporary
reduction of human action to the manipulation of objects, and the re-

48 duction of rationality to instrumental calculation. He urges that these only exist in the broader context of communicative action and rationality whose liberation is the true modern project.

For Lyotard "the issue in modernity . . . was not, and is not, . . . simply the Enlightenment; it was, and is, the institution of will into reason" (1986b, 216). Rational calculation is now at the service of a will to power that has only its own infinite productive expansion at heart. Measure and efficiency spread domination everywhere, but there are no dominating individuals or classes. Habermas opposes this Heideggerean description of the modern scene; for him the symptoms Lyotard discusses show not a sickness at the heart of reason and will, but the effects of current capitalist economic and social structures, which allow "systemic" considerations of efficiency and productivity to invade areas of life which should be managed by consensual methods.

Both Habermas and Lyotard oppose the standard modern purified notion of the individual. Such individuals populate many philosophical and social scientific theories; they consist of a set of preferences coupled with abilities to choose. These individuals use their freedom to maximize their success in realizing their preferred goals. Their social relations are chosen or constructed with these interests in mind. Social reality results from the aggregation of these individuals and their negotiations. Both Habermas and Lyotard believe in "thicker" individuals whose relations to community are more intimate because individuality is itself a social construct.[7]

Habermas's individuals strive not simply to realize individual preferences, but to question and validate their preferences amid a social process of clarification and reason-giving. That process is not something added to their already finished individuality; it is in the process of rational interaction that they become fully individualized. When we take time out to reflect and collect ourselves, it is our dialogically constituted selves we recover. Society is not an aggregation of independent atoms.

Lyotard's individuals are also more complex than modern preference machines. Individuals are constituted by their social relations in the varied language games they play. But they do not have a unified center either individually or in community; there is no one "self" constituted by one drive for truth and consensus. Neither the individual nor the community can get itself together to the degree Habermas would require. The social bond has many strands; we play many roles in many games; there is no overarching or underlying unity, only the need to be involved in games and to play them well. Language games do not emerge from one unified play in us or one unified "we" among us bound by one set of rules of discourse. Indeed, "the human" could well be "replaced by a complex and aleatory assemblage of (nondenumerable operators) transforming messages" (Lyotard 1986b, 217–18). Yet Lyotard still shares Habermas's demand for judgment: not every game should be allowed. Lyotard labors to impose conditions of justice on this multiplicity of games without decreeing either a central self or a unified meta-game.

Both Habermas and Lyotard would agree that there is no way to avoid making judgments case by case on conflicts and novel forms of life. They disagree about which Idea opens the space within which judgment functions. The controversy is between Lyotard's aesthetic judgment and Habermas's rational consensus. It is here that the Sophists and Plato appear yet again, in the old fight between poetry and philosophy.

Habermas aims at showing that we have ideals and goals built into language that give us a chance to criticize apparent truths. It is this he thinks Lyotard and the postmoderns do not provide, leaving us in the hands of the Sophists. Lyotard suggests that a combination of individual judgment and aesthetic novelty can do the job that needs to be done.

But what is the job that needs doing? I argued that the hopes and fears that motivate Plato's strong distinction between reason and rhetoric involve metaphysical fantasies on both sides. If we cannot deploy a perfect method neither do we have to avoid some shapeless persuasive force. Yet even if the Sophists are not so powerful as Plato thought, there is critique to be done. The job is not necessarily that of getting free of all conditioning and opacity, but rather of criticizing and building as best we can. But can that be done without at least aiming at some full self-knowledge and self-transparency? What kind of self-criticism is possible for use in a world that is neither Platonic nor Sophistic? When we are building or rebuilding our world or our city, when we are facing one another and our differing traditions, how do we talk to each other in a way that is self-critical and not merely talking "to have an effect"?

My approach in the later chapters will be broadly pragmatic. I will not try to defend the existence of some one structure that is the key to self-criticism, so I will not be offering a master argument for such a structure. I will instead make a series of observations and claims that are meant to keep open the variety and heterogeneity of our modes of self-criticism and their practical import. Later, in discussing changes in architectural vocabularies, I will propose something more similar to

50 Lyotard's innovation than to Habermas's consensual process; but still later, in discussing the city as a whole, I will come back to Habermas and agree that Lyotard's mode of self-criticism does not allow the mutual dialogue that is necessary for living and building in the finite spaces we must share.

] 5 [

SELF-CRITICISM IN A BROKEN
MIRROR

If we are trying to make or remake places for ourselves, whether through city planning or cultural criticism, we need some idea of who we are and what we want. But what can we know of ourselves?

Modern philosophers and social scientists tended to think of the self as able to capture reflectively the structure and conditions of its activity. At least in principle the self could become transparent to its inner gaze. Modern artists tended rather to find the self opaque and inaccessible to reflection. Now that oppositional trend is strengthened by postmodern thinkers influenced by Nietzsche and Freud.

From the Greeks on, "know yourself" has been a cardinal maxim, but its import has varied. In many ages the principal message was to know your station in life (in relation to your betters, to the gods, to your mortality). That station was shared by members of your group or class. In modern times the emphasis has shifted to knowing special facts about yourself: to know yourself is to tell your own particular story, with its uniquely contingent history, its dreams, desires, aspirations, faults, and so on. Socrates would not have considered personal facts to be true self-knowledge; such a list would have formed only the starting point for the real quest that would take you from such particulars to the more universal conditions and goals common to all selves. For him, self-help begins when we can see beyond our individual particularities. Today's popular self-help books practice self-examination, but without suggesting a goal beyond our particular desires. In Foucault's disciplinary society we are all constantly checking our particular qualities; supposedly this helps us grow; mostly it just keeps us in line.

As modernity developed the self was treated both as more empty and as more filled with personal content than in earlier societies. According to modern theory, making places together should be a matter of looking into ourselves to understand our individual needs and goals, then negotiating ways to coordinate with others according to general principles. It becomes important to overcome anything that blocks or distorts our access to our true selves or to true social needs. Where the ancients would have seen flaws of character, we see false consciousness.

But what if we cannot look into our individual or collective self-consciousness and read our desires and goals? If we doubt the ideal of

52 transparent self-reflection, how do we assure enough space for discernment and self-criticism?

In this chapter I ask whether giving up modern self-transparency means we cannot criticize ourselves. In the next chapter I argue that not only the content but also the act of self-evaluation always stems from a particular context and tradition. Later I will try to provide examples of this kind of judgment as it might be involved in extending architectural vocabularies or building a city together.

What if there is some kind of influence on our selves or our community such that the influence can never be gathered up and examined "objectively"? Martin Jay reports that "Like Lyotard, Foucault would hold that power (and language) are prior to the self and could never be overcome in the name of perfectly transparent intersubjectivity" (Jay 1984, 51–52).

Among others the target here is Habermas, who insists on the ideal of a totally self-evaluated community. No factor or force is to be outside the reach of our critical activity. For the usual modern view, we must keep everything in view and get the total picture so that nothing will get behind our backs where we cannot see it coming. Society must look in all directions to make sure that nothing is surreptitiously affecting it. Habermas denies this subject-centered approach. He proposes instead an intersubjective method; it is not our vision that we must clear but our talk. Ideology is not a distortion of our vision but a blockage to our communication; it silences us on crucial topics and questions. We are to aim not so much for clear sight as for justified statement. The result will not be a total picture of ourselves, but rather a total discourse that can encompass and evaluate everything about a society and all the factors shaping its activity.

PRIOR CONDITIONS

For postmodernists such as Foucault and Lyotard our language and tradition, our social relations and the power they present cannot be made transparently rational or be encompassed by discourse even in the ideal limit. The self cannot dominate them either by individual reflection or by intersubjective discussion. Symbolic systems and language games and power relations are prior to the self, constituting it in a way that cannot be gotten behind.

This notion of *priority* needs to be examined. I want to suggest that even when (and in part because) we give up the idea of complete self-reflection, even when we deny the possibility of a totalizing individual or social discourse about self or society, there is still nothing so "prior" that it cannot be talked about. Whether it can also be evaluated and changed will depend on the facts of the case, but nothing is in principle immune. The supposed opaque factors are conceptual twins of the idea of a totally transparent discourse, since it is only when all ways of talking and criticizing can be totalized under some unified principles that one can suggest there might be something outside the reach of any and all discourse constituted (and limited) by those principles. If there is less unity to the critical discourse, it has fewer limits.

There is an old argument in Greek philosophy that is relevant here because it shows us how not to think about these matters. We find the argument first in Anaxagoras:

> Other things all contain a part of everything, but mind is infinite and self-ruling, and is mixed with no thing, but is alone by itself. If it were not by itself, but were mixed with anything else . . . the things mixed would have prevented it from ruling over any thing in the same way as it can, being alone by itself. (Fragment 12)

Anaxagoras says that if the mind were mixed, it could not rule all things. The argument Jay reports accepts the connection Anaxagoras is making: because mind is mixed with something (constituted by social or linguistic or whatever factors) it cannot rule all things (cannot dominate those factors by self-reflection).

Aristotle makes the same connection when discussing the intellect. "Since everything is a possible object of thought, mind, in order (as Anaxagoras says) to dominate, that is, to know, must be pure from all admixture" (*On the Soul* 429b 16–20). Aristotle starts with the assurance that the mind can know everything; this comes from his metaphysics of form and from his doctrine that the proper object of knowledge is the universal. Aristotle then affirms (and contraposes) Anaxagoras's connection: since the mind can dominate all things it must be unmixed and pure of any material admixture.

The opinion Jay reports restates Anaxagoras: the scope of the mind's ability to criticize depends on the degree of its self-activity. The ancient quotations testify to an emphasis on purity; for Anaxagoras it is a matter of keeping some foreign stuff out of the mind. For Aristotle the mind can have no qualitative shape; colored glass does not admit all colors of light. In the postmoderns the Greek emphasis on matter and form changes to a Kantian emphasis on the necessary conditions that let an activity be what it is. The influences in question shape the self not by being something alien mixed into it, but by being the conditions

54   that make a certain kind of activity possible. In so doing they limit it to the definiteness of that kind. Language, social relations, power relations, and other factors are not outside forces worming their way into the intimacy of an already existing self. They are forces and relations that by being in play in certain ways let there be a self. So the influence here is more subtle than the Greek argument conceives.

But just how are we to take the claim that the self cannot overcome the factors that make it a self in the first place? There are three progressively weaker ways of reading this claim. The first would be that the self cannot even know such factors, and therefore cannot overcome them in any way. The second would be that the self may know about the factors but cannot criticize or control them. The third would be that the self can know and to some degree change these factors in their particulars, but cannot do without them in general. Only the third reading is the defensible claim.

If we interpret the claim reported by Jay as saying that we have no access to the factors that constitute the self, then we are still caught up with the ideal of pure self-presence. As long as the Greek connection between purity and domination is accepted, then any opaqueness in the self prevents full self-reflection. Or, in more postmodern terms, some dispersion and lack of center in the self prevents the self from re-centering itself in full presence to itself. This presupposes that self-knowledge demands that the self coincide with itself, and that if such self-communion is impossible then self-criticism is impossible. To contend that there sulks behind all aspects of the self we can talk about some prior influence we can never trap or escape raises a specter akin to the power of persuasion we cannot locate, which I discussed earlier.

If we give up the Greek link between knowledge and transparency then claims of "priority" become less useful. In fact, when the model of transparent self-presence is removed and all the necessary softenings and impurities are allowed into the notion of self-knowledge, we become even more able to talk about presuppositions and constituting factors. If the self cannot be seen in an overview or summed up in one total discourse, that does not mean that we cannot talk about ourselves. Quite the contrary. Diversity and dispersion within the self increase our ability to talk about ourselves. If we had to rely on a pure view or a special method we might worry about what was constituting and so limiting that one method, but if our ability to talk about ourselves is multiple, indirect, metaphorizing, and unregulated by any fixed principles or patterns, it is not limited a priori to any particular sphere.[1]

The opinion Jay reports is open to a second reading: that we can know but not influence the factors constituting our selfhood. It is ruefully true that merely being able to talk about something does not mean we can criticize and change it; this is especially true of our own habits and dispositions. But this commonplace does not justify the claim that we can in no way change. To recognize the possibility of change requires that we be able to recognize alternatives. It is this, rather than some supposed self-transparency, which is the crucial issue. Even if we agree with the many thinkers who argue that there is no way of conceiving a self without language, history, culture, and the like, that does not mean that we cannot recognize possible alternative ways of language or culture.

We can distinguish two ways of questioning. One is to wonder at our condition, without any particular alternative in mind, a wonderment that things are the way they are, but without any definite doubt about them. We can wonder about something that we take for granted, or some standard, or some self-evident practice. Such wonder is a source of philosophy but it is not yet a definite question. The other occurs in Plato's dialogues, where that wonderment is taken up and given a name and a direction in the Socratic quest. The move is graceful, but it is a move; the prior wonderment could be specified in other ways. Epistemological skepticism probably fascinates us most when it is kept as a wonder that avoids any specific challenges. Just wondering "maybe we are completely mistaken" produces a thrill that does not give any direction to discourse. As soon as skeptics actually offer alternatives (the world is a mental representation, we are brains in a vat, there is an Evil Genius deceiving us) then arguments begin and critical decisions get made. The same is true for ethical skepticism.

So, we might roughly distinguish two kinds of descriptions: one that suffices to identify an item in question, and another that locates it in a way that has some consequences. Skepticism might identify its topic as "all our beliefs" or "all our experience" and ask vaguely whether these were "true." But the discussion would really begin once some meaning had been given to the notion that our beliefs could be false, by locating them on one side of a powerful duality such as mental/external or spontaneous/imposed.

Again, someone in a traditional society might wonder at its hierarchical distribution of power, without really envisioning alternatives. Then later the traditional hierarchy could be located on one side of a duality such as just/unjust or equitable/inequitable, with some description of what a society on the other side might be like. With the availability of alternatives the initial disquiet could become a force for change.

Self-criticism demands that we be able to delimit some area of our life and describe it with concepts that have implications we can argue about. If this is so, then we can see one sense in which Habermas is right to consider postmodern irony to be a conservative move. Irony locates some practice and distances itself from that practice, but does not necessarily insert it within a network of other concepts that provide critical leverage.

Thus the third reading of the opinion reported by Jay seems to be the correct one. Even if there are factors constitutive of our selfhood, we are not blocked from considering changes in their particulars. Even if we cannot conceive a self without language and history, we may envision different languages and histories.

True, this provides at best a strategy for piecemeal self-awareness. We cannot be sure we will come to know *all* the factors conditioning us. (Obviously there can be no argument that will prove that we can never know some particular factor; the fact that we could make the argument would refute it.) The fear remains that in criticizing our situation we appeal to standards that themselves are the effects on us of some as yet undiscerned particular influence.

How can we be sure this is not happening? I think there is no way we can be sure, but is this so bad? If our fear of being influenced stays general and provides no indication of what kind of factors we should worry about, then it is no different from the generalized fear of the Sophist I spoke about earlier, or the vague skepticism mentioned above. If the fear has some specific focus, then we can examine it.

Besides conceiving alternatives, we have to be able to actually effect changes. These do not always go together. We can conceive of spaces of more than three dimensions, but no one has suggested a way of adding a dimension to our space in order to provide more real estate. Still, we do not know the limits of our power to effect changes in nature or society. It is not clear that social and economic "laws" are as fixed as our current analogies with natural science make them seen.

We have all had the experience of being aware of how we are shaped by cultural or historical influences but not being able able to change as we think we should. The women's movement has afforded both men and women many occasions for being aware of influences that seem difficult to escape. There is no single answer to this predicament anymore than there is a single weapon to be used against Sophistic persuasion, but once there is awareness and a vision of alternatives we can work at changing.

Traits of character and historical conditioning can be changed only with difficulty. They cannot be altered by merely willing them to be different, yet in many cases we could change over time by being alert for their effects and by developing new habits. Aristotle's *Ethics* describes the process for cases where drastic social change is not needed. Achieving such re-habituation we would not have escaped language and culture, but we would have somewhat altered their particular constellations.

DISCIPLINE AND APPROPRIATE JUDGMENT

If we are going to build together, criticisms and changes must be agreed on by many people. Unless we want to reduce communal dialogue to nothing but strategic bargaining on the part of individual interests, some communal criticism and discernment will be necessary. If we have trouble understanding ourselves individually, won't that be even more difficult in society? And what kind of "we" do we want to make a place for? Is our goal to become modern self-transparent autonomous detached selves? We should not presume that the only alternatives are modern distance or a helpless subservience to factors we cannot control.

Influenced by Plato's fears, controversies over the form of public discourse too often presuppose that rational discussion and forceful manipulation are the only alternatives. But any argument we can propose will always remain surrounded, located, and made relevant by that shifting discourse I spoke of in earlier chapters, the discourse that is not itself structured as an argument. While that shifting discourse has no first principles to rely on, it is not undisciplined. And other modes of discourse can have their own disciplines that are not the same as rational argument.[2]

From Socrates to Kohlberg and Habermas, the ideals of mature selfhood and developed community have almost always been linked to the ideals of rational discourse and justified self-criticism. It is the mark of a mature person or a mature society that a process of inner or outer dialogue replace the pressure of impulses and images. But perhaps the notions of person and community should not be so tightly linked with the notion of speaking and acting according to reasons.

Maturity in a self or society should certainly depend on being able to resist the pressure of impulse toward arbitrary and inappropriate ac-

58   tion. But "appropriateness" is a wider category than "justified rational belief," and "rational" is not the only opposite of "arbitrary." Also opposed to arbitrariness is discipline. In place of seeing a mature person as a source of rational discourse and decision one might see them as capable of reacting *appropriately* to situations, where "appropriateness" is not defined in terms of rules or justifications but in terms of disciplined perception.[3]

After Foucault, there is some danger in using the word "discipline," since it has become one more name for a supposed essence of modern society. But the word has an older resonance from the discipline one learns as one learns a craft, for instance how to center clay on the wheel, and what shapes a particular clay allows you to attempt. This is not a matter of learning a set of justified rules; it is more like learning a dance, or how to inhabit a particular locale. There are also the disciplines of the traditional spiritual paths. These involve kinds of self-discernment and unity that are not matters of justified true belief. Certainly these older disciplines are ancestors of the modern one described by Foucault, but they do not connote its ubiquity and standardization.[4]

We are often told that rational criticism is "impersonal" and thus escapes being bound by the particularities of individual feeling and preference. But it is possible to escape the details of individual preference without demanding rational universality. The discipline of a craft is "impersonal" to the extent that anyone properly trained in that context and situation would judge in a similar, if not identical, manner. Yet that discipline is context-bound and not applicable in all situations.

Thus it might not be by studying the processes of argument leading to conclusions but by studying the processes of discipline leading to graceful skill and insight (in the crafts and in some traditions of spiritual development) that we might come to understand what it means to be a developed person or society.

This is not an academic matter; the classical notion of mature personhood tied to rational discourse and action has become fundamental to so much of our ethical and political theory, and so interwoven with our legal and social practices, that we have only the dimmest ideas about what personal and institutional relations might be if personhood were thought and lived differently. It would be necessary to rethink the ultimacy of the opposition between rational and irrational actions. It would also be necessary to work out what it means to have a mutual discussion that is disciplined without necessarily following standard patterns of argument. This would mean finding ways of opening the disciplined appropriateness of actions and words to interpersonal evaluations rather than individual appreciation, though not to rule-governed decision procedures and transparent public discussion. Contemporary feminist thought most directly attempts to address the task of rethinking personhood and institutions along these lines. As feminists suggest, we can find the wider notions of discipline and appropriateness already present in repressed corners of our own experience.[5]

Community demands mutuality, and Habermas is right to demand that participants to a discussion aimed at coordinating mutual action should be able to challenge the appropriateness of one another's judgments and values. But his claim that this implies self-transparent rational evaluation may actually narrow our possibilities for social self-criticism. As I said above concerning individual self-knowledge: as our methods of self-discussion become more varied, indirect, and metaphorical, there are fewer limits on what we can come to know about ourselves. It may seem that Habermas demands too much of discussion; perhaps he demands too little.

Yet while it is true that the crafts, the arts, and the traditions of spiritual development have means of disciplined discussion and evaluation that are not arbitrary even though they do not demand universal rationality, it is also true that these activities have been riven with conflicts and forceful interventions. The disciplines they offer are not enough to insure peaceful agreement. But this does not imply that they must be subject to a higher uniform set of rules. It may be that disciplined communal judgments of appropriateness can be reached by some weaker version of Habermas's dialogue. Habermas himself may suggest something along these lines when he speaks of the reintegration of artworks into the lifeworld.[6] It is not the case that our only alternatives are rational universality or arbitrary force.

There are kinds of encounter that lie between the standoff produced by liberal tolerance, and the shared rational project Habermas encourages. Examples of such discussion can be found in the best intercultural and interreligious dialogue.[7] The crossings of traditions with one another and with the everyday world can further self-critical processes at work in the traditions, without being part of a universal project of self-criticism.[8] There is a mutual project involved in such dialogue, but it is neither the goal of liberal coexistence nor Habermas's universal rational agreement. Rather it is what I will call a care for the whole that does not involve a total vision of the whole. This, with the problem of discerning our communal identity, is taken up in the final two chapters, which concern the problem of building together in cities.

Self-evaluation should not be conceived as a process elevated above

60 history.[9] My notions of appropriateness and discipline may seem vague; they can even seem dangerously empty if we persist in looking for criteria or processes of judgment that can be applied to *any* situation. Appropriateness and discipline only make sense in context; unlike "rationality" they cannot be defined in a purely formal way. If we generalize the notion of discipline and appropriateness too much we lose the specificity that makes particular judgments possible; at most the discussion should be supplemented with descriptions of intellectual virtues. This does not insure peaceful agreement, but can anything guarantee that?

] 6 [

FORM AND CONTENT IN UTOPIA

In this chapter I discuss some reasons why Habermas insists that our common dialogue and joint building must be done on modern terms; then I ask if his views give an adequate account of the place of tradition. The reading I offer is an attempt to force Habermas where he does not want to go. His doctrines are designed to maintain a delicate balance between our particular roots and our universal critical project. I argue that this position is unstable, and that it leans heavily toward universality and distorts our relation to history.

Reflective distance from traditional ways and values allows one to use traditional material for one's own purposes: this is the Sophist at work, picking and choosing what strands of tradition to emphasize in order to achieve personal or party goals. This is also Habermas's ideal community at work, picking and choosing what strands of tradition to emphasize in order to achieve what they take to be universally justifiable goals. If the universality of those goals were to be questioned, then Habermas would look more like the Sophist. He means to look more like Plato, who tests and corrects traditional material. But Plato hoped to find substantive values and not just procedural rules to keep his use of tradition from being willful. Habermas does not mean the use of tradition to be willful, but perhaps that is an effect of the very formal rules and goals he suggests (cf. Bubner 1982, who accuses Habermas of being too close to the Sophists).

MODERNITY AND TRADITION

Habermas does not believe in the distinction between modernity and postmodernity; for him the crucial distinction is between the modern and the traditional. What does modernity have that traditional society lacked? Habermas summarizes the difference as follows:

> We have discussed the "closedness" of mythological world views from two points of view: the insufficient differentiation among fundamental attitudes to the objective, social, and subjective worlds; and the lack of reflexivity in world-views that cannot be identified *as* world-views, as cultural traditions. Mythical world-views are not understood by members as interpretive systems that

61

62   are attached to cultural traditions, constituted by internal interrelations of meaning, symbolically related to reality, and connected
with validity claims—and thus exposed to criticism and open to
revision. In this way we can in fact discover through the quite contrasting structures of "the savage mind" important presuppositions of the modern understanding of the world. (Habermas
1981b, 52–53)

When Habermas speaks of mythological worldviews he has in mind
the classic examples cited by anthropologists: the Nuer, the Azande,
and so on. On this scale the Greek myths are not purely traditional;
they represent an already changing system that is on the road to modernity. Fully modern society has learned to distinguish "the objective,
social, and subjective worlds" and has institutionalized expert ways of
dealing with these worlds.

For Habermas there is a story to tell about the gradual differentiation that leads to modern society. The modern spheres of science, law,
and art work according to their own evolving rules and become independent of political or religious control. This may resemble Lyotard's
insistence on a postmodern plurality of language games, but Habermas's differentiated spheres fit together into a synthetic whole which
Lyotard would be the first to attack. Unlike Lyotard's discontinuous
proliferation, the expert spheres Habermas talks about each have their
own developmental logic that guides them as evolving systems with
continuing identities. There is no logic to the genesis of Lyotard's language games from one another, nor for changes within a given game.

In the story of modernization, the key trend is the gradual coming
into focus of a distinction between nature (as something given) and
culture (as something made). Less developed societies, we are told, see
culture a natural given and nature as something made by super-
persons. Separating nature and culture means developing institutions
that can distinguish and treat differently such things as ineptitude and
guilt, causes and motives, harm and evil. This separation means seeing
the difference between natural health and moral goodness. It means
moving from a magical to a technological approach to nature, which
brings a higher level of productive forces and more mastery of the
environment.

These developments do not proceed haphazardly; Habermas likens
them to the maturation of an individual, and he makes connections
between Kohlberg's stages of moral development and the changing or-
ganizational principles of historical societies. He sees these developments as genuine improvements in a species-wide learning process that

helps us fulfill our needs. Modernity is an advance, not just a change. Traditional society tends to be static and repressive, because without distinguishing the social and the natural order there is no room for envisioning alternative social arrangements as something that people could bring about on their own (Habermas 1981b, 51).

Above all, modernity requires us to separate the world from language about the world. Habermas argues that as the distinctions he lists become available they allow people to make semantic distinctions between the referent, the content, and the sign in linguistic acts. This enables them to conceptualize linguistic acts *as* linguistic rather than natural acts, and to distinguish connections due to the rules of meaning from connections due to the causal relations among objects.

This destroys the magical function of language. But it opens up the possibility of understanding how some statements might be valid locally just because of their connection with the rules of a particular language game. And other statements might be valid universally just because of their connection with the rules for communication in general. This allows us to distinguish various spheres of validity and the appropriate rules and type of rationality for each sphere. In working out these conditions and rules in detail Habermas arrives at his ethical and political conclusions.

THE THREE-WORLD STORY

These distinctions establish a picture of the world that explicitly distinguishes the world from its pictures. We can distinguish the content of a worldview from the presumed order of the world it is trying to describe. We become able to talk about a worldview as a cultural construct with its own rules for connecting statements. The logical structure of the worldview is distinct from the causal patterns it reveals in the world. We can also separate the logical structure of the worldview from the subjective qualities of our experiences. Once these three elements (world, worldview, and subjective experience) are seen as separate, we can imagine alternatives and criticize our traditions in more radical ways than ever before.

I call this overall framework "the three-world story." The three worlds are the "objective, social, and subjective worlds" mentioned above. There is the world of objective fact (linked by causal connections), the world of cultural constructions (linked by logical and other rule-governed connections), and the world of inner experience (linked in aesthetic and temporal connections, but not a realm of mental entities:

64   cf. Habermas 1981b, 91). Each of these three worlds makes sense in reference to the others, and they interact to provide a framework for language and understanding. "Taken together the worlds form a reference system that is mutually presupposed in communication processes. With this reference system participants lay down what there can possibly be understanding about *at all*" (Habermas 1981b, 84).

Each of the three worlds fills a different function in our communication and action. It is important to see that the three worlds are completely defined by these functional roles. The cultural world that lies between experience and the objective world fulfills a certain function of structuring and unifying and guiding, and it does so for every culture, regardless of the particular constructs involved. Some cultures are more developed and differentiated, some less so, but there is a cultural world in every case, defined by its function rather than its content.

The three-world story is perfectly general. Since the function of each world within the overall story is not tied to any particular content for that world, a modern person can think about the nature and function of cultural constructs without necessarily referring to the constructs typical of his or her own culture. Moderns can talk about worldviews or the role of inner experience without indicating any particular view or experience.

This generality allows modern people to criticize existing cultural constructs or experiences. Since we understand the differentiated roles of the three worlds, and the functions each world fulfills in the story, we can examine particular cultures or experiences to see if they fulfill their roles well. The story suggests the goal of making the three worlds function better together. That goal belongs to the three-world story itself rather than to any particular culture or worldview. In terms of this goal we can criticize culture and experience from a perspective that has no particular content it must hold sacred at the cost of its own identity.

Thus the abstract and formal quality of the three-world story allows it to be in principle shared by all cultures despite their differences. This should encourage consensus-building that will improve the functioning of the worlds of experience and culture in general. Of course this can only happen once people are able to make the distinctions on which the three-world story is based. They can share in the story once they have moved beyond the stage of seeing a particular tradition as "natural." Only *modern* people can tell themselves the three-world story.

The three-world story provides a self-image for modernity. The story includes a history of how people developed so that they became able to tell the three-world story: this gives a direction to the story and helps define its goals. What it means to be a modern person is to live in a society that is so structured as to make the three-world story basic to one's identity. "We have to face the question, whether there is not a formal stock of universal structures of consciousness. . . . Every culture must share certain *formal properties* of the modern understanding of the world, if it is at all to attain a certain degree of 'conscious awareness'" (Habermas 1981b, 180). Instead of a founding myth, moderns have the three-world story.[1] The story defines a place for modern individuals to stand and judge how well any tradition measures up to the ideal of smooth functioning expressed in the story. And because the story gives the *form* of modern culture rather than any particular content, it completes the development of self-consciousness that has been occurring throughout history. These features allow the three-world story to make normative claims that demand universal acceptance.

Because we moderns have seen how culture and the world fit together, there is no turning back. We cannot again sanctify any particular cultural or experiential content. There is no return to traditional forms of culture, for this would mean losing the differentiation that gives modern persons their distinct perspective. This could only be a regressive step.

As far as Habermas can see such regression is just what many postmodern thinkers are suggesting. When Lyotard says that grand narratives of liberation and progress have lost their credibility he is claiming that we no longer believe in something like Habermas's three-world story with its built-in goal of perfect function and transparency among the three worlds. Yet Lyotard offers his own story that also involves a formal characterization of our relation to each other and to history, this time in terms of multiple language games and the possibility of novelty. Like Habermas's story it provides a self-image, one closer to artistic than to social and scientific modernism. This story differs from Habermas's story because it does not invoke rational criticism, and because it does not lead to a final unity. Habermas stresses these differences in his critique of Lyotard, claiming they make Lyotard unable properly to criticize distorted and manipulative communication. Yet the results of both stories for our attitudes toward history may not be all that different in Lyotard and Habermas.

FORM AND CONTENT

Is the three-world story the only way we have left to describe our relation to tradition and the past? It will be worth examining the distinction of form and content in the three-world story as it applies to our dealings with history.

If one defines as traditional a society with no self-consciousness at all about the status and nature of tradition, the roster becomes vanishingly small. Self-awareness of the society's relation to its traditions can emerge in many ways connected with changing patterns of trade, religious innovation, new agricultural technology, and so on. The decisive distinction between traditional and modern societies lies not in the presence but in the institutionalization of modes of self-reflection that may have existed in previous societies but were not made part of the standard modes of interaction among members of those societies.[2] Those new institutions include modern political arrangements, and the specialized spheres of science, law, and art which were mentioned earlier. Each of these deals with the past in a different way, but they share an objectifying attitude.[3]

Habermas claims that because of modern differentiations we find ourselves no longer able to stand in immediate unity with the traditions we have received. We interact with our traditions as with tools that we have made and whose function we must improve. The three-world story gives us a formally defined place to stand independent of the content of any particular tradition, and it gives us a universal project with goals independent of any particular historical project.

It may appear, though, that the goals of the three-world story are indeed those of a particular culture and tradition. Despite its apparent universality the three-world story appears to be a European story, and the cultural forms Habermas draws from the story are typically European. Habermas argues that this ethnocentrism is only apparent. While the modern structures emerged in Europe for contingent historical reasons, taken as abstract structures they are not Western but universal since they concern action and communication in general.

More importantly, Habermas argues that what is described abstractly in the three-world story is not a European cultural project or form of life because it is not a full cultural project or form of life at all. It is a structure of distinctions, relations, rules, and values that must undergird any self-aware form of life. But that structure cannot be lived by itself. It provides necessary conditions for any modern form of life, but in order to be sufficient for actual life it must be supplemented by historical content.

The three-world story suggests a life where all three worlds relate in smooth functional interchange. But the rules and structures required for this functioning do not make a blueprint for a perfect society. In his earlier works it sometimes appeared that Habermas was suggesting that it was possible to define a utopian society based merely on the conditions for perfect communication. More recently he insists that his discussions of the conditions of communicative action are meant to provide only the formal necessary conditions that make possible a modern society. They are not meant to outline sufficient conditions for a utopia. He defines utopian thinking as "the confusion of a highly developed infrastructure of possible forms of life with the concrete historical totality of a successful form of life" (Habermas 1981b, 74).

There is another reason why Habermas does not want the three-world story to be a sketch for a complete culture. While he wants to affirm the modern trends towards universal norms, differentiated institutions, and the creation of more flexible individual identities, he does not want to say that we could have a purely procedural society made up of what I earlier called "thin" individuals.

In a society of such individuals, people would be characterized only by their lists of preferences, and by a drive to maximize satisfactions. Institutions would be set up to facilitate trades in goods and services, or in rewards and punishments, that would help the aggregate goals. This subordinates everything about persons to the gathering of satisfactions, and everything about society to the efficient functioning of one kind of interaction. Many theorists approve this picture. Others attack it from the right and left. Hegel and Marx attacked such a picture (of "civil society"), and later Weber feared that modernity was developing in precisely this direction. Habermas's predecessors at Frankfurt, Max Horkheimer and Theodor Adorno, shared Weber's fear. They saw a "dialectic of enlightenment" whereby differentiation and rationalization paradoxically develop into a homogeneous society where all life is subordinated to an inhuman rationality of production and efficiency (cf. Horkheimer and Adorno 1972, Connerton 1980). Those early Frankfurt thinkers would concur with some recent postmoderns in seeing rationalization as ultimately repressive, and in hoping for aesthetic or instinctive means to counter the dominance of modern rationality.

The three-world story is meant to provide the resources to counter

68　　such pessimistic accounts; it allows Habermas to develop a subtle theory about different types of rationalization that function in the
separation and in the integration of the three worlds. He argues that
there is no fatal flaw in the process of rationalization itself, but there is
a dynamic by which certain types of rationalization tend to dominate
others due to their position in the current economic structure. We must
favor the principles of rationalization and differentiation if we are to be
self-critical. What we need is a more differentiated study of rationalization. The bad effects cited by Horkheimer and Adorno are effects of
capitalist modes of rationalization, not a necessary consequence of rationalization in general.

There are kinds of rational development operating in the various expert spheres of culture. There is also a more general rationality operating in the consensual dialogue found in the everyday lifeworld. This
latter works to reintegrate the results achieved in differentiated spheres
of culture back into the everyday world. These kinds of rationality involve our dealings with one another in communal dialogue and the
exchange of justifications for beliefs and decisions; they are not oppressive; they liberate us from the shackles of traditional roles and
values.

What is oppressive about modern society is that yet another sort of
rationality has become too dominant. Our dealings with nature have
been made vastly more efficient by a means-end instrumental rationality that replaced traditional magical and emotional dealings
with nature. Habermas agrees with his predecessors that in capitalist
society this kind of rationality has come to dominate life. Impersonal
mechanisms such as market forces and bureaucratic efficiency break
into interpersonal relations where they are inappropriate, thus allowing one kind of rationality to repress others that are necessary for the
reproduction of a full human life and world. Habermas calls this the
colonization of the interpersonal lifeworld by impersonal systemic imperatives and their instrumental rationality.

Ideally speaking, in a differentiated modern society described by the
three-world story, the structures making society possible would be so
general that they should be open to an immense variety of particular
content. Such a society should support more different lives and a richer
mix of goals and projects than any traditional society could ever
achieve. Traditional society needed to stabilize definite values and ways
of life in order to maintain its identity. Modern society finds its identify
in the formal structures of the three-world story and so it can be more
accepting and flexible.

Our society does not fulfill this ideal. What may appear as greater variety is partly a matter of differentiation and mostly a matter of the consumption of commodified life-styles. The dominance of instrumental rationality is reducing our possibilities and blanking out rather than transforming traditional content. We are sacrificing the richness of human life to the flashy surfaces of consumerist efficiency. In this Habermas is at one with postmodern critiques of our contemporary world.

I will return to the influence of system on lifeworld in the later chapters devoted to the problem of building livable places today. For now I want to concentrate on Habermas's positive alternative, and indicate its problems in dealing with the past.

Habermas wants life to have content as well as form. The three-world story must be supplemented by historical material for its processes to work on. If there were no historical "substance" to consciousness that was more than purely procedural, something very like the "dialectic of enlightenment" might indeed take place (Habermas 1985a, 401–2).[4]

It is here, though, that the relation of formal process and particular content becomes problematic. Habermas says that historical material needs to be respected, yet the three-world story possesses goals independent of any particular historical project.

The past influences us "from behind" as our stock of pre-interpreted unquestioned beliefs and values. Habermas holds that our cognitive (and other) activities all take place within the lifeworld, which is a network of undoubted background beliefs that act as a fund of meaning. Every explicit act presupposes the lifeworld, though modern cognitive endeavors do so in a particularly self-conscious way.

Although for Habermas our belonging to the lifeworld we do is not something at our arbitrary disposal, it is available for communal reflection and correction. A traditional society would equate passing on the received background with passing on the truth, but what it means to be modern is to make a distinction at that point. The lifeworld supplies a fund of meaning, but the process of establishing the validity of propositions is distinguished, in modern societies, from the process of reproducing the lifeworld.

The lifeworld is composed of linguistically structured units, but it does not form a structured whole that can be seen or reviewed as a totality. Still, any particular belief in the lifeworld may be raised into explicit consciousness and have its validity claims tested. Such criticism might lead to a new consensus based on testing the past against objective criteria or communally accepted values (which can them-

70 selves be tested). The lifeworld may thus be changed piece by piece, though not as a whole.[5] Thus although we always act from out of a background, there is nothing in that tradition which is sacrosanct, nothing that cannot be questioned and revised by conscious mutual agreement (Habermas 1985a, 82). It cannot be judged all at once, but any part of it is available for judgment.

This is reminiscent of Otto Neurath's famous image of the ship. We are like ships under way. We cannot tear the ship down and rebuild it on the open sea, but we can repair or change it part by part while we travel, working on one part while relying on the other parts to sustain us. The crew is quite modern; they relate to their ship in a purely instrumental manner. The present state of the ship only imposes the requirement that the steps from its current condition to some envisioned future state be carefully worked out. Possibilities are unlimited except by scarcity of materials.

In this image, as in Habermas's three-world story, tradition sets no goals and imposes no constraints. Neurath's ship has no destination; it is a philosophical Flying Dutchman. Any real ship is not traveling simply for the purpose of being remodeled to travel better. Habermas's three-world story sometimes makes it seem as if the purpose of living together were to purify the conditions for living together. All particular contents that might provide goals for living are subject to judgment and remaking in light of the formal goals implicit in the three-world story.[6]

While Habermas looks to the historical lifeworlds for some solid content for living that is different from the purely formal structures in the three-world story, it turns out that the historical content serves only as material to be used in allowing the formal activity to continue (Habermas 1985a, 401–402). Like the planking on the ship it is there to be remodeled. In itself the historical content sets no goals and imposes no restraints. Habermas cannot allow particular historical projects to set the goals of our self-criticism, for he fears that this would remove them from criticism. Only universal goals will do. But is this the only mode of self-criticism?

Habermas is rightly concerned to avoid the unity of the universal and the particular that can lead (as in Hegel) to sanctifying some particular arrangements as the final rational structure for society. So Habermas points out how general structure and particular content do not form a unity (Habermas 1985a, 397–99). But when the structure and the content remain separate, there is danger of the complete dominance of efficiency and instrumental calculation. Habermas tries to ward this off

by refusing to allow the modern formal structures to be, on their own, 71
a complete blueprint for social living. What is to prevent instrumental
dominance of social content is the requirement that there always be
some historical content for the formal process to work on. But this is
not enough to avoid the dominance of instrumental rationality and the
dialectic of enlightenment, because the historical content is present
only as material to be examined and reworked.

Habermas does invoke distinct kinds of rationalization that do not
reduce to instrumental reason, but all his types of rationalization share
the distinction of form from content. All content is to be judged by
reflection and mutually constituted in a process guided by the formal
goals in the three-world story. All identity is to be a made identity.
Radical autonomy is the modern project. Historical goals and identities endure as cases of believing because it is good for you.

Habermas's problem is the purity of the overall goals given in the
three-world story. They have to be free of historical contamination so
that they can be available on all occasions as tools for critiquing any
tradition.

The difficulties with the three-world story are similar to the problems concerning the transcendental and empirical levels in Habermas's
earlier writings: he seemed to be proposing conditions so transcendental that they had no critical bite. Or, if the principles had critical power,
their own universality seemed in question. In his newer writings
Habermas claims that the developmental logic of human growth leads
to the three-world story and its associated norms. While not strictly
universal these do give the pattern common to any sufficiently developed human community. In so doing they indicate that only certain
historical contents are able to support the three-world story, so the
principles have some critical power. But in attaining this power the
story so dominates particular content that it raises again the specter of
the dialectic of enlightenment.

In his description of the modern situation Habermas makes use of
many controversial principles. In claiming that there is an overriding
unity to language that enforces rules that are valid for any form of discourse, Habermas must distinguish relations of pure formal validity
from relations dependent on material forces or cultural particularities.
In analytic philosophy the attack on pure relations of validity has been
going on since the late Wittgenstein (1963), through Quine (1969),
and now again in Rorty (1982). In continental philosophy as well the
notion of a purely formal mode of being has been attacked repeatedly
since Heidegger, usually by analyzing or deconstructing candidates to

72   show their substantive roots and their inner betrayals of their supposed purity. Habermas is fully aware of these attacks and mounts spirited defenses against them. I will not try to rehearse these debates here, but will side with the critics who contend that what may appear to be pure relations of validity are always supported by ongoing community practices that are not themselves describable in purely formal terms.

Many postmodern thinkers endorse the general direction of Horkheimer and Adorno's theories about the oppressive nature of the process of rationalization. It might therefore seem that someone like Lyotard could give us more real historical connection than Habermas can allow. Certainly Lyotard vehemently denies any overall goal such as the three-world story proposes, and he insists on the independence of our various cultural games from any universal norms. But the fact is that Lyotard's creation of new language games, and the irony in much postmodern art and architecture, embody virtually the same attitude toward historical content as we find in Habermas. Historical content is only material for the play of postmodern signification. This is not Habermas's rational process of judgment and criticism, but it maintains the same general separation of a formally described process from its particular historical content. What may appear a reimmersion in history turns out to be an celebration of our distance from history.[7]

It is the purity and totality in Habermas's story that ought to be questioned. Can we separate a level of pure formal validity from the forms of life and historical development of practices? And even if a formal description of cultural constructs is possible, can it generate goals that give a critical perspective transcending all historical projects?[8] If, on the other hand, we are more deeply historical, if we are set in many different motions by traditions, if what distinctions of form and content we can draw are either quite local or so universal that they provide no critical bite, then the pure process Habermas describes needs to be revised.

Its totality, transparency, and formally described goals make the three-world story thoroughly modern. The story prescribes an activity of communal self-criticism that ascends above the history that gave it birth. I have been urging that this underestimates our immersion in history, but Habermas has a powerful retort. Only the modern project, he argues, can free us from historical distortions. Because in a traditional society the various cognitive and social domains in the three worlds are not functionally differentiated, mythical discussions can blend them so that relations of things and power substitute for relations of reasons and argument. People are swayed by bad arguments blended with power relations; there is no free rational criticism and consensus. The three-world story provides the goal of unmasking claims where power substitutes for reasons. As far as Habermas can see, theorists of postmodernity are working to collapse the differentiations and blend argument back with rhetoric, thus opening the door to the Sophists.

This is not to say that in the modern world all is clarity and argument. Myth is not the only way to befuddle the critical faculties. Modern society has its own ways to hide the relations of power, and Habermas's deepest intent is to unmask and criticize our present world. But he thinks that the principles that enable us to do so are now implicit in our modern projects.

While we have good reason to worry about ideological distortions, Habermas's way of approaching the issue employs the same basic distinctions that I criticized in the earlier chapter about the Sophists. Since the three-world story demands self-transparency, ideological pressure can only be thought of as an outside force distorting a fundamentally self-active process of communication. In traditional societies there was no separation between the self that sought pure validity and the self constituted by social and causal pressures. But once modernity arrives with its formal process of rationality described in the three-world story, ideology can be seen as an alien force. This is because the process of intersubjective relations has become formal and empty. Habermas does not endorse the modern empty self, but he replaces it with the formally defined community for whom historical tradition can only be material. Against this, we need to rethink the categories of ideology and criticism to take account of our connections and impurities. We need to reconsider how the disciplines of craft and language might allow communal self-criticism without rational universality.

My argument has been that if the universality described in the three-world story could be really established, any rootedness in the past would be destroyed, despite Habermas's attempt to have it both ways. I treat the three-world story as an impossible attempt to rise above history. The other side of this claim would be the diagnosis that the three-world story itself remains particular. This might be made plausible if we could show that there are other ways to move away from primitive social structures. There might be alternatives that are neither modern nor postmodern, other routes away from myth, other kinds of differentiation, and perhaps other strategies than differentiation. Perhaps with these one would have to characterize traditional society in other ways

74   than as "non-differentiated." In the West such other alternatives would have been subdued by the Socratic story. But there may be paths that lead from myth to other kinds of self-reflection about tradition, ways that do not go by way of a confrontation with the Sophists and the establishment of universal criteria. These ways might not share all the presuppositions of our modern mentality. For example, the Buddhist notion of emptiness, as it expands into a critique of propositional truth, claims a self-awareness that is distanced from myth, but in a different manner than the western critiques.

Any story about us and the past needs some distinction of form from content; to talk about tradition at all is already to make such a distinction. The question is whether that distinction must support a critical practice with its own pure goals, as Habermas desires. Habermas sometimes speaks as if the alternatives were either his critical practice or a Sophistic pragmatism. But these both share a presupposition that the self or community stands outside tradition using it for its own particular or universal goals. Our immersion in language and tradition is stronger than that, and we have no goals given outside of all traditions. But because of the distances and multiplicities involved in being "in" our past, we are not so restricted and uncritical as Habermas suggests in his modern picture of the premodern world.

] 7 [
LIFE IN A BALLOON

Here is a thought-experiment; deciding whether it is really possible may lead to questioning our notion of the premodern. Imagine that in exploring New Guinea, or Mars, we discover a tribe of people who have all the correct equations engraved in shining gold on the walls of their temple. They have better equations than we do. Using these equations they can explain and predict phenomena with amazing accuracy. They employ this power to control the local environment for successful agriculture and a quiet, serene life. They have wonderful machines and when the machines break down the people go to the temple, where there is a great Book. The Book contains the equations, plans for the machines, and directions for repairing them. Everyone is free to consult the Book, though there are hereditary experts who know where to find particular sorts of advice. Tribe members are happy and prosperous.

In the neighboring valleys are other groups who worship a variety of gods and use a variety of techniques to control nature. They slash and burn; they recite spells; they use machines of their own, with varying results. When we ask members of the tribe we've met about those neighbors, they say "those people are not us; they do not have the Book; our ways were given to us alone."

If we ask tribe members why they rely on their particular equations and machines, they reply "because these equations and machines are in the Book!" They give the same answer when we ask them why the equations and the machines are so successful. If we ask where the Book itself comes from, they say "it has always been here with us." When pressed on the matter they recite stories, in many variants, about how the Book was handed to their first ancestors in the morning of the world, or how it is a description of God's intentions, or of God herself. If we ask them why they believe in the Book they look askance at us as if they do not fully understand the question. "It has always been like this," they say, "we and the Book, together."

Premodern Ancestors

This tribe has what we want: the equations and the techniques. They have what we often claim separates us from our ignorant ancestors:

76 they have the truth about nature. It seems that they have more truth than we do. Yet they are not like us. While we would be glad to copy their equations, perhaps we would not wish to live their lives. Somehow they seem more like our ancestors than like us, even though they have the truth.

Perhaps something is wrong or incomplete about the standard divisions between us and our premodern ancestors. According to the easiest version of that division we are modern, scientific; we have literal, clear, full truth (or pieces of it, or at least the ideal of literal truth), while our ancestors had analogous, metaphorical, unconscious, disguised, partial truth. This contrast and its convenient two-stage theory of history have been popular since the Enlightenment. Our ancestors had myths and fables, with their distorted figurative truths. Their myths can be studied in many ways; they can be sociologized, structuralized, psychoanalyzed, and so on, but in all of these there appears the same contrast: we are the ones who make the distinctions; we can distinguish psychology from physics, and nature from society, but our ancestors muddled them together. Even when writers delve into old myths for analogues of current ideas, finding the Big Bang in Hindu scriptures or quantum mechanics in Buddhism, there is still the old division of us from them. We extract our truth from their myths.

We are supposed to be the people who live by the literal truth instead of by superstition and myth. But the tribe has more truth, and yet they "possess" it differently. They treat it as we imagine our ancestors treated their myths. They seem to lack something which sets us apart from our ancestors, something which is not just truth as opposed to myth.

What is it that we have that the tribe lacks? Perhaps they are too placid? They have the information to enable an aggressive expansion; they could have come exploring to us, but they do not care to expand. We like to think that our truth comes from our acquisitive inquisitive attitude toward nature. But it seems possible that the truth could be possessed more serenely.

Perhaps they lack Research, the organized drive to know more and still more? But they already have the equations; why should they want to do research as an end in itself?

Perhaps they should be curious about the origin of the Book? But they know that it has been with them forever, part of their identity as a people. Imagine that it was left behind by alien astronauts, if you want; it is not the factual origin that bothers us but their unthinking trust. Shouldn't the people worry about the Book's origin? Shouldn't they keep testing it to see if it might be mistaken? But suppose that for thousands of years there has never been any evidence of mistakes; why should they bother with fruitless tests?

Yet this last suggestion does indicate what bothers us. It is hard to speak of the tribe members having a reason for believing in the Book. They don't "believe in" the Book; they just live defined by it. Their relation to the Book is not the result of inquiry and justification. But does this matter? Isn't the goal of inquiry to get the truth? And in the knowledge of nature do we have any more basic criterion than pragmatic success? They have the success, so why inquire?

We feel that if we had such a Book we would believe in it because we had reasons to believe in it. We would not believe just because it had always been part of our identity as a people. Our own Book can't claim that role anymore. If we had their Book we would trust it because it works, but we would keep the option not to believe, even as we had a reason to believe. We would hold that the Book was *true*, not just that it was *ours*. We would test its limits; we would distance ourselves a little from the Book and believe in it because doing so fit with our criteria, and with our purposes and desires.

The tribe inhabits their truth simply and neatly. We would like to see a little more distance there. We would prefer that the tribe have a sense of its identity separate from the Book, and use the Book as a tool. Then there would be space for research and distrust, even if these were never needed. Tribe members would be more self-conscious about their stance toward the truth, and they would make a distinction between accepting a belief because it is part of their ancient identity, and accepting it because there were reasons for doing so. They could distinguish, in Habermas's terms, between reproducing their lifeworld and justifying their beliefs. If the tribe members had more distance from their traditional identity they, like us, could explore the joys of epistemology, and come to describe their own beliefs and their neighbors' beliefs in more complex ways than by opposing their own identity to that of the other peoples.

Then they would have found their identity in something else than their Book's description of the world. That seems to be what we moderns do: we find our identity not in any definite set of beliefs but in our inquiring attitude toward beliefs. Habermas seems right when he argues that part of the modern self-definition is our refusal to be simply defined by any of our beliefs. Yet he does refer to an ideal community that finds all of its beliefs completely justified according to any standards it can imagine. Could that community be this tribe?

I created this thought-experiment in order to dramatize how the cru-

78 cial components of our contrast between premodern and modern life can be separated from questions about truth and pragmatic success. I modeled the tribe on what Hegel says when he discusses the Greeks of the heroic age (Hegel 1977, chap. 6). He pictures an individual like Achilles as having no distance from his social roles. Achilles becomes who he is by embodying given duties and roles; there is no secret inner self that is calculating the utility of those roles. Modern persons have become separate individuals who judge roles and values. That change began with tensions within Greek society, and when the Sophists began to teach a rhetoric which involved distance from traditional beliefs combined with a manipulative attitude towards them. The change was complete in the modern world of democratic governments, free markets, and romantic subjectivity. Hegel does not regard this change as altogether happy, and he suggests that history finally comes to incorporate the best features of both stages while avoiding their limitations.

The tribe of my thought-experiment relates to their cognitive beliefs in the way Hegel imagined the heroic Greeks related to their social roles. There is no reflective or critical distance, just immediate identity. But what may be different in the cognitive case is that it is not so clear that distance is still needed if the truth is possessed. A simple identity with social roles and values feels to us like a restriction on our freedom, even if we sometimes yearn for such definiteness and security. But does a simple identity with a complete science seem restrictive in the same way?

In creating the tribe I also had an eye on C. S. Peirce and Wilfrid Sellars, who claim that science moves toward a final state of complete predictive success and social agreement; Habermas incorporates a version of this ideal. My tribe has the success and agreement, but without any distance from themselves. Is such distance only a condition of the journey and not of the goal? If we could abandon self-awareness about our cognitive state once we had the truth, would something be missing? Or is something missing in the description of the premoderns as lacking self-aware distance?

THE PROBLEM OF SIMPLE INHABITATION

We can define the issue better by examining some typical ways of describing the difference between us and our ancestors. The first suggestion is straightforward: we have the truth and they did not. We are the simple inhabitants of the truth while our ancestors were simple inhabitants of error or figurative truth. But if this were the case we would be like the tribe, and we are not.

So we have a second suggestion: we are the self-conscious ones. We are conscious of how we relate to beliefs; we make distinctions between literal and figurative truth, between our beliefs and our identity as believers. We apply criteria and make judgments. It is likely that we have more truth than our ancestors, but what is crucial is our self-reflective distance. This distance is more basic than our commitment to any program of research or inquiry; it is what makes such commitment possible. Other institutions of ours also embody this distance. Nowhere do we plant our feet and stand as our ancestors did.

This picture, too, is oversimplified. It makes us completely critical while our ancestors were completely credulous. It makes us creatures of distance unable to rest in any beliefs but only in our own relation to them.

So we might propose a third model combining the distanced self with the simple believer. This resembles Habermas's interplay of the accepted lifeworld and critical reflection. It is tempting to see us as having added a layer of self-reflection to some persisting ancestral simple inhabitation. This model has several versions. Sometimes we think of science as the distanced critic whose purified view corrects a simple childish believer that persists in each of us. The simple believer is swayed by rhetoric; the keen-eyed critic knows philosophy or science or semiotics. On the other hand sometimes we think of science itself as part of the simple belief, subject to ironic comments from a distanced self-awareness that acknowledges no home. Popular culture tends to the first of these versions, literary and philosophical culture to the second. Education is sometimes viewed as transferring people from the popular to the literary version. "Growing up" then means, for the individual as for the group, finding distance, refusing to find one's identity in a Book (even a scientific book), learning ironic distance, correcting the child-self.

Many see this inner split between the simple believer and the distanced critic as our modern plight, and they try to absorb one side of the split into the other, telling us we can win peace through returning to simple faith, or that we can win freedom by becoming totally critical or ironic. Others look for a simple but deep inhabitation in some region of the self prior to the split. Still others tell us to stop fighting the split, since it is ultimate, in the name of Freud, or Weber, or the two halves of the brain.

The first suggestion pictured our ancestors as living simply in error, while we live simply in the truth. The second suggestion produced wholly credulous ancestors and wholly critical moderns. The third sug-

80 gestion has distinguished one-piece ancestors from split moderns who combine a simple inhabitant and a detached critic. Science gets assigned to one or the other side of this split; what remains constant is the division.

There is something to all these models, but the diagnosis is mistaken. The distinction between a simple believer and a distanced critic is wrong whether applied across time or within the individual. No one, premodern or modern, stands simply inside any framework, nor simply outside. All the models proposed so far are wrong: simple inhabitation, pure distance, and their combination. They are all wrong for the same reason: they imagine that distance is created by an act of reflection added to some framework of life or beliefs which is simply accepted.

Part of the problem lies in the use of spatial metaphors like "distance" and "split." These images are dangerous because they can express only a few kinds of external relations. Play for a moment with my image of "simple inhabitation"; it suggests that we are in our beliefs or our language the way we could be in France or Belgium. Were we in Paris we would be surrounded by French territory and its faraway borders. The internal landscape of France would fill our horizon. Over there, beyond the borders but invisible from within, would be Belgium. Truth here, myth there, and foreign relations. Transport across the border would be possible. Although some currencies of belief have to be left behind, others could be brought across and exchanged, at a slight discount. France is more advanced and regards what is deemed essential in Belgium as only local color to be noted for its similarity to French ways. With this model the relation between truth and myth is external. No changes in Belgium would affect France, though they might hinder the importation of curios.

If the French were in the truth the way they are in France, they would be much like my imagined tribe. If we were to translate the other suggestions into spatial metaphors we would put the modern critic in a balloon, surveying all and distant from all. But this is too rarefied and detached, so we tie the balloon to the people below. The critic in the balloon now functions as a spotter for the others on the ground. The critic is pure and unsullied by the prejudices that come from being on one part of the ground as opposed to another. The balloonist can see clearly. That vision tells the people below what ways can be taken, and where they lead. The balloonist's sight does not show which way should or must be taken; for that the balloonist and the people on the ground must confer, joining their desires to the balloonist's vision of possibilities and consequences. The balloonist may not be able to ex-

plain precisely what he sees to his earthbound colleagues, so he may   81
have to use a kind of persuasive rhetoric, under scientific control, in a
good cause.

This picture renders some ideas of Max Weber which provide a so-
phisticated example of what I called the popular version of the modern
split. Science is the neutral critic above, providing clear views of the
facts and consequences, while the simple inhabitants provide the motivating values and desires. We are not our ancestors because we have
found out how to elevate the balloon and we know it for what it is.

But this picture purchases the purity of the balloonist's view at the
expense of affirming desires and values in a simple inhabitation below.
Weber thought science could rise to objective vision, but values could
not be rationally criticized. Opposing this, perhaps we could imagine
the elevated critic to have some values implicit in that very elevation
and in the universality of the view from above. This would be to go
beyond Weber to Kant and Habermas. But there has always been the
question whether Kantian formal principles really recommend
particular paths of action and overcome the fact/value distinction.
Analogous problems remain in Habermas's scheme. The critical self
still does not have its feet on the ground.

Spacious Systems

All the images suggested so far make distance an external addition. We
need to understand what it means to be *in* a tradition or a place, and
how self-discernment and self-criticism do not need to be added from
outside. One way to approach this issue is to ask whether my tribe
could have their Book include social as well as physical sciences. They
might be able to use physics and run machines without modern self-
distance, but could they use sociology and run polls?

Imagine that the Book of the tribe contained information on the society, blueprints for how it should be organized, even a plan for some
changes. Tribe members could carry out surveys to determine which
social equations to apply, could criticize current events according to the
standards of the Book, could intervene in the society according to the
directions of the Book, without thereby creating the typical inner distance which we value so much.

This shows that our distance comes from more than having information about social roles or intervening in society according to a vision of
its structure. Priests and nobles and traders have been knowing and

82 doing these things for a long time; the Book would just let them be done more efficiently.

In fact, even if the Book contained a self-referential account of the tribe's way of living according to the Book, the tribe members might not automatically become modern distanced selves. Tribe members are already aware of how they depend on various physical laws; why should they not take various social laws in a similarly accepting spirit? The tribe members are not thereby *required* to stand at a reflective distance from their own identity and way of life, which may seem all the more complete for including such self-information. Members need not adopt a new identity as free inquirers or choosers among ways of life. Information alone would not constitute a change of identity. What would be required would be new ways of interacting, a set of social institutions that would make living new roles possible. The mere possession of self-referential descriptions does not create new forms of life.

We find it hard to imagine that social knowledge could come about except through self-reflective distance. Yet our ancestors and we ourselves have developed such an impure social inquiry; we have called it "history." In many of its styles the telling of history has resisted the typical modern dichotomies that the social sciences have accepted. History's circles can both undermine and deepen our social identity without turning us into pure detached observers. Again, we must ask what it means to be *in* a tradition or a place.

There is a kind of inner spaciousness that is part of being in a way of life or a set of beliefs. The tribe I described can get along without modern self-reflection, but it is their lack of that inner room to move that makes them unreal. This shows in that they have no politics and they make no metaphors. Would any power arrangements set up by the Book remain as unself-conscious and uncontested as I claim for their technology and knowledge? I isolated my tribe and made them peaceful, to avoid issues about the relation of knowledge and power, but this is unconvincing. And could any system of meaning remain as stolid and unchanging as my tribe's? They could not avoid differences in interpretation, and new ways of using the Book's language.

No one has ever claimed that politics and power struggles, or differences of interpretation and new metaphors, are distinctively modern. What kind of distance makes them possible? Is any dispute or self-criticism or change already an anticipation of modern reflective distance?

The root mistake in these matters is the idea that distance is created by adding movement to something that is already solidly present. This immediately present something might be social roles and values, economic distinctions, beliefs and desires, or personal identity, or even scientific results. In my thought-experiment I tried to push simple identity as far as it would go; the results should make us unhappy with that whole way of thinking.

If we imagine that there is some simple inhabitation of solid systems of meaning, then we have to complement this by imagining some pure, empty process of reflection, which can be defined by its form alone without reference to any content. But if identity and inhabitation have their own motion and distance built-in, then we will not need external reflection. What if nothing is simply given, if there is no neat system (or compact self) for reflection to add space to? What if beliefs and selves already contain their own spaciousness?

Define some notation consisting of a few symbols in contrast with one another, and specify some rules that say how to combine them in "grammatical" ways. Then look again and see how the symbols persist in suggesting ways of going beyond the rules you have set up (cf. Caputo 1987, chap. 5). New contrasts and illicit combinations are suggested just by the differences of the symbols. You do not have to bring in some external force to pry open space to envision alternatives. Nor is there any wall you can build which will stop the possibility of new combinations. You can declare them ungrammatical, but you cannot declare them unusable; they can create or be taken into new contexts. Your walls around the system become new items within the play of oppositions and combinations. Even though the possibilities the system generates are qualitatively limited, there is always already room to play and to extend the system by what I will later call metaphorical moves. This excessive play of contrast and combination was in motion from the beginning. What makes systems of meaning and belief possible also keeps them from ever being the delimited and simply identical wholes we imagine our ancestors possessing.

Our science, too, was described by the logical positivists as having a simple identity. Some have since read Kuhn as picturing scientists as simply inhabiting a normal science paradigm, then in times of crisis frantically sending up balloons in all directions, which provide views but no norms for decision. I suspect Kuhn may be closer to the ways of extending language which I describe later in terms of architectural metaphor. In any case, some have begun describing science as having a certain native spaciousness. Scientific theories, once seen as tight de-

84 ductive systems hovered over by the detached judging self, are being talked about as looser assemblages of images, metaphors, concepts, and techniques, as well as the important nets of propositions. Scientists find themselves within these historical assemblages, not above them, and the scientists can take advantage of the spaciousness within the theory to extend and question it. The scientist is a member of a community which gives and is given space by a loosely defined traditional assemblage. The tradition and the scientists help define each other; there is always already space to move.

As soon as we have anything (a word, an act) which might be meaningful, we have possible differences and instabilities.[1] Instead of opening a space where none existed before, modern self-reflection tries to restrict that native spaciousness and tame the generation of wild meanings.

DOUBTING MODERN DISTANCE

Who then are we? Are we the simple inhabitants of the truth? The tight self-distanced modern ones? A split-level compromise? All and none of these. If nothing is simply given, then neither are we. This playing with systems and keeping them open is not something we do from above. We are within it as we are within language and culture, as much products as makers. There is no simple inhabitation.

But even granting that our ancestors were not without play and inquiry, and that our distance and research is less pure than we imagine, there is still something different about us. We have *institutionalized* distance. Some of our ancestors might have thought as we do; none of them could have lived our lives, for the world was not changed to fit. Our ways of relating to one another are more formal, more flexible. We pay a price; our ways are also more empty, less measured and less in contact with the life beyond and around our reflections.

We find ourselves within new institutions that allow a freer identity, and this is no illusion. The illusion comes when we make this difference something total, when we imagine that our ancestors had no space to move, when we think that our self-reflection is the origin of freedom, and forget the motion and difference that was already there. We have roles and interactions that identify us with the process of reflection and choice, while we imagine our ancestors identified with some fixed unreflective structure. Neither is correct. They had more space to move; we are not really outside. Habermas is right that our society has new differentiations, but he conceives of the distinct spheres as places of simple inhabitation, which are then to be united by a dialogue which surrounds them from outside.

We are both less and more naive than our ancestors: less naive because we have more distinctions to make, more naive because we reduce our freedom of movement to a few modes of irony and reflection. We take the simplicities that come from our reflection as if they were its basis, projecting back on our ancestors closed systems they never lived, though neither did they live our divisions. Our ancestors moved more freely than we think. Medievals, for example, were no simple inhabitants of their beliefs. The huge systems of philosophy and theology had an aspect of play about them, even more so the songs and jokes that parodied sacred things and solemn disciplines without the superior ironic tone of so much of our humor. We have trouble achieving friendly parody that does not destroy connection.

Usually, we take the presumed simplicity of our ancestors as a mark of inferiority. Sometimes, though, when choice and inquiry become threatening, we find their imagined naiveté appealing. Then simple inhabitation becomes the ideal we can never return to: immediate awareness, union without question, integrity and fullness of motive and belief. Then the division between us and our ancestors becomes our own myth of origins, the story of a long-ago beginning of thought when beliefs were whole and innocent, an Eden from which we have been exiled when we ate of the tree of the knowledge of truth and falsehood.[2]

If we break away from that modern myth, and see the spaciousness native to any system of meaning, then perhaps modernity, for all its crucial freedoms, can seem a hardening of oppositions and a constriction of movement. It only maintains itself by insisting on splits and levels. If we criticize these splits, Habermas may protest that we seek a nostalgic return to premodern undifferentiated life. But it need not be so. We could live in science and myth and art and our attempts to relate them, without demanding that one of these be our true and simple home. We need not give up our reflection, our research, our distance, but we should compromise their purity. To suspect the purity of the differentiated spheres of culture is not to demand they be melted down into some romantic wholeness.

There is more than one way to be self-aware. Modern reflection, represented variously by Descartes' method and by sociological studies, can itself be put in context by an awareness in motion that does not

86   stand off, that sees sideways without the direct fixed stare, that speaks
many ways without one official voice. The shifting discourse need not
be a meta-language. The realm of language and culture has no center
where we could be in secure possession, and no border where we could
be in exile. The free-floating balloon still moves with the wind.

The Pantheon in Rome. A classical building that has continued through changes of context and use. Photo by Philip Isaacson. See pp. 125–27.

Crown Hall at the Illinois Institute of Technology in Chicago, designed by Mies van der Rohe. Modernist poetry of pure form and flexible space, presented in the name of functionalism. Photo by Hedrich Blessing, courtesy of Illinois Institute of Technology. See p. 88.

The Hirschorn Museum in Washington, designed by Gordon Bunshaft.
An abstract grid stares at the inner court. Photo by Philip Isaacson.
See p. 88.

Bouygues World headquarters in Paris, France, designed by Kevin Roche. Versailles redone for the corporate age.

Photo courtesy of Kevin Roche John Dinkeloo and Associates. See p. 118.

The Piazza d'Italia in New Orleans, designed by Charles Moore. Celebrating the local community's traditions with ironic references and twists. Photo courtesy of Centerbrook Architects. See pp. 132, 178.

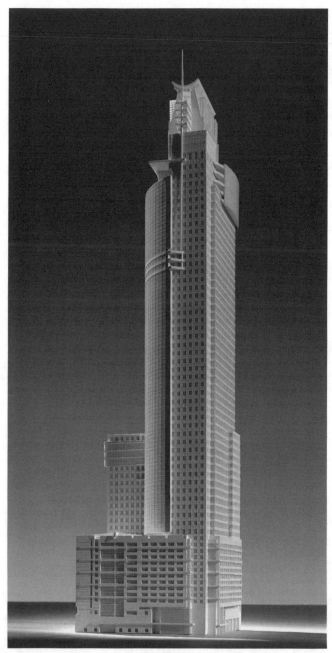

Model of the Ameritrust Tower in Cleveland, designed by Kohn Pedersen Fox. A collage of modern, postmodern, and local references, this building becomes a miniature cityscape that frustrates our expectations of unity; it can only "make sense" in context, and even then not as a single monument. Photo by Jock Pottle, courtesy of Kohn Pedersen Fox Associates. See p. 118.

Model of The National Gallery in London, with the main building, this addition fits into its monumental context. Sainsbury Wing designed by Venturi, Rauch, and Scott Photo by Heini Schneebeli, courtesy of Venturi, Rauch, and Brown. By displaying on its surface some fragments of the Scott Brown. See pp. 177–78.

Model of the Whitney Museum in New York, with the addition designed by Michael Graves. Breuer's museum (lower left) is upstaged by references to classical architecture, Rudolph, Schinkel, and others. Photo by William Taylor, courtesy of Michael Graves, Architect. See p. 119.

San Juan Capistrano Library in California, designed by Michael — a less ironic manner. Photo by Proto Acme Photo, courtesy of Graves. The Spanish Mission style modernized and extended in — Michael Graves, Architect. See p. 141.

Hillingdon Civic Centre, London, designed by Andrew Derbyshire, of Robert Matthew, Johnson, Marshall. A governmental building reusing in new ways, but without notable irony, architectural elements already familiar to its users. Photo by Keith Gibson, courtesy of RMJM. See p. 166.

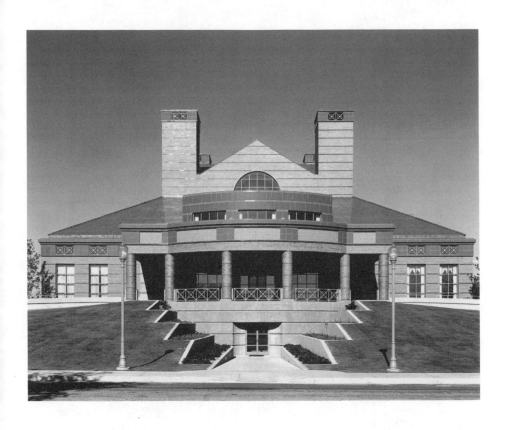

The River Crest Country Club in Fort Worth, designed by TAFT Architects. Historical blending with contemporary materials: a Georgian estate mated with Richardson. Photo courtesy of TAFT Architects. See p. 166.

The World Financial Center in Manhattan, designed by Cesar Pelli. Everyone's filmic dream of New York City. While their tops refer to the older buildings of the financial district, the shafts try to link the mammoth towers behind them into the city's scale. Photo by Peter Aaron/Esto, courtesy of Cesar Pelli and Associates. See p. 179.

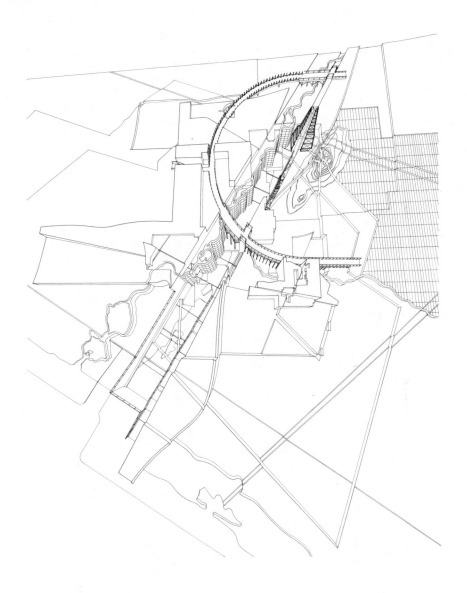

The University Art Museum, Long Beach, California, designed by Peter Eisenman. Denying both the building as monument and the building as part of nature, this design accumulates traces of the local natural, historical, and cultural networks, without resolving the gaps between them and without declaring any one code to be primary. Axonometric drawing courtesy of Eisenman Architects. See pp. 156–57.

] 8 [
MODERN ARCHITECTURE FROM PILLAR TO POST

The boldness of the best modern architects continues to inspire us even as we disagree. In appropriate mythic fashion, as the modern architects took over the schools and devoured their nineteenth-century parents, they assured their own eventual overthrow. Their large claims eventually generated equally sweeping counterclaims. For many, the great liberation proposed in the modern manifestos became the tyranny we must escape; for others, the pronouncements of the masters became the clichés of an aging father whose limitations have become all too obvious.

In this chapter I start with a conventional portrayal of the differences between modern and postmodern architecture. Then I argue that despite these differences they are deeply alike. That conclusion is often accepted today; my particular strategy will be to support it with a description of modernization drawn from the social sciences and philosophy. I examine how postmodernism and its modernist parents share a purified and distanced role for subjectivity, which distorts architecture's relation with history whether that relation is affirmed or denied.

The cluster of related trends in architecture that we call "the modern movement" was more varied than it declared itself to be. It was important for the modern revolution that its leaders be seen as standing together rejecting a narrow past. And now there is a narrow "modern architecture" to oppose. The debased versions of the International Style that fill our cities cannot be adequate emblems for the works of the modernist masters, or for the national and vernacular and compromise attempts that built so much of what surrounds us.[1]

Nonetheless, if we are going to talk about postmodernism, we need to recall the polemical picture of modernism. On the side of theory, most commentators take as canonically modern the international organization CIAM and its manifestos, the Bauhaus ideals as expressed by Gropius, Le Corbusier's *Towards a New Architecture,* and Giedion's historical accounts.

According to these documents, modern architecture liberated us by freeing us from the dead weight of traditional styles. This freedom came at the price of new restrictions: historical references were forbidden, and decoration was a crime. These restrictions were to open up

88　　possibilities that had been denied by the tyranny of the historical styles. Architecture could now progress according to its own free aesthetic impulses, and because of the unity of life, this would solve questions of function as well. Architecture shared with other modernist movements the break from tradition, but while architectural modernism stressed certain aspects of artistic modernism, it de-emphasized others. With the avant-garde, it strove to begin art anew with pure forms. But those forms were to be rational and controlled. Given the enthusiasm of some of its founders for technology, and architecture's perennial need to make friends with those in power, architectural modernism tied itself to those very rationalizing tendencies that were being opposed in avant-garde literature and painting (see the photo of IIT).[2]

While they proclaimed a revolution against nineteenth-century historicizing, the founders of the modern movement agreed with the nineteenth century that the architect must try to express the spirit of the age. There was a new age with a new spirit marked by technology and unlimited possibilities. A new self-consciousness had arrived. A modern building "must be true to itself, logically transparent and virginal of lies or trivialities, as befits a direct affirmation of our contemporary world of mechanization and rapid transit." It must represent "not the personal whims of a handful of architects avid for innovation at all cost, but simply the inevitable logical product of the intellectual, social, and technical conditions of our age." It must be devoid of reference to historical styles. "A breach has been made with the past, which allows us to envisage a new aspect of architecture corresponding to the technical civilization of the age we live in; the morphology of dead style has been destroyed; and we are returning to honesty of thought and feeling." That honesty should be embodied "not in stylistic imitation or ornamental frippery, but in those simple and sharply modelled designs in which every part merges naturally into the comprehensive volume of the whole." Modern architecture was not to be a new style but what architecture became when it was stripped of styles and was pure functional form, "the discovery of the ideal type of building " (see the Hirschorn Museum photo).[3]

POSTMODERN ARCHITECTURE

The great modern architects thought we were growing into a unified technological world that would express itself in an architecture that was direct and honest with its forms. Most postmodern architects claim the dramatic simple forms of modern architecture are passé, and we

cannot recapture the straightforward spirit in which they were built.
We postmoderns see how codes and cultures multiply and transgress, and we are not at home in any of them. When we build we must express the spirit of our age by manifesting the limits of any vocabulary through some ironic twist or mixture of different idioms.

The phrase *postmodern architecture* now has too many uses, but it still has some value. In general it connotes the end of the modern ideal of pure form, and the removal of the modernist barriers to historical reference. In the popular press the word seems most often applied to designer tall buildings that have historical ornament and some gestures toward the local context. For smaller buildings the word often connotes a certain vocabulary of arches, curved windows, smooth but blocky shapes with historical appliqué, and the like.

There is a postmodern ironic historicism in the buildings of Charles Moore and Robert Stern and Ricardo Bofill. There is a deconstructive architecture in recent projects of Peter Eisenman and Bernard Tschumi. There is the postmodernism of images and simulacra; a shopping mall might capture this, though the most appropriate architecture for this vision of our world would be a simple cube whose surfaces, inside and out, provided screens for projections that would change the building into any and every style.

Charles Jencks, who helped popularize the term *postmodern* in architecture, urged applying it to buildings, such as many designed by Charles Moore, that use historical forms and ornament without belonging to any one definite historical style, and have a self-consciously ironic or playful tone. Jencks calls this *double coding,* where a building speaks in a local vernacular but also makes ironic commentary upon its own language. In more recent writings Jencks seeks to appropriate the term especially for buildings that rework the classical and neoclassical vocabularies (cf. Jencks 1987b, esp. 352). Jencks's proposed meanings for the term apply to those buildings that have received the most press, such as Moore's Piazza d'Italia, Michael Graves's Portland and Humana buildings, and recent works by James Stirling.

A somewhat wider meaning was given the term by Paolo Portoghesi, who defines as postmodern any building that breaks the modern prohibition against historical reference, whether with ironic self-commentary or with vernacular earnestness. A still wider sense would include all of the above as well as buildings that break other modern prohibitions. A building with applied decoration that was neither ironic nor historical would still be postmodern by this wide criterion.[4]

If we wished to include deconstructive architecture under the label

90   *postmodern,* we would have to extend that term even further. All the senses thus far considered involve some movement away from abstraction and towards representation (cf. Klotz 1988, 4). Deconstructive architecture contests both sides of that duality. Thus I suggest that we distinguish between postmodern and deconstructive architecture, even though in philosophy and criticism the label *postmodern* is used by proponents of deconstruction to describe their own thought.

Most of what I say in this chapter is aimed at the "standard" postmodernism described by Jencks and Portoghesi. My concern is with the reentry of history into architecture, whether this is in a revivalist or ironic manner. I am not claiming that this is *the* important feature of current architecture, but whatever the fate of the current styles that receive the label *postmodern,* the modernist prejudice against history will no longer dominate design. As in the earlier chapters, I will be questioning theories that view our relation to history as either simple inhabitation or as detached criticism and ironic manipulation.

THE MODERN WORLD: WEBER

It is important to situate modern architecture and its aftermath within the wider process of modernization in society. That process reached a culmination in the last hundred years. Modernization's central achievement was the creation of relatively free (because they were formal and abstract) social processes inhabited by relatively free-floating individuals. Modern people are less attached to the naturally or culturally determined details of their identity than were people in more traditional societies, who identified more closely with their social roles and values. While it can be debated whether this detachment is as widespread as is claimed, modernity has brought the ideal of the detached individual, capable of judging his or her life and taking charge of its content by beginning anew.

Early in our century Max Weber studied the process of modernization from many perspectives, and his influence continues today. For Weber, modernity brings a rationalized world. In one area after another tradition gives way to modes of living based on disciplined efficiency and calculation. Substantive rationality is replaced by formal rationality. In traditional societies certain social patterns, values, and ends are taken as substantial poles fixed in the nature of things. Rational action in a traditional society consists of working consistently and efficiently according to those patterns to achieve those goals. Planning and choice are guided—and limited—by substantial social content contained in fixed values and ways of life. As societies modernize, the substantiality evaporates and rationality demands only that people maximize the fit of their means to their ends, whatever those ends may be. New possibilities are opened when substantive restrictions fall away. The process by which this happens is complex, but the result is a greater freedom of choice and a greater number of differentiated ways of dealing with the world and with our experience. The effect of modernization is to increase our available possibilities, and we choose among those so that we can best maximize our goals.

The modern spirit of maximization is at work, for example, in Gropius's arguments about the ideal size of a residence block. The entire argument depends on finding forms that maximize a combination of variables (population per unit area, but also the ideal amounts of light, air, and so on). Among other conclusions, Gropius declares that height restrictions on city buildings are "irrational" (Gropius 1965, 107). His argument makes use of what he takes to be sufficiently abstract natural goals so that no cultural specificity need be given to the investigation of density or light requirements. The results should be valid at all times and places.

Modern functional thought makes a break with history. Premodern tradition is seen as limiting human possibilities. Now, nothing is to be accepted or ruled out just because it has always been so. The widest possible field of options is open for our judgment. Modern architects saw themselves as sweeping like a storm through received ways of designing, building, and living; the new architects judged the worth of the old ways according to new universal criteria and opened up the field of choice.

Such willingness to judge traditional modes of life demands a new style of human selfhood, more flexible, self-critical, and internally disciplined than before, able to stand at a distance from what was previously taken as fixed. Weber traces the development of this new modern self and the social relations and institutions that it demands. The new self is a process of choice and control, a process without any particular substantive content. Accidents of birth, class, social role, none of these define what the self is or may become. Modern people must fashion their own lives, choosing patterns and values amid myriad possibilities, without any substantial reasons for the choices. There may be functional, instrumental reasons, but these refer to further ends that are themselves chosen, or at least reviewed, by the self. Modern self-

92   consciousness shows a process that can be described quite formally, without reference to social content. The social sciences depend on and promote this new self-consciousness. Their "methodological individualism" is for Weber a reflection of the true nature of selfhood, now stripped of the encrustations by which traditional society restricted freedom.

Weber sees this as the product of many related historical changes. Once it is achieved there is no way to bring back some privileged content that can guide or limit the process of choice. The separation of form and content cannot be undone; to return to a traditional mentality would involve either playacting or a loss of self-awareness, perhaps through religious conversion, which Weber called "the intellectual sacrifice."

If we cannot go back, neither can we advance beyond modern self-awareness, which is final because it has stripped down our identity as far as possible. Once we live in a society that has uncovered the pure form of our selfhood there seems nowhere else to go.

For Weber the structure of our social institutions can be judged only in terms of the goals the institutions serve, and not by received values or standards. Form should follow function. This allows institutions of unparalleled efficiency that liberate humanity from many of our historic scourges. Since these institutions can no longer be defined by the old historical limitations, the purified building forms of modern architecture might be their appropriate palaces.

But Weber might agree with those who criticize modern architecture for delivering a message of indifferent power and impersonal bureaucracy. Weber worries that modernity will betray the liberation it promises, leading beyond liberation to a bureaucratically administered flatness of life. Efficient administration encourages uniformity, and the inner discipline required to sustain modern selfhood tends to repress the variety which that selfhood could make possible. Weber expects a gray society, rational but stifling, disturbed from time to time by bursts of charismatic novelty that give way once again to rationalized routine. He offers little hope of relief; there is no content for life that can be insulated from the corrosive effects of efficiency and instrumental reason. The best he thinks we can do is to linger privately in warm humane pockets of culture and historical memory that escape, for a time, the spreading uniformity. This private realm is the modern space for art. We might see Weber's prescription acted out by a postmodern architecture that plays with historical references for ironic domestic enclaves, while decorating the surfaces of the bureaucratic control towers.

Could there be a way of thinking that was true to the essence of modernity yet denied Weber's pessimistic vision? Could we show that the primacy of instrumental reason and the loss of social content are not the whole story? This would mean showing that analyses such as Weber's, which see modernity in terms of a separation of the form of the social process from its particular content, are not the last word about the modern condition. This is what Hegel tried to do in the 1820s.

Hegel is a loyal partisan of modernity, believing that the changes of the last few centuries represent the culmination of history. Nonetheless he criticizes many features of the society of his day. There are two phases to his discussion of modern society, corresponding to two social forms, civil society and the state. Civil society is Hegel's term for the social relations that arise when traditional roles and values no longer define what it means to be an individual. With the growth of self-reflection and inner division come new forms of selfhood demanding that all the content of life be mediated through the insights and decisions of self-sufficient individuals. Such modern selves can exist only through social relations that are free of any fixed substantial content. Hegel sees such patterns of interaction coming into being through the Reformation, the growth of the free market, and other modernizing trends. The process is not accidental; it expresses a necessary sequence derived from the logical principles that structure any complex historical totality.

The modern self is not identified with any particular historical mode of being. In civil society no tradition dictates how one should live; modern selves can use what Hegel (like Weber) calls "formal rationality" in the choice of goals and means. Civil society separates the formal process of choice from the particularities of content. This results in a vast increase in our possibilities. In the idealized free market, for example, the forms of contract and exchange are clearly defined, but contracts can have any content, with no traditional (and only a few procedural) restrictions. Hegel analyzes the market and its supporting institutions and argues that these enact an essential human liberation.

But they also contain deep problems. Civil society has in itself no particular goal, only the expansion of its system of exchange and satisfaction. Hegel sees a whole catalog of economic and social harms stemming from the unrestricted growth of commodity exchange and the endless multiplication of needs characteristic of civil society. In ad-

94   dition there are cultural problems. Within civil society's abstracted
way of life traditional ways and values can at best be considered as hob-
bies. The modern self cannot be defined by them. If civil society were
the whole of human community then shared human identity would be
reduced to the lowest denominator of needs, and would be dominated
by capricious fashion and artificial needs.

There are some profound differences from Weber in just how Hegel
connects the self with social relations, but so far his general picture
seems remarkably like Weber's. Yet Hegel would not accept Weber's
pessimism. He argues that the structures characteristic of civil society
(the separation of the universal form of interaction from the particular
content) can operate only if inserted into a larger context. Civil society
describes itself using categories that it thinks are ultimate but which are
not. They can only be thought, and the reality they describe can only
exist, in a larger context described in more dialectical categories.

Hegel analyzes the overarching movement of spirit in history
through stages where the whole is formed by an immediate fusion of
form and content (traditional society), where the whole is dominated by
an acknowledged separation of form and content (civil society), and
finally where the whole is articulated into a process that has its own form
for content (the fully developed modern state). Concretely this means
that civil society is not the last word in social relations. It actually exists as
the economic side of a more comprehensive social whole, the state,
which holds civil society's expansion in check and corrects many of its
bad effects.

In the state individual and social whole come together in more complex mutual dependencies than would be found in civil society alone.
Hegel is often accused of subordinating the individual to the whole,
and the particular institutions he describes do have that effect, but
such was not his intent. He was trying to find a way to realize individual freedom without moving backward to a traditional fusion of
form and content, but also without affirming as ultimate the splits
found in civil society. This did necessitate a different concept of individuality from that characteristic of the liberal thought that glorifies
civil society, but Hegel is far from reducing the individual to a mere
expression of the state's wholeness.

Hegel studied the categories of being and thought, and he described
the necessary motions and interdependencies needed for any self-sufficient whole to exist, in society or in nature. He then attempted to
translate those descriptions into institutions whose principles he could
discern already coming to birth in his contemporary world.

Thus Hegel provided his own notion of the postmodern, or rather, of the perfected modern. He tried to do what Weber would deem impossible: to join modern freedom to some privileged social content. The efficient operations of instrumental reason and the endless possibilities opened by modernity were to be restricted by certain social structures that could be affirmed as rational in and of themselves. These structures were derived from the properties of any rationally comprehensible society. They were not purely procedural; they included concrete historical content. On the most basic level that content would be the particular spirit of the nation, for instance, the Frenchness of the French. But within the state were many subcommunities (mostly stemming from the division of labor) each with its own associated roles and ways of life. Hegel's task was to show how the purely rational categories and the historical content come together. He did this by assigning the various subcommunities and national spirits to different stages in the self-reflection of spirit. Because that structure of spirit's self-development can be independently known apart from society and politics, the historical content of modern life becomes rationally justified. This allows the modern individual to feel at home both as a reasoning modern self and as a person with a particular historical tradition, which can be seen to have its place in the development of the self-transparent universal process.[5]

Like Weber, Hegel emphasizes that modernity brings a new self-consciousness that changes our relation to history. Unlike Weber, Hegel allows a relation to tradition that goes beyond instrumental calculations of efficiency, though the traditional content stays within a self-awareness dominated by modern freedom.

For Hegel, art traditionally embodied the vision and ideals that were the core of a people's identity. Traditional artists expressed the deepest principles and values of their age. But art can no longer express directly what it means to live in our world. To dwell at home in the modern world we must comprehend how the oppositions and splits that threaten the unity of modern life are in fact reconciled and contained. This requires a knowledge of the process by which spirit achieves its unity through opposition and contradiction. Such knowledge cannot be expressed by images, or by traditional concepts; it demands the dialectical method, whose motions cannot be revealed except in its own terms. So art, which by Hegel's definition embodies its insights in matter or images, can no longer contain our most developed self-awareness. Besides, modern distance and self-reflection have touched the artist, who is now too self-aware for straightforward identification

96 with the objects and values portrayed. This results in an art that lacks the heroic side of classical art, and that portrays ordinary objects, exhibiting in them the artist's own technique or ironic humor.

While his discussion of architecture does not go beyond the Gothic (which was then being revived), Hegel's description of the painters of his time might be applied to the postmodern architect today:

> No content, no form, is any longer immediately identical with the inwardness, the nature, the unconscious substantial essence of the artist. . . . The artist's attitude to his topic is on the whole much the same as the dramatist's who brings on the scene and delineates different characters who are strangers to him. The artist does still put his genius into them, he weaves his web out of his own resources but only out of what is purely universal or quite accidental there, whereas its more detailed individualization is not his. For this purpose he needs his supply of pictures, modes of configuration, earlier forms of art which, taken in themselves, are indifferent to him and only become important if they seem to him to be those most suitable for precisely this or that material. Moreover . . . the topic comes to the artist from the outside; he works to a commission. . . . However much he puts his heart into the given topic, that topic yet always remains to him a material which is not in itself directly the substance of his own consciousness. (Hegel 1975, 605–6)[6]

For Hegel there is no longer any subject matter that art can take perfectly seriously. The difference between Hegel and ironic or deconstructive postmodernism is that for Hegel there remains something else that still is "the substance" of the artist's consciousness and can be regarded with "an inherently affirmative interest."[7] The motion of spirit, described in logical terms, lies at the heart of consciousness and is known as such. It is taken quite seriously in religion and philosophy. For the postmodern who refuses to admit that core (or refuses to make it self-transparent as Hegel does), the artist's activity becomes more empty and ironic than Hegel envisioned. But, lacking Hegel's substance, does this irony only return us to the distanced selfhood Hegel is trying to overcome?

THE MODERN WORLD: HEIDEGGER

Is it possible to share the goal of moderating Weber's complete separation of the self from all particular content and yet avoid Hegel's completely reconciled whole? Doing so would demand new ways of thinking about the issues on which Hegel differed from Weber: the nature of identity, the relation of the self to history, the place of reason, and so on. Martin Heidegger sought these new ways.

Where Hegel is upbeat about modernity, Heidegger is gloomy. But he does not recommend escape. Heidegger describes our world in two related ways, in terms of subjectivity and in terms of technology. In his first view he sees an ever increasing emphasis on the individual self as the foundation of truth and value. Descartes and Nietzsche exemplify this trend. Our contemporary technical, scientific, and artistic world is structured around the self as the center affirming its own being through control of all other things. Modern freedom is the self-assertion of a will that dominates through knowledge and power in order to secure its own empty self-certainty.

Heidegger challenges this modern view of the self and develops a rival description that emphasizes the temporality of experience, an account in which the pure unified modern self appears as derivative rather than foundational. He does not deny the modern experience of the self and its world but he asserts that this is only one way self and world may be revealed, a way that depends on the tensions and dispersions of our temporalized existence that the modern experience fails to grasp.

Later, Heidegger somewhat changes his description of modernity and its overcoming. The description in terms of subjectivity is now seen as too "metaphysical." In the new description (in terms of technology and *das Gestell*) the contemporary world has no center. The will to order and form affects us all but is not rooted in individual selves, who now are seen as themselves subject to the demand that they be available for ordering. Rather than being material for the will of the self, other things stand as the reserve available for a general call to order and control.

In these new terms we will be freed from modernity, to the extent we can be, when we realize that the conditions that make possible the call to modern control are not themselves describable in its terms. This frees us from thinking and acting as if the modern mode were the only or the ultimate way to be. In this Heidegger rejects the ultimacy of the terms in which Weber analyzes our situation. But the realization Heidegger talks about, the "thinking" it enables, does not provide any new way to be. There is nothing in Heidegger parallel to Hegel's prescriptions for a perfected modernity.

Heidegger sometimes sounds as if some conversion on our part, some change of attitude or concepts, might enable us to escape the rule

98 of modern ordering and technology. His essays "The Thing" and "Building, Dwelling, Thinking," among others, have been taken as describing a way to dwell at home in a unified world of places whose deep meaning is articulated and supported in appropriate buildings and artifacts. In this interpretation modern life is seen as having covered over a primal world of human dwelling, which if we but change ourselves somehow we can rediscover or rebuild. But this reading is misleading; according to Heidegger all we can do is think through our relation to our present world while awaiting the coming of new revelations of beings and world. There is nothing we can do on our own to overcome modernity; if there were, that very action would only replay modern control. We can, however, acknowledge our helplessness. Paradoxically, in doing so we will partially escape the modern definition of our selves.

This is possible because of the un-centered universal demand for ordering and control that claims us in the modern world. There is no highest being we can cite as the source of our predicament. Thinking in the proper manner we can come to realize that the way beings stand revealed does not itself stem from any of the beings that surround us; it is prior, defining us and how things come to presence with us. If we realize how the basic meaning things are revealed as having does not depend on our subjective doings, we will begin to realize how the modern definitions of human life are not the whole story. They are part of one historical fate; there could be others, and the "event" by which those fates are delivered is not itself something that can be described in modern terms of a relation between subjects and objects. That event is not a being to be charted, planned or manipulated (as in Weber), nor is it an inner motion we can be at one with (as in Hegel, whose grand reconciliation Heidegger sees as one more manifestation of the modern principles of subjectivity and order).

Modern subjectivity is not the source of its own meaning, and the modern call to order is not the last word. The seemingly endless possibilities opened in the modern world are themselves qualitatively limited, though not by any subjective act of ours. Experiencing this does not start a new age, though it does urge us to delve into our historical tradition. While this will not suggest any particular privileged content for our lives, it does free us to live with a self-understanding that is different from the modern definition of us as wills, workers, consumers, and manipulated manipulators available for ordering.

Heidegger criticized the modern world while clinging to the landscape of a provincial Germany that he knew was being destroyed even as he wrote. There is an ambiguity about his essays on art and architecture that encourages the romantic hope that we might pierce the technological skin of our world and discover a rich dwelling still available to us. In several later chapters I discuss this hope for a recovery of our sense of place. But officially Heidegger, like Hegel, believes that in the modern world art has lost whatever power it once had. It has been reduced to the business of supplying stimuli on demand, and machines for living. Unlike Hegel, Heidegger hints that perhaps the power of art might be restored, though not by our creating some new style. Art today cannot renew the barren modern landscape, but it can still awaken in us the sense of the withdrawn happening by which we are destined to live in the modern world. Once awakened, that sense changes our relation to our world. The change, however, is not an escape. It remains an ambivalent mixture of complicity and understanding.

THE POSTMODERN WORLD

If the cosmic pillar of early shrines speaks of the centered fixity attributed to traditional society, modernity finds its emblem in the functional pilotis of Le Corbusier, and postmodernity in the oversized columns of Bofill and the invisible hitching posts in the parking lots of Las Vegas.

While in architecture the term *postmodern* has had its vogue and is beginning to fracture, in philosophy the phrase *postmodern thought* has been increasingly used to describe movements that have been influenced by Nietzsche and Heidegger. I mentioned in an earlier chapter the "metaphysics" that these movements attack; modern architecture, with its rational forms and technological purism, is seen as one more expression of the metaphysical search for unity, pure presence, and firm grounds.

Among the movements loosely labeled postmodern, deconstructive thought is the closest to Heidegger. It refuses to proclaim a postmodern era, for that would be to fall into the modern pattern of seeking continual novelty. Rather, we come to experience the limits and the self-undermining of modernity, without being able to escape into a new age.[8]

Going on from what Heidegger says concerning the finitude of any revelation of the being of things, deconstruction sees a permanent tension between the modern claim to unity and its own self-limitation within a dispersion that escapes such unification, while making it possible. Showing this tension and self-transgression within the very texts

100 and claims of the tradition, deconstructive thought helps undermine modern claims to control, order, and transparent rationality. But it does not replace them. Rather it attempts to locate them within a space that they do not dominate. This has the effect of critique, though not one that proceeds from rival first principles.

Deconstruction concerns our manner of dwelling and does not itself provide any substantial meaning for a new home. There is no home in which we can dwell as we desire. Instead of inventing new styles, we maneuver the pieces of the old to express and undermine their unities. Gianni Vattimo (1988) discusses the kind of changes that might be expected from this process. In architecture this can lead to the deliberately frustrated centerings and self-references in Peter Eisenman's House X, or to the divergences from unified form and the traditional goals of building in the projects of Bernard Tschumi. I will argue later that such works have a crucial though marginal role to play in the postmodern city.

The most self-proclaimed postmodern thought is identified with Lyotard, who at times speaks confidently of a new age (although he is more circumspect than many of his followers). As we saw in an earlier chapter, for Lyotard our age is losing the total meanings characteristic of both tradition and modernity. The central self is a myth, and its pure rationality gives way to a diversity of language games and practices that are irreducible to each other. Amid this plurality we should play our games lightly and ironically, inventing new rules as we go. No one game can define us and there is no pure meta-game above them all. Innovation is possible, and we need, for our liberation, constantly to invent new moves, new language games, new ways of being. We are caught within the infinite displacement of images (or of signifiers, simulacra, surfaces, intensities, and so on) and we should swim buoyantly in that flow rather than seeking firm ground.

Lyotard's postmodernity is an explicit extension of the avant-garde modernism that insisted on continual novelty, at the expense of the modernism that urged rationality and control. This is the reverse of the modern architect's preference for rationality over avant-garde experimentation. For Lyotard the rational society is the terror we must battle. In its concrete form that terror is the impersonal flow of international capital and its technology of control. Lyotard does not see this in orthodox Marxist terms, which still accept one grand story that aligns all history. Lyotard does not reject technology, which he sees as potentially liberating. Computer technology played a central role in the exhibition of our postmodern sensibility that Lyotard organized in

Paris. Lyotard's vision of a fragmented yet technologically connected 101
postmodern world resembles that of Jean Baudrillard, who is hardly so
optimistic about our chances for creative innovation, because for him
the play of simulacra washes out the differences (between language
games) that Lyotard wants to promote.

To express and support this new age postmodern architecture needs
a proliferation of styles, and new games played with the old pieces.
While Lyotard's thought can be taken as calling for more novelty than
deconstructive thought, both have been used to justify an architecture
that uses historical reference ironically. For the most part, however,
postmodern ironic historicism does not need Lyotard and Heidegger;
its theories speak the language of semiotics and structuralism.[9]

Hegel's description of the painter who has no substantive identity
with the content of his art seems appropriate for these architects. Now
the question returns: if there is no deep dwelling to be rediscovered
and integrated into our building, if we are to be deconstructive or to
invent new moves and games, if, in Hegel's terms, there is no substance
of our consciousness, then have we escaped the distanced modern selfhood described by Weber and Hegel? Or is postmodernism just modern subjectivism with a stylish costume?

Irony and the Suspended Architect

We might have expected that when the modern prohibition against historical references weakened, architects would relax into the older
traditions, or begin new ones, and get on with building readable structures that fit our world. Vernacular and "invisible" architecture could
be approved again. Give architecture back to the people!

Such slogans have been heard, but they have not set the trend. We
see distanced subjects playing with history, double coding, irony, applied decoration, complexity and contradiction. This is different from
modernist planners banishing history, but the distance remains. Why
don't we find architects being praised in the media for devoting themselves to non-ironic development of traditional motifs?

> While postmodernists acknowledge history, many seem compelled
> to torture it until an "original" contribution to artistic Progress
> has been made. . . . A tangible burden of guilt still weighs on those
> who would deal with the past un-self-consciously, without coyness
> or irony. To regain fluency in the traditional language of design—
> and to make the product of such a collaboration with past cen-
> turies accessible to a broad cross section of society . . . requires a

redefinition of the very heart of artistic creativity. (Brolin 1985, 292, 309–10)

What are we to make of this? Is it just a passing condition soon to change once a residual modernist sensibility wears off? Or is it a matter of media bias and marketing strategies, to last as long as ironic buildings can charge higher rents? (cf. Blake 1984). Or is it because the architects are trained to play elitist games and can't settle down with the people? (cf. Wolfe 1981). Or are the architects victims of bad philosophy turned into dogma? (Cf. Brolin 1976 and 1985.) Or is it perhaps because our world itself is multiply coded, ironic, complex and contradictory? It is the last alternative that links architectural practice to postmodern philosophy and criticism. I partly agree with this diagnosis, though in a later chapter I stress the difference between claiming that we must express the unified spirit of our plural age, and claiming that there is no unified spirit of our age that we must express. For now, we need to look at the self-consciousness implicit in the ironic imperative.

Buildings that play ironic games lead a risky life. Suppose that a building has been carefully designed with ironic references to past styles. As time goes on and the building is used, do the ironic references and undertones survive? Or are they smoothed out as the building takes on its own immediate identity?

Still, it can be argued that if postmodern irony is not always perceived by the average user, it continues to be evident to the informed professional. Jencks canonized this division with his notion of double coding.

> One must start by defining a basic opposition in coding between the inhabitant and the professional, perhaps taking as one departure point Basil Bernstein's fundamental distinction between "restricted" and "elaborated" codes . . . a popular, traditional one which like spoken language is slow-changing, full of clichés and rooted in family life, and secondly a modern one full of neologisms and responding to quick changes in technology, art and fashion as well as the avant-garde of architecture. (Jencks 1977, 129–130)[10]

Notice that Jencks has here almost reproduced the division between traditional and modern consciousness that furnished the basis for the story of modernity told by Weber and others. Jencks differs from the modern story in that he allows the postmodern artist no pure language or formally neutral point of view. But the fast-moving professional

code holds a position above local tradition just as the modern architect's rationality placed him above history.

The concepts Jencks uses in his argument for double coding are basically modern. This can be seen in his argument on why we cannot ever
return to a single level of coding.

> There is an unbridgeable gap between the elite and popular codes,
> the professional and traditional values, the modern and vernacular
> language, and since there is no way to abolish this gap without a
> drastic curtailment in possibilities, a totalitarian maneuver, it
> seems desirable that architects recognize the schizophrenia and
> code their buildings on two levels. (1977, 130)

A return to one-level coding, such as was urged by Brolin in the quotation above, is impossible because double coding *allows more possibilities*.
This argument resembles Weber's: the special professional self-
consciousness keeps us apart from premodern methods of building and
increases our freedom.

Some who talk about postmodern architecture speak as if with the
modernist barriers down we can roam freely through the past, taking
historical allusions and forms from where we will for our double coding or ironic enjoyment. The fall of the modernist prohibition against
historical reference coincides with a new world where history is available but we are not restricted by the premodern traditions. We, in our
self-consciousness, can use all of history as our material.

> Architecture can now recycle in new syntactic contexts traditional
> forms, taken from anywhere. The world now emerging is search-
> ing freely in memory, because it knows how to find its own
> "difference" in the removed repetition and utilization of the entire
> past. . . . History is the "material" of logical and constructive op-
> erations, whose only purpose is that of joining the real and the
> imaginary through communication mechanisms whose effective-
> ness can be verified. (Portoghesi 1983, 13, 26, 31)
>
> Why, if one can afford to live in different ages and cultures, restrict
> oneself to the present, the locale? Eclecticism is the natural evolu-
> tion of a culture with choice. (Jencks 1977, 127)

We recognize here the Nietzschean will to power that appropriates the
already formed and revalues it into a new meaning. This attitude gets
results: Venturi puts a temple in the garden; Isozaki puts the Campidoglio at Tsukuba; Krier wants to put a ziggurat at La Villette. The
architects seem to roam freely. And they are creatively changing their
historical originals for the new context: the temple is a decorated shed;

the Japanese Campidoglio conspicuously lacks a heroic central focus; the ziggurat would be a hotel.

We are told that we can do this because we hold historical content within a new self-consciousness. Unlike our literal-minded ancestors and eclectic nineteenth-century grandparents (not to mention our narrow modern parents), we understand the nature of coding and the semiotics of architecture and, in that awareness, can use all of history as material for play. Our eclecticism is different; in Jencks's terms it is "radical" rather than "weak" because we can choose styles based on a developed semiotic theory.[11]

All this sounds suspiciously similar to the earlier quotations from Gropius implying that the modern style was not a style at all but a free creation based on logic and technology, which one arrived at by abandoning styles and following the strict logic of function. For the postmodern theorists quoted above, history provides a space for free movement. Of course they are not saying that we should follow a strict logic of function. What they are saying is that the postmodern architect stands toward history differently because of a special self-consciousness. But that is what the modern movement claimed. Moderns and postmoderns disagree about historical reference, but is that significant? No style, all styles, what's the difference?

Polemics against modern architecture attacked as naive the modern belief that its forms would fit the new industrial world everywhere. This missionary and colonizing attitude is said to have reduced architecture to a few mute words about power and efficiency. Postmodern architecture is supposed to respect local semiotic codes and taste cultures. Architects and theorists speak of the need to adopt (and adapt) the language of the community and its unavoidable cultural archetypes. The free play of imagination is to be tempered by the need to communicate, to make a legible architecture that fits its context, to be, in Venturi's words, "expert in current conventions."

This seems to leave the architect curiously suspended, dipping into "their" context for a particular commission. Once the architect understands the client's vocabulary and codes, the building can use conventional elements for legibility, with "high art" supplying the twists and ironies that delight other architects.

This chameleon facility with local codes, this ability to understand the native tribe and its language while remaining above it all, doesn't it sound suspiciously like Weber's social scientist, who dwells nowhere, even in his modern home?

The modern architect disdained historical codes, believing our civilization had advanced to a universal pure language of form. The postmodern architect sees through all historical codes, believing our civilization has advanced to a vision of ironic plurality. Is the postmodern architect just another distant modern self who happens to have other goals for the exercise of instrumental rationality?

If we would escape the modern, we must avoid the temptation of saying that after the complete barrier between the architect and history we now have a complete freedom with history. To flip from no access to total access is to stay within the modern. Perhaps we need to envision more carefully what would be truly beyond the modern: the switch from "all or none" to "some."

The really nonmodern idea would be that the architect's inhabitation of the world does not involve the modern ideal of total freedom and flexibility, even in its postmodern guises.[12] We have to understand differential availability. Not every local code can be entered into. We are not modern detached subjects, and yet we do live in a self-consciously multiple world. Trying to understand this will be the burden of the subsequent chapters.

If we try to think through just how the architect's own activity is located and finite, we may find that we can have styles and contents of our own, yet with awareness and practices that do not reduce either to traditional fixity or to modern distance. We may find our historical dwelling, one that is not unified, but one for which we care in a way that is neither rational administration nor ironic play.

] 9 [
WHERE DO THE ARCHITECTS LIVE?

We hear a great deal about local context these days. Even the jet-set creators of signature buildings deliver some words about context before they drop their creations into the midst of our cities. Architects flit here and there, checking out native languages. Perhaps the architects' designs treat a language ironically; perhaps they treat it earnestly. But where do the architects live?

In this chapter I will argue against universalism in architecture, whether modern or postmodern. Changing the modern "no!" against history into the postmodern "let it all in!" solves nothing. The significant move would be to accept *some* languages, some design vocabularies, as *native,* without saying that the architect lives in the fixed, bounded space of possibilities we attribute to the traditional, premodern mentality.

In the heyday of modernism architecture school often began with a course devised at the Bauhaus, in which students worked through a series of exercises whose purpose was to make them confront colors, shapes, and materials directly. The students were to learn to deal with colors and materials in a way free from traditional ideas about appropriate design. The course was to help them begin anew, without historical prejudice, as pure designers confronting pure problems. Thus the students could develop that universal design language that modernism sought for the new civilization.

In his theories about modernization Max Weber claimed that any remaining pockets of substantive traditional values were being pushed to the edges of life by the triumphant march of instrumental rationality. The modern movement in architecture made similar claims. There might be external constraints on the new universal culture and its designs, but there were no intrinsic limitations within the new culture itself, since it was not based on prescribed substantive values and social roles.

The modernist universal language has become suspect in recent years, but it is not clear what is supposed to replace it. Almost no one suggests a simple revival of the traditional styles. Instead, we have ironic reuse of traditional materials. This postmodern irony also appears to have no particular shape of its own and no internal limits. It replays modern universalism with the signs reversed. But where do the architects live?

We need to think about the location of the architects, not just about the clients' semiotic codes or taste cultures. What does it mean for the architect to have limits and native languages? A limit is where something ends, but it is also, like a native language, where something begins.

Modernism presupposes that once the self or society has been purified of traditional restriction it will face an unlimited field of possible actions. There may be contingent constraints of many kinds, but in principle our purified vision and actions begin afresh with the widest field of possibilities. In contrast I want to assert that history opens only limited possibilities. The architect lives somewhere definite.

At first glance it seems a cliché to say the architect lives in a definite place. There are a host of factors, none of which seem especially dramatic, which locate the architect: her early experience and education, books she has read and buildings she has seen; what is current in the profession, what the public will pay for, regional taste; available materials, the quality of local construction skills, and the like. For example, to be an architect in Maine where I live means you are surrounded by the historical presence of northern New England villages and mill towns, several typical styles of wood construction, including plain farmhouses and shingle-style cottages, the cold climate, and other factors all of which are quite different from what might influence an architect working in Atlanta. The Maine architect may sketch a form but decide it was not saleable, or that the materials were not available, or that it would not fit in with the rest of the town. We all live somewhere and suffer various influences. So what?

What is at stake is this: could the Maine architect, though in fact limited by various regional factors, in principle access an unlimited field of possible forms and styles? This is the modern (and often the postmodern) claim that presupposes the detached modern self and society.

We need to examine how the architect relates to possibilities. In one sense, this is a very abstract issue. For the architect does not relate to "possibilities;" the architect deals with designs that are acceptable to the client or not, constructible or not, and other practical limitations that cannot be easily joined into some master list of what is "possible."

But the mundane issues hide a deeper question. In deciding what the client could be persuaded to accept, or what shapes the local trades could construct, the architect relates to a certain background. What is the *repertory* from which the recommended form is drawn? What are

108   the limits, if any, of the field of possible forms that the architect works from?

I will explore this question by considering several suggestions. In deciding what is concretely possible the architect might draw from a repertory that consists of all *possible* forms, or all *historical* forms, or all forms the architect has *experienced*. None of these suggestions will prove adequate, but examining them will help our understanding of limits to the language of architecture.

DOES ARCHITECTURE SPEAK A LANGUAGE?

Concerning limits, in this and later chapters I will be referring to architectural *languages* and *vocabularies*. Though this is a common way of speaking about architecture, the practice needs some defense.[1] It seems clear that if we define language strictly then architecture does not possess a language. (Though it is also true that in many of its uses language itself is less "language"-like than some philosophers would have us believe.) Current discussions about the nature of language mostly center around the structure of sentences and what constitutes their meaning. Architecture contains no sentences; buildings do not combine their parts to make predicative or relational assertions.[2]

However, architecture does have something analogous to words, namely the elements in architectural design that stand in mutual contrasts within chains of substitution and combination. For example, consider the classical orders, or the varied modernist types of windows. When a Doric column or a strip window is present, it is experienced as there in place of some other order or window that could have been used. When the user experiences a building in this way the user "understands" the building as one possible expression using a vocabulary or code that is capable of other expressions. This is similar to someone who understands the meaning of a word, or a move in a game, through knowing the other possible words or moves that could have been used.

While architectural elements stand in mutual contrasts that are organized loosely into vocabularies, and they combine in ways guided by conventions, those conventions are not like the strict rules for combining words into sentences. They are more analogous to the flexible rules for combining sentences into paragraphs and texts (cp. Donougho 1987, 62). A column supporting a lintel, or a wall and a window, do not make a sentence that predicates some quality of an object. But such subgroupings can combine with each other into a whole that has many of the qualities of a text. Like a text, a building makes a separate object that may or may not be a "whole" and that can be analyzed and read in different ways. While a building cannot make one precise point about one object, it can act as a text might in opening up a whole world of activity and meaning. Also, more like a text than a sentence, a building can violate the modes of organization usual for its "genre," though those modes remain present as what has been departed from.[3]

Like linguistic expressions, a building may be a move in many games at once. The choice of architectural vocabulary and the way that vocabulary is handled is also a social and political statement. No language game exists alone, though they all have some independence. We exist as the intersection of many codes and games, at once constrained and constituted by that multiplicity.

Buildings also have an involvement and bodily presence that cannot be captured by speaking about signs and communication systems. Living a building is not like reading a message. Some would take this as severely limiting the use of terms like "language" and "vocabulary" in discussing architecture (cf. Klotz 1988, 420). I would rather say that this points up the mistake in conceiving language as only a matter of signs and communication systems.

The Master Language

Consider now the first suggestion mentioned above for how an architect might decide what is feasible in a given context: she draws from a repertory consisting of all possible architectural forms. To describe that repertory we might use geometry. Any building occupies a volume; imagine all possible volumes. The task is difficult; there is an uncountably infinite number of shapes a volume could have. Combine these with the similar number of possible surfaces. Even granting that not all the shapes would be perceptibly different to us and that fewer still would stay upright if built, the number would still be non-denumerably infinite. Such a repertory is un-surveyable, and so useless to us; we need a catalog.

Yet given the aim of making all possible forms available, we cannot use any specific architectural vocabulary to provide a catalog of the possible forms. In terms of the suggestion we are considering, specific architectural vocabularies would present subsets of the larger collection. What we would need is a master language that makes the total set available.

It would seem that geometry should provide the master language. The Platonic solids and other simple shapes can be discerned in most

110   constructions; perhaps some suitable geometric language could be devised for the total shape of all buildings. But this is doubtful; what set
of purely geometric elements would serve equally well to analyze, say,
Isozaki's Los Angeles Museum of Contemporary Art (whose decomposition into simpler solids seems straightforward), Hagia Sophia
(where the decomposition is ambiguous), a New England farmhouse
(where the small deviations from regular shapes are important in the
design), and Porre's Cuban Center (where the historical and biological
associations overwhelm any purely geometric analysis). A great many
abstract geometrical analyses can be applied to these buildings, but it is
not clear how we would select *the* basic analysis; there is no one clear
canonical decomposition of the total shape suitable for every case. Even
if this were possible, such analysis would be more relevant to some
buildings than to others.

Other purported master languages have been based on functional
analyses. Units such as entrances, walls, stairs, windows, or functions
such as entering, supporting, extending, ascending, and so on, have
been suggested. Though none of these proposals have been worked
out in sufficient detail, they all run into problems. Either the number of
basic units multiplies without clear boundaries, or else the language is
applied with great difficulty to the variety of styles, periods, and
cultures already available. As heuristic methods of analysis such proposals have their merits, but when employed by architects as a supposedly universal language, the proposals merely become more local
dialects.

It is certainly possible to point out formal features that show up in
virtually all architecture. Symmetry, balance, scale, flow of space, and
so on, are present (as affirmed or as denied) in any building. But these
formal characteristics do not make a universal vocabulary; they are features that can be exhibited in different ways by different vocabularies.
They are analogous not to elements of a vocabulary but to features of a
text; texts can be described as balanced or symmetrical no matter in
what language or genre they are written.

Those inclined to structuralism have sought another kind of universal
language by seeking basic elements from which the various architectural
vocabularies might be generated. If one gives up the attempt to find one
master vocabulary for architecture (as people gave up the quest to find
some basic vocabulary underlying all the languages spoken in the
world), one might still seek some kind of elements which, while not
themselves vocabulary items, still are universally present. The parallel
here is phonetic analysis. For example, aspirated and unaspirated "k" (as

in "kick" vs. "skin") are not distinguished in English (they are allophones of one phoneme), but they can be used to differentiate words in ancient Greek or Chinese (there they belong to different phonemes). The linguist searches for basic contrasts in terms of which the phonemes of all languages are constituted: voiced/unvoiced, aspirated/ unaspirated, tongue placement positions, and many others. Phonemes of any language can be analyzed into bundles of these contrasts. Though no languages share exactly the same phonemes they all employ the same sub-phonemic contrasts.

Phonetic analysis is astoundingly successful. Attempts to perform the same analysis on the lexical level by finding basic "sememes" behind all words have met with less success. If there were architectural parallels to these kinds of analysis they would not themselves be items in any architect's vocabulary but rather those basic elements from which any vocabulary was constituted. One might imagine perhaps items such as horizontality/verticality or enclosure/openness. Although some analyses of individual styles along these lines have been offered, no convincing universal proposal has been constructed.

Even if successful, such analyses are only useful retrospectively. Phonetic analysis provides analyses of existing sound systems, not a list of all possible languages. We could form such a list by making all possible combinations of the characteristics, but since the list would be produced by exponential multiplication applied twice over (once to generate the phonemes and once to collect them into possible languages) the results would be, while finite in number, inconveniently large. The same difficulty would hamper any proposal to find a usable scheme of elements behind all architectural vocabularies.

There is a still more basic difficulty in the architectural case. The success of phonetic analysis depends on the limited number of ways a stream of air can be modified by our human vocal organs. It would not be possible to analyze with the same concepts the speech of an alien who produced sounds by a tympanum that did not use a stream of air. The primitives of phonetic analysis cannot analyze musical sounds in all their variety. Although there are many constraints on architectural form, the possible variations are not so constricted as to be likened to the limited possibilities of human speech. They are like the wider possibilities of musical sound.

Another suggestion is to develop a master language from building types (market, church, meeting hall, city office, home, and so on). But types do not form a language. Building types have more independence than words, because they get their identity not only from relations to

112   one another but from references to our social activities. But our social
activities involve too much bricolage for them to fit into a useful master
language. New building types are invented when the underlying activities change, as we can see from the efforts of the modern movement
to find architectural forms for new industrial and commercial activities
that had already developed independently. So no master list of building types is possible.

Thus there seems to be no useful sense in which we can say that the
architect draws concrete possibilities from some repertory that includes all possible architectural forms.

EQUAL ACCESS TO HISTORY

The second suggestion was to limit the architect's repertory to all historical forms, or at least to all documented historical forms. This
suggestion runs into a number of problems. It does not mean much to
say that historical forms are available until one has specified a mode of
presentation that will make them accessible to the design process. But
if there is no master language, no mode of presentation will be sure to
present "all" the historical forms. (And would it do justice to those
novel forms that enlarge the historical repertory? I will be discussing
the enlargement of architectural possibilities in a later chapter, so I
leave this question aside.)

Even granting for the sake of argument that there is some system for
making historical forms available, there are still grave problems. Only if
it could all be kept at an equal distance would all history be equally
available. But some historical forms are unavailable to us.

It seems strange to claim that some parts of history are not available
to us. Can't we build any form we know about? We could build a Gothic
cathedral, reproduce the temple at Jerusalem, build a ziggurat.

But could we really reproduce the ancient buildings? We could certainly build a copy of a Gothic cathedral. It would have the same
geometrical form. We would not likely use the same system of construction; it would be very expensive to build the cathedral as they were
once built, and we are not sure of all the details of the process. But we
could make a copy that would look the same. Or would it? Our exact
copy would not be in the right place. Even surviving Gothic cathedrals
no longer have the same look now that they are embedded in a new
society. Even believers must see them differently now. For one thing
they no longer dominate the skyline of their cities. Nor are their plazas
used in the same way. We cannot live a Gothic cathedral in the old way,

because we do not live the life the building originally fitted into. Nor do we have the fertility cults or royal hierarchy to "do" a ziggurat. Religious buildings are the most obvious examples of this lack of fit, but an Indian bazaar, a Greek theater, or a Renaissance piazza would do as well. Our copy would stand in our space, surrounded by our buildings and activities. It would not shape lives in the old way.

There is an additional problem if we try to build in an ancient genre but do not make an exact copy. We may work from documents and surviving buildings, but we cannot be sure we know how to build a new shape that would fit the old rules. It takes an ongoing form of life, Wittgenstein would say, to decide whether a proposed example extends the series or violates the rules. That ongoing community is not available to us. Even when the rules are written down, as in the case of Vitruvius, there still needs to be a community to decide what counts as following the rules.

These are limits we cannot will away. We have no equal access to history. On the other hand, we are not imprisoned within fixed limits; we can envision other forms of life, but we cannot on our own make the decisions such a community might enact.

My argument so far has presupposed that we want access to history that will allow us to continue the past. What if we gave up the ideal of continuity, paid no attention to how the past lived or analyzed their forms, broke historical forms into parts in any way we chose, and used those parts in our current ironic play and parody? Then would not history be equally available, with all its distances abolished?

This would be postmodernism with a vengeance (a vengeance against time, as Nietzsche would say), replacing any hermeneutical ideal of continuity or understanding with the parodic manipulation of text fragments. But whatever the success of this in literary art, it cannot succeed in architecture, since buildings are to fit into ongoing activities. If the architect's dealings with past forms were as free of the need to understand the past as the parody method suggests, then there would be no need to deal with the past at all. One might as well use a random number table to generate the forms, but randomness abolishes parody. If the past becomes *only* a repertory of abstract shapes and building fragments, it is true that we are freed from the obligation to understand it, but neither is there any longer a second level of meaning to play with. Unless the fragments of historical forms carry *some* understanding of their use in their home environment, they cannot be twisted to produce parody or irony. The composition becomes a flat assemblage with no interaction between meanings. Parodic use requires understanding. But if any

114   understanding of the historical forms of life is required, then there is no
        equal access to history.

VOCABULARIES AND MEMORIES

Our third suggestion is that the repertory that forms the background
of the architect's work is simply those forms and styles that the architect
has experienced. In some sense this has to be correct, but how does the
architect relate to those possibilities?

Imagine an assiduous architect who has photographed every angle of
every building she has ever seen, has kept a copy of every architectural
journal, and photocopied every picture in every book she has read.
This architect's memory of buildings and types is available; it can be
surveyed and cross-indexed. Is that archive the field of forms the architect works from? No, for we would have to add the architect's dreams,
reveries, the flitting dance of possibilities as the pencil hovers. Even if
there were some way to catch all these forms, how would we organize
them? Any order we come up with is unstable, for tomorrow the architect might see her memories in a new light. It happens in literature:
Joyce changes the way we read Virgil. It happens in architecture: Venturi makes us see Luytens again, Gaudi becomes important and old
memories are rearranged. The past, even the personally experienced
past, does not stay fixed enough to provide a secure base.

Architectural possibilities do not line up neatly for inspection, and
there is no algorithm that will generate them in a surveyable order.
Whether we are talking about abstractly possible forms, historically realized forms, or personally experienced forms, the architect needs some
mode of organization and presentation to define a useful repertory.
The architect needs a vocabulary that generates a set of basic forms or
types and suggests ways of combining and decomposing them.

I have been arguing that the architect cannot relate to possible forms
without a vocabulary, for only by mutual contrast are possibilities
made definite. Yet no architect today knows only one vocabulary.
Again we can ask where the architect lives: If I can build in five vocabularies where am I? Hovering over them in empty space? No, for once
again there is no equal access; there are relative differences in availability. There will be saliences and distances, with some styles or vocabularies taking a foreground position.

These differences of availability are not an unimportant by-product;
they are part of what allows there to be a repertory of styles. There are
multiple causes of such saliences and distances, and of the particular
axes along which the contrasts run. Few of those causes are matters

over which the architect has much control. And if the architect deliberately goes against the currently salient vocabularies, the desired effect
will depend on the accepted configuration retaining its hold.

Speaking of the classic orders, Jencks quotes Gombrich's point that
"within the medium at the architects' disposal, Doric is clearly more
virile than Corinthian" (Jencks 1977, 118). The orders exist as orders
by standing in relations to one another along a variety of axes. But, as
Jencks also points out, the intrusion of a new style (the Gothic-Hindu
as Nash used it) disrupts the relations and changes the relative positions of the styles along the same axes (72).

There must be a limited number of salient styles or vocabularies related along accepted axes of contrast. If there were an indefinite
plurality of styles and none were particularly salient as the highest in
this or that quality, then the problems we saw earlier with suggestions
about all possible forms would recur on this level. Without differences
there are no meanings. It is true that the notion of fixed meanings may
need deconstructive therapy, but that will not mash all styles together
into some vague identity.

Such a mash of styles is where some fear postmodern architecture is
leading us. This is rightly condemned even as we admit that we always
have it with us. Just as no language can avoid the possibility of flabby
metaphors, so no configuration of styles can avoid the possibility of
bland mixtures. But this does not mean that above the various styles
there is some universal platform from which the architect can perform
the mixtures well or badly. I have been arguing that the architect does
not float freely over an unlimited field of possibilities but must live
somewhere within a limited configuration of styles and vocabularies. A
universalism that banishes history for the sake of the master language
fails, as does a universalism that declares ironic equal access to all
history.

The plurality of architectural vocabularies means that we should suspect claims to universality, but also that we should use what historical
contrasts and continuities we do find, since these are all there is to architectural language. If we cannot base ourselves on some master
vocabulary, neither can we wish away what meanings are already embodied in our ongoing local practices. That is what the modern
movement tried and failed to do.

This conclusion may seem to suggest we are in the imagined situation of the premodern builder imprisoned within a small compass of
styles, without the self-consciousness we value so highly. How do we
avoid being imprisoned by our limits? In the following chapters I examine how we extend our limits and criticize ourselves.

] 10 [

EXTENDING ARCHITECTURAL
VOCABULARIES

Architects work within a field of design possibilities, but we should avoid conceiving them as surveyors of that field instead of its inhabitants. Limits look different when you live within them rather than look down on them from above.

Modernist theory celebrates the breaking of limits; the modern self, freed from the blinders of traditional culture, becomes capable of exploring an endless field of creative possibilities. If not all these possibilities can be realized, this is because we do not possess a perfect science or infinite resources, but such restrictions function quite differently than did the traditional limitations that kept people from surveying the wider field.

I argued in the last chapter that no architect really works within an unlimited field of possibilities. My point was that a vocabulary is needed to open possibilities for knowledge and creativity, and those possibilities remain qualitatively limited. But the vocabulary is only one third of the story. There is also the question how we are to conceive change and self-criticism in architectural vocabularies, if there is no steady conquest of unlimited possibilities. And there is the question of self-conscious multiplicity: how do we build differently together?

Of all this century's arts architecture has been the most infected with the notion of progress and with the idea that tradition as such could be put behind us. It has also most actively retained the nineteenth-century ideal of the form-giving genius. In reaction there have been discussions of architectural semiotics that emphasize the importance of the vocabularies within which architects work. Many of these discussions, unfortunately, reinforce the picture of the architect as a floating subjectivity rather than an inhabitant. If we avoid that danger we still face the problems of change and multiplicity. In this chapter I address the question of change.

Limits

A limit is where something ends, or where something begins. It depends which way you are going. Experienced as an end a limit is a frustration, as when we come to a wall or a coastline and want to continue. A limit can only be experienced as an end if we want to go farther, if, as Hegel says, we are already in some way beyond the limit. A limit that does not block a desire is not experienced as a shock. As a beginning, when you walk in through the gate, a limit opens possibilities. This is the deeper function; without limits as beginnings we could not experience the definite desires and objects that bring limits as endings.

For the moderns, any traditional architectural vocabulary restricted the possibilities for design solutions; by contrast, modern architecture was to open all possibilities to the desire for rational control and elegant function. For the ironic postmoderns, both traditional styles and the modern ban on history are felt to restrict the play of reference and quotation; postmodern architecture is to access all styles while belonging to none. In both modernism and ironic postmodernism traditional vocabularies are seen as imposing limitations on some wider field.

But vocabularies also work as beginnings; they set up the contrasts that open possibilities. Language rules may cut the field of possible word sequences down to those that are grammatical. But language rules could not select the grammatical sequences if other limits as beginnings had not set up the contrasts that differentiated the words from one another. This allowed operations that generated the field in the first place. Limits as beginnings make possible limits as endings.

If possibilities depend on contrasts, and if there is no master language to provide the definitive set of contrasting basic elements, then there is no total, widest field of possibilities containing as subsets all the more limited vocabularies.[1]

Architects use more than one vocabulary and those vocabularies relate along axes of comparison with salience and distance, as I discussed in the last chapter. The resulting complex of vocabularies does not form a strict system but a loosely related assemblage that is itself limited and in contrast with other personal or regional assemblages. These in turn allow moves in various larger social codes and games. Such assemblages are not selections from some master list of possibilities; they are what open possibilities for the architect. They are something the architect inhabits, not something the architect stares at.

The architect is aware of the existence of other vocabularies and complexes of styles. Influenced by "the tradition of the new," we seek for novel solutions. So, as the limits of the current vocabularies open possibilities, they also function as barriers. But merely willing that it happen will not create a new style nor change the current relations between vocabularies. The emphasis on novelty can distort everyday

118 practice. The success of organized science proves that it is possible to set up training and institutional arrangements that encourage large-scale change while preserving a high level of everyday "normal science." It is doubtful whether current architectural training and institutional arrangements succeed so well at this double goal.

CHANGES AND METAPHORS

How then do the limits change and new possibilities emerge? We do not merely step across the limits as we might climb over a stone wall into a neighboring field that we could see all along. But neither do we make a sally into empty space. Our steps firm up the ground as we move, as firm as it ever is, and we move from and with what we already are. We do not create out of nothing; and we do not choose the influences and connections of our creation. But though there are always connections, there are no rules, no algorithms to generate the new possibilities. Rules and algorithms operate within languages; they need already distinguished and contrasting elements to operate upon. Changing the set of elements requires another kind of operation.

I will call that operation *metaphor*. This use of the term stems from Max Black, and has been developed by Nelson Goodman and Paul Ricoeur. They have enlarged the theory of metaphor to include more than the striking use of names and adjectives that since Aristotle has been taken as central to metaphor. That older conception makes metaphor a deviant operation of substitution within an already established set of elements and rules. In the newer theory, systems interact in an operation by which new elements and rules can be created through deviant use of the old (see the Bouygues headquarters photo).[2]

Metaphor in this sense expands the limits of what can be said. This does not involve simple importation of a foreign element. If Venturi's country house quotes an English original, that is not in itself a metaphor. What is necessary, in Ricoeur's words, is that some *impertinence* be committed. Some expectations become frustrated, some systems broken, or two systems collided. This impertinence leads to new pertinence (see the Ameritrust Tower photo).

For instance, in Portland, Maine, a renovation of some row houses blended references (in the mansard roof) to the houses in the neighborhood with references (in the facade) to the Greek Revival granite post and lintel storefronts common elsewhere in Portland.

> During the design process the U.S. Department of the Interior, which was involved in the financing and historic-preservation ap-

proval of the project, brought objection to the roof form on the 119
grounds that it was inappropriate to the period references of the
building's facade. . . . I would suggest that the composition is exciting precisely because it is "incorrect." It demands of the
historian as well as of the passerby a reexamination of the building's parts in order to discover the significance of their juxtaposi-
tion. (S. Moore 1983, 11)

This is a case where incorrectness, "impertinence" in Ricoeur's terms,
seems to be in the process of creating new pertinence. Notice that this
mixture of vocabularies is not an ironic comment about the vocabularies in question, but an attempt to expand signification.

We can distinguish several kinds of intersection that create new
meaning. One transfers a single item (for example, we speak of a blue
mood but not of green and violet moods). The second transfers a whole
set of interrelated items (for example, we might begin to talk of moods
using the full range of color predicates; this would also reinvigorate
the dead metaphor about blue).

Examples of the transfer of single elements might include the quotations in Graves's Riverbend or in the new Olin library at Wesleyan
University. It is possible for such transfers to become normalized and
no longer commit the impertinence that creates meaning. Such rou-
tinization enlarges the target vocabulary. As Ricoeur says, in the
dictionary there are no metaphors, only multiple meanings (1977, 96).

The second, more complex type of change brings into a vocabulary a
whole field of elements already interrelated by their own rules. This is a
more productive transfer. For example, in Bofill's huge apartment
blocks the classical orders and French royal styles are put into the vocabulary of modern modular housing. Kenzo Tange combined the
béton brut of late Le Corbusier with traditional Japanese protruding
beams and other shapes from native wooden architecture. In these
cases, new possibilities were created that permitted whole families of
new forms.

We can distinguish these transfers from another operation that
changes the combination rules. For instance, when the classical orders
began to be built on top of one another something new was created out
of the old contrasts. Such an operation can also twist, fragment, and
recombine the relations within a given system.[3] This move is seen in
many postmodern buildings, since it allows for ironic and parodic
effects (see the Whitney Museum photo).

There is still another type of operation, one that is akin to the creation of a new language. This has no immediate parallel in literary

120   operations on the level of the word or sentence, but it resembles the way a new genre of text might be created by a creative misunderstanding of an earlier genre. Sometimes architects create new vocabularies that rely on former buildings but are not directly composed of the intended elements of the original vocabularies. Buildings are experienced in many ways other than through architectural analysis. So we might "cut up" a building differently than was intended. For instance, an architect might visit Bali and bring home new forms. The traveler might not have transferred directly from the intended vocabulary of Borobudur, but nonetheless the architect might develop new forms for home use.

The modern movement itself perhaps involved such a transfer. Architects visited factories, railroad stations, and industrial yards. When they came home they developed a new analysis of wall, support, and function. They had not necessarily learned the vocabularies of the engineers who built industrial buildings. Perhaps those builders were thinking in terms of an older vocabulary where steel beams were akin to columns. Someone might build something very close to a curtain wall while still seeing it as a version of columns and masonry. A visitor might reanalyze the construction and come up with new forms and vocabularies. This type of change differs from the earlier ones in that it does not involve the intersection of already differentiated prior vocabularies.

The various operations I have discussed can be combined with one another. All of them change the current vocabulary or the relations of salience among vocabularies. The result is new possibilities. This does not mean, however, that our architectural possibilities keep on expanding. For when languages change, possibilities are lost as well as gained. If limits are beginnings as well as endings, changing the limits can destroy meanings and combinations made possible by the old differences. In the context of today's styles, we cannot use the classical orders with the meanings Vitruvius found in them. This is a story that discussions of architectural change seldom tell.

In none of these cases does the architect create out of nothing. Though they cannot be programmed or predicted, such innovations become retrospectively comprehensible. Like any metaphor they can be traced back, if not exhaustively paraphrased. Also, like any metaphor they do not respect previous divisions between what is essential and what is accidental. One vocabulary may define a division between the essence of the building and some accidental added decoration, but this may be twisted or abolished by a metaphorical change.[4]

It might seem that architectural metaphor cannot provide self-criticism. As Klotz says, "playing with an order is predicated on one's acceptance of it" (1988, 392). But this is to mistake irony for metaphor. As I pointed out earlier, irony establishes distance from some order, perhaps reverses it, but does not challenge its internal structure. Habermas is right to see in this a conservative move. Metaphor, on the other hand, reaches into the order and changes the internal relations. It makes new spaces for thought and life; the old order is challenged when its limits are transgressed into a different space. Criticism need not be located above the language or work being criticized. It can take place through an extension from within, or a crossbreeding from without, that wins new territory. Criticism need not be aimed at some unitary future goal; as Kuhn would say concerning the advance of science, criticism is *from*, not *to*.

My concern has been with extending architectural vocabularies. However, there are other kinds of operations that can be performed on those vocabularies. They can be manipulated for ironic or parodic effects that do not extend the language. They can also be combined and transgressed in ways which bring into prominence, and perhaps question, not so much the architectural vocabulary itself, but the boundaries and oppositions within the wider social codes and games into which the architectural moves are always inserted. This last is an important operation for helping us discover where we live.[5]

There are dangers in conceiving of change as I have suggested. This way of thinking fits all too well into the standard modern discussion of subjects and objects, intended meanings and unitary forms, where all the initiative is on the side of the powerful self that organizes and reorganizes a world of neutral data.

But there is no self above it all; we are set in motion by and within our languages. We are more at the mercy of language than we are its masters, and insofar as architecture involves something akin to language it shares the devious ways language has with us. Nor is there a master language, nor a first language without traces of previous metaphorical construction. Nor, finally, do the operations I described have to be intentional in order to produce new meaning. Juxtapositions and crossings happen, and there is no way to avoid unintended contrasts. We may by an effort of abstraction perceive the older buildings in lower Manhattan as they looked before the World Trade Center changed their scale, but we cannot will away the new contrasts.[6]

MANY FORMS

In the remainder of this chapter I will soften the discussion of architectural vocabularies by pointing out how little the form and meaning of

122   buildings depend on our intentions. I argued in the last chapter against the idea that there is a master language of architecture. All buildings do not share a basic vocabulary. Now I want to argue that even a single building does not have a unique form or vocabulary, either over time or in the present.

My discussion will concern the geometric and perceptual properties of buildings and the receptions they undergo. There are more radical things to be said about architectural form and intention. But the ordinary concepts are much used, and even in their terms there is no unique form (or intention) belonging to a building. This means that there is no unique signifier that is the building.

There are several varieties of form that a building may possess. I will distinguish, first, the *operative form* or structure of a building; this includes the particular way the loads are carried, heat and ventilation are distributed, and other "engineering" problems solved. This form could be described through diagrams of stress and bracing, maps of duct work, and so on.

There is also the *geometric form* of the building as a total volume; this could be described by an equation, though the mathematics would be too complex to be useful. This form includes everything: the exterior volume and detail, and the interior spaces with their detail. A description of the geometric form of a building is not from any particular point of view. We cannot directly perceive a volume this way, but we can build it up by repeated viewings from various angles.

Then there is what I will call the *presented form* of the building; this is a projection of the geometric form from a particular perspective or a particular route through the building, and in a particular built context of other shapes. The presented form could be recorded by photographs of a building in context.

Also there is the *perceived form(s)* of the building; this is how the presented form is taken by a person who interacts with it with a given history and background of community practices and architectural vocabularies. This background provides the contrasts within which the building is perceived. The perceived form also involves routes through and sequences within the building. There is no way of picturing this form, but it can be suggested by montage techniques.

There is in addition what might be called the *lived form* of the building, which is not describable in the subject-object terms used for the others. This belongs to the inhabiting body and its movements as a sense of possible motions, gestures, and styles of action. This form is not perceived; it is present in our habitual patterns and ways of interacting with the building. It is tempting to regard this as the basis from which the other forms are abstracted, but the sets of contrasts that involve the other forms have their own independence. And a lived gesture has no meaning apart from its own sets of contrasts.

A building can have only one operative form, but that could change without affecting the other forms (for instance, the heating system could be redesigned or new bracing introduced without any visible effect). The geometric form of a building is by definition total and unique, but it has no single decomposition into component forms. A building may have many presented forms from different points of view, and from the same point of view over time, depending on changes in the environment. A building can have many perceived forms at once, depending on the history, practices, and vocabularies of those who use it.

Whatever theory of the meaning of architecture one adopts, the perceived form (and in some ways the lived form) is its visual and spatial signifier, not the meaning signified. Signifiers are constituted by contrast; for example, the letter "p" could remain the same shape while those of its features that stand in contrasts might vary from one system to another. In the Roman alphabet "p" is distinguished from "o" by the stem's presence, from "b" by the stem's position. In other alphabets the same shape might be distinguished perhaps by the size of the loop, or by a circular rather than oval loop, or by being on the line rather than above it. A building has many features that can stand in different contrasts, so the building can be or include many different signifiers. The total geometric form of the building may remain constant, but the building does not stand in signifying contrasts by virtue of its total geometric form. It "means" by virtue of this or that feature. A building's total geometric form can be analyzed into features and routes in many ways, which can stand in many contrasts, so a building can be a variety of signifiers.

Operative form concerns how the building works at its material tasks of keeping erect, resisting the wind, providing light and ventilation, and so on. There might be several operative systems of bracing, or several systems of ventilation, but these add together in the one operative form. Operative form is what buildings share with machines. An automobile transmission works as it does because of the shape of the various gears and the mountings that bring them into contact with one another in definite ways. So also a building's steel skeleton or flying buttresses or duct work functions through its shape and arrangement. Operative form is defined by contrasts with other technical means of achieving the same goals.

124   There is little ambiguity about operative form but its status is not quite so straightforward as it might seem. Part of the modern movement's aim was to reduce the difference between operative and perceived form. If that difference could be reduced to zero the operative structural form would stand honestly revealed. But this cannot be achieved. In the Seagram building, for example, fire regulations prevented Mies from expressing the structural beams directly; the steel beams visible on the facade are added doubles of the actual supports. But even if the actual beams could have been exposed, the operative form would not have been "honestly" expressed. The presentation of operative form, perhaps by uncovering trusses and duct work, immediately puts those items into other contrasts. They are now visually involved; they now contrast with other ways the building might look, not just with other ways of supporting loads or distributing air. They stand implicated with history, and with other ways of expressing or not expressing the operative structure. Then there are the associations gathered from similar buildings, from the use, and from conventional meanings of the resulting form.

Foster's Hong Kong and Shanghai Bank building makes dramatic use of an external supporting structure from which the building is visibly suspended, and of the "sunscoop" that brings light to the atrium. But these structural elements are doubled when they are presented. They are available in different contexts at once; the play of the contexts and meanings is enjoyable, but it is not the harmonious perception of a unitary form.

Turning the point around, we can imagine a building with its operative form hidden and the appearance of another structural system pasted on (perhaps a modern Gothic cathedral with a hidden steel frame and the look of masonry construction). It could be arranged that people knew about the hidden operative form; this would change the perceived form of the building even though nothing about the visually presented form was different. Or it could be arranged that the hidden operative form was truly hidden, and everything about the building felt and said that it was supported in the traditional Gothic way. In terms of perceived form such a perfect deception would *be* the imitated kind of structure. This would be dishonest (in modernist terms) but there is no reason to deny that it might be sometimes desirable.[7]

We saw in the last chapter that constancy of geometric form begs the question of architectural vocabulary. The complex shape of the whole does not specify any particular decomposition into simpler units, no matter how simple and intuitive they might appear. Indeed, various architectural vocabularies can specify different *kinds* of analyses of geometric form. When Wojtowicz and Fawcett say "architectural form is exact and precise because it is expressed with geometry" (Wojtowicz and Fawcett 1986, 15), they confuse precision with uniqueness. What I have called the geometric form of a building is precise and exact, but the analysis and contrasts that control the perceived form will vary.

Furthermore, constant geometric form cannot stabilize the presented form of a building, since that depends on the environment. Consider the case of Hagia Sophia. When the basilica was changed into a mosque its overall geometric form was not altered much. But the balance of the composition and the presented form of the domes were altered because the church was enclosed within the angular volume created by the added minarets. The same geometric form now produces different presented and perceived forms. This kind of change happens all the time, as when the World Trade Center grossly affected the perceived form of the older buildings in lower Manhattan. Analogous changes happen in literature, when novels or poems are read in new contexts.

The perceived form of a building gives architects the most trouble. Dependent on the reception of the building, it cannot be controlled very well. (Why architects might want to control it is a separate question, treated below.) For example, the Pantheon in Rome has endured for a long time. It became a Christian church, then more of a museum. While it is still made of the same bricks in the same positions, the building's presented and perceived forms have changed as the building's context and uses have changed. As the sets of contrasts into which the building is inserted change, the building provides different signifiers; the signifieds also change as the building finds itself within different forms of life.

This example, however, forces me to qualify and extend my claims. After all, in many ways the meaning of the Pantheon does not seem to have changed so much. Furthermore, the decomposition of the building into parts seems easy: the dome and its oculus, the large enclosed space, the entry with its columns and portico. Doesn't this challenge my claims about the variability of form?

Christian Norberg-Schultz argues that the Pantheon embodies a basic Roman combination: the man-made world is oriented toward the cardinal points of the compass in a way that claims cosmic validity. The horizontal axes from the cardinal points meet in the rotunda un-

126 der a dome where "the vertical axis which rises up from this center through the large opening in the zenith" unifies earth and heaven (Norberg-Schulz 1980, 52, 165; see the photo of the Pantheon).

But for Germanic invaders in the fifth century who had never experienced a dome, the "meaning" of domes in general would not be clear and the particular qualities of the Pantheon's dome would not be naturally obvious. For an eighteenth-century Roman who routinely lived with the large Roman churches, the Pantheon stood in new contrasts; a modern who has experienced even larger open interiors spanned by steel trusses finds the Pantheon within yet another set. These examples are not matters of subjective interpretation; as the building fits into those different forms of life it stands within different sets of contrasts and "makes different moves."

Still there is something right about what Norberg-Schulz says. In claiming that a building's geometric form has no one definitive way of being analyzed I mean to encourage doubts about other less sweeping claims to continuity as well. But that is not to deny continuity. Some ways of analyzing buildings are very deeply ingrained in our culture. The Platonic solids seem almost unavoidable. And Norberg-Schulz is correct to point to other continuities of form and signification that may tie to racial features such as our erect posture and our common experience of the heavens and the weather (cf. Norberg-Schulz 1984, 1985). Karsten Harries has written about these and other "natural" sets of contrasts stemming from our posture and location and common experiences such as gravity and support, light and dark, enclosure and openness (Cf. Harries 1980, 1983, 1984b, 1988a, 1988b.)[8]

An even stronger argument might be made for certain sorts of "analysis" of edges and volumes that seem to be inherent in our brain's visual systems. For instance it is probably unavoidable that we perceive a surface with a molding not as a rumpled surface but as a plane with a molding laid over it.

Such continuities are important, but there is no universal language to be garnered from them. To whatever degree they are universal, such natural contrasts are facts about us that need to be taken into account, but they are not the basic elements of any vocabulary. They may be involved in the constitution of an architectural vocabulary without themselves being elements within it. They can guide choices of and within vocabularies, when that is appropriate. Or they can be ignored or played against, when that is appropriate. In either case the judgment of appropriateness is something beyond these "natural" contrasts and meanings.

MANY INTENTIONS

There is another question to be raised in connection with the example of the Pantheon. We know enough about Roman society and architecture to be fairly clear about the original context and use of the Pantheon, and how a Roman would have analyzed its form and meaning. Granted there have been other ways the Pantheon has been lived with, the Roman way seems to have a certain priority, since they built it; they got there first. Just what importance do we give to the original intention? Does it limit the plurality of forms and meanings?

Whatever the status of intended meaning in literature, it is alive and well in current architectural practice. Because there are many coworkers who may have their own ideas, the architect will often be consulted about the intention behind features of the design. At least for buildings in the media's eye, questions whether the design successfully realized the original intentions often dominate critical discussion. There are usually records of what the owner or corporation or town committee wanted; likely the architect's presentations involved statements of intention. So architectural intentions have a more public existence than intentions in the other arts.

Furthermore, an architect is routinely expected to take more precautions against variant interpretations than is a novelist or painter. The architect knows that the building will sooner or later find new functions beyond those specified in the owner's program. The building will likely outlast the saliency of its particular vocabulary. Eventually the intended meaning and function will become less important, perhaps even unknown. But the owner wants the building's meaning to endure as long as possible. The architect is urged to control the perceived form of the building.

The architect, too, wants to emphasize the success of particular solutions to particular design problems, and likely to emphasize a particular vocabulary. Within narrow limits it might be possible to design using aleatory techniques, or to make a building whose uses and meanings are intentionally left open. Some architects have experimented in these directions.[9] But commissions are set and buildings financed by people with definite ends in view. The current buildings

128 that most clearly show that their uses are left open are wide Miesian spaces, but these, like empty stages, do not offer a wealth of meaning for multiple interpretation.

The same Charles Jencks who showed how buildings in the International Style spoke in an unintended vocabulary (not about purity and function but about power, indifference, and bureaucracy [1977, 19–37]) is anxious that this not happen to postmodern buildings. Jencks talks of the importance of coding the intended meanings of a building in multiply redundant ways so that they will survive future changes of use and context for as long as possible. This suggests that even the postmodern architect thinks of intended meaning as crucial, a conclusion that is borne out by the conversations recorded in the Charlottesville and Chicago symposia, where architects argued vociferously in favor of their authorial intentions and against the alternate interpretations of their buildings advanced by other architects (cf. Robertson 1985, Tigerman 1987, and the analysis in Soltan 1987).

For all this, a building has its own stubborn independence. The author never has complete control of the work. Architecture involves many more compromises than are required of a novelist or painter. There are other people working on the project. Once finished, buildings go their own way. They last and they are unavoidable. People can put down novels or avoid picking them up. Paintings can viewed by selective audiences. Buildings intrude upon users and interpreters of all kinds. They get reused and reworked.

Public discussion about buildings makes their intended meaning more prominent than in the other arts, but it is the community's practices, not the architect's intentions, that are finally important. Buildings fit into established patterns of living that are not changeable by critical or architectural fiat. We cannot automatically assume that what the architect intended does in fact rule the interpretation of a building.

Consider the case of Isozaki's plaza at the Government Center at Tsukuba. The plaza makes clear reference to the Campidoglio, but in the center where the Roman original has the statue of an emperor, Isozaki places an empty space, with a drain from a nearby fountain pool. Isozaki has said that his intention was to assert that Japanese society lost a center when the old imperial figure was rejected, and that the society has not found a new center (cf. Jencks 1987b, 292–98). But if this is his intended meaning, must one know the Roman original in order to read it? Is Isozaki coding this for the cultural elite? Or is the intended meaning somehow there in the lines of the plaza to be felt by anyone?

To decide this we would have to look at how public spaces in Japan are organized. We would find that celebratory central monuments seldom appear in Japanese public spaces, which are usually organized in a linear fashion with the culminating point at the far end, often out of view. This weakens Isozaki's statement at Tsukuba since the absence of a central figure will be less salient in the Japanese context.[10]

And, in Europe, what about the lack of a strong center in many plazas inside Bofill's residential groupings? Is this a statement about a lack of center in modern European civilization? As far as we can tell Bofill intended no such meaning, but with Roman and French plazas in the contrasts at play, that meaning is there whatever the architect's intentions.

This is not to say the original intentions can be completely ignored. If we look at discussions of the Gehry house in Los Angeles we see critics applying their own standards to a house intended to challenge their way of reading (cf. Macrae-Gibson 1985, 104). Here the silence about Gehry's intentions is not due to a change of community practice but to critical special pleading.

Part of the dispute among the interpreters of Gehry's house concerns just what standards are appropriate for criticizing a "home." But this is a dangerous question. Architectural theorists spend too much time looking for essences in order to be able to issue norms. We should look instead for continuities and discontinuities of practice and interpretation in which we find ourselves already involved, and which we can use or modify by metaphorical moves.

Building is like writing. Letters joined together can be used for many different purposes; a laundry bill is not a wedding invitation or a newspaper article or a novel. But that is not to say that there is no accepted way of approaching a laundry list or a newspaper article. If there is no one correct way to approach laundry lists, there is a way we generally do approach them. We are already on the move within such conventions. They must be taken into account, which is not to say that they must be followed. But they cannot be ignored since they will influence community practice with the final product no matter what the artist wishes.

To take something into account is not the same as being ruled by it. We can always make a metaphor. What we cannot do is step into empty space, either to get the god's eye view or to create form out of nothing but our supposedly unique intentions.

] 11 [

HAUGHTY AND HUMBLE
IRONIES

Irony has become a buzzword in postmodern circles; nowadays even buildings are ironic. Whom can you trust?

The word *irony* comes from the Greek noun *eiron,* which describes a sly dissembler, a person with a smooth way of taking people in by hiding his strengths. Aristotle speaks of a quality he calls *eironeia* that consists of understating one's own good qualities. He considers this the vice at the other extreme from boastfulness. The virtue of straightforwardness stands between these two. Irony in Aristotle has more to do with a trait of character than with a literary turn. Maybe in the end it still does.

Classical rhetoric defines irony as calling something by an opposed name, for instance blaming someone through praising them, as Socrates praises his opponent while deprecating himself. After a long history in commentaries and books on rhetoric, during which the word was used to discuss a wide variety of attitudes and tropes, irony moved into discussions of art, especially in the nineteenth century with the Schlegels, Solger, Kierkegaard, and others.[1] Most recently Charles Jencks has called "ironies or complexities of reference . . . the defining characteristic of postmodernism" (Jencks 1987b, 196, also 330–350).

My concern in this chapter is to understand some varieties of postmodern irony. Much of what goes under the name postmodern irony still presupposes something like the superior distanced selfhood typical of modernity, though some deconstructive irony escapes this connection. However, the irony we find so far in postmodern architecture is not as subtle as the irony in postmodern literature and critical theory.

I will start by discussing the everyday notion of irony and some conditions for the success of irony as a speech act. Features of the everyday notion extend quite far into the refined philosophical and artistic meanings. I will be following two such features: the need of a firm platform from which to be ironic, and an act of superior judgment. Later in the discussion we will come to types of irony that question these features.

JUDGMENTAL IRONY

One popular dictionary describes irony as occurring when the literal meaning of a statement is the opposite of the intended meaning, especially when this understates the intended meaning.[2] The dictionary goes on to speak of irony as, "especially in contemporary writing, a manner of organizing a work so as to give full expression to contradictory or complementary impulses, attitudes, etc., especially as a means of indicating detachment from a subject, theme, or emotion." It is also described as an indirect presentation of a contradiction between an action or expression and the context in which it occurs. Irony is linked to distance and detachment. Typical thesaurus entries relating to irony include "sarcasm, satire, sardonicism, ambiguity, equivocation, doubletalk, sophistry, casuistry, double entendre," and the thesaurus suggests related notions are under such headings as "confusion, misinterpretation, uncertainty, contempt, detraction, disrespect, insult."[3]

So in the dictionary and thesaurus irony is a negative attitude on the part of a haughty ironist who looks down on those who are the butt of the ironical gesture. These "ordinary" reference works portray irony as a surprisingly negative and judgmental act, considering the positive tone the word has in academic circles.[4] These ordinary references also emphasize the contrast between the literal and the intended meaning of a statement, and between appearance and reality. In the more refined concepts of irony that descend from the nineteenth century these features become problematic, but they do not entirely disappear.

Irony as a speech act depends on intended meaning. I say one thing and intend that you (or some bystanders) understand another. This contrast calls attention to itself. By some signal the intention is conveyed that I want you to know I am being ironic—or at least I want someone to know, not necessarily you. Undetectable irony would fail; a hoax is not irony (Muecke 1985, 36).[5]

Notice that since successful irony demands that I signal to you the intention that my words be taken ironically, the signal itself must be non-ironic, on pain of an infinite regress. There must be the possibility that the audience can compare the literal meaning to the ironic meaning. If all acts of communication are ironic, then none are.

This does not preclude my being ironic about the *platform* from which I am passing my ironic judgment; it precludes that the *act* of communicating irony can be endlessly doubled on itself. Irony in the ordinary sense requires that the ironist have some higher place to

132   stand. The later developments of irony try to abolish this requirement; I will discuss to what degree they succeed in doing so. My point here is that no matter how recondite the self-irony may become, there still must be some signal that irony is going on, and that signal cannot itself be ironical.

Irony also demands the possibility of being misunderstood by being taken literally. Part of the experience of irony is the realization that I could have understood it too simply and missed the point. If that possibility is not acknowledged, then there would be only a one-level communication, which is sarcasm, not irony.

Irony fails if it is not understood as irony; when the context required to recognize the double communication is no longer available, the irony disappears. That context might be restricted to a select few (as are the meanings of the ironic names of characters in Plato's dialogues) or no longer available (as we might lack the context to decide whether some statement in the epic of Gilgamesh was meant ironically).

Irony can also fail by excess. Ordinary factual reports and requests are undermined if they are done with too much ironic comment. If I sense irony in your request to open the door I will be unsure whether I should open the door. Performatives, too, cannot be overly ironic. How ironically could I say "I do" and still get married? There is a limit to how far I could engage in self-parody of the act and still accomplish it. At some point I would cease being a groom and become someone putting on the role of a groom, and so fail to promise or marry. Yet works of art are more resilient, and can comment ironically on their own happening to almost unlimited degrees without vitiating their performance.

Italo Calvino's *If on a Winter's Night a Traveler* (1981) can overload and multiply self-referential narrative in a manner that can be called ironic, without ceasing to be a novel. Charles Moore's Piazza d'Italia in New Orleans can ironically overload and multiply references to its own assertions of Italian identity and festive character, and still be a successful public space (see photo). But there are some limits: a house will not succeed as a house if its roof makes ironic and self-referential gestures about shelter that do not actually keep out the rain.[6]

Irony can also fail through repetition, as the ironic gesture becomes standardized. What is the irony equivalent of dead metaphor? Some metaphors are living, some have grown stale, some have disappeared and become only another "literal" meaning of the word. As Ricoeur says, in the dictionary there are no metaphors, only multiple meanings (1977, 97). Can there be ironies in the dictionary? A dead irony would be one that has become sarcasm. In sarcasm there is no intended possibility of missing the meaning. So it loses "the curious special feeling of paradox, of the ambivalent and the ambiguous, of the impossible made actual, of a double contradictory reality" (Muecke 1985, 45). It ceases to be irony and becomes direct attack. Ironic gestures degrade with time; they need to be renewed; hence ironic art is driven to extremes.

Irony in the judgmental sense demands distance and double reference. The ironist refuses to be simply identified with a straightforward meaning. "There is more to me and to what I say than the literal meaning of my words. I use this code and know it as a code. I see further; I am not just blindly following rules that are immediately one with my consciousness. I know this and you know it too." There is detachment, and a put-down. Other types of irony keep the distance but are less judgmental.

On the other hand, there are kinds of distance and complexities of reference that are not irony. For instance, *play* suggests a motion that is freed from strictures or rules but is not standing off and putting them down. Play has no other place to stand. *Self-reflection* involves a double awareness, but not necessarily the distance that brings criticism. Self-reflective persons recognize their codes and languages, but self-reflection has no particular tone; it makes possible a variety of attitudes and judgments. One such attitude would be *self-consciousness* in the sense of an uneasy awareness of one's own actions that gets in the way of their successful performance. This disquieted self-consciousness need not be ironic.

The most prominent of irony's cousins is *parody*. Parody demands some shared community understanding to begin with, as well as some signal that parody is being performed. But parody can take that community in at least two directions. As a kind of bitter satire, parody can be a weapon used by one group against another to create divisions within a community. Or it can be a playful affirmation of community. Consider, for example, the parody of medieval liturgy and theology in the Carmina Burana drinking song "In taberna quando sumus," or the political parody of Saturday Night Live. In this situation we stand together as members of a community; a distance is created so that we can look at ourselves, but it does not create a superior position for some of us to occupy.[7]

Much of what goes by the name of postmodern irony tries to be parody of this latter sort, though often it remains on the level of judgmental irony. In particular, postmodern architectural irony often

134   ends up reaffirming the dexterous superiority of the distanced architect who has dropped by to learn a bit of the natives' language.

There are many kinds of double reference and self-awareness. Too many critics and philosophers class every kind of doubling as irony. This collapses a wide variety of attitudes and stances into one opposition between simple inhabitation and ironic distance. The result in architectural criticism has been to run together wit, humor, parody, playfulness, self-awareness, self-consciousness, irony, and the like. But then, to the extent that irony carries connotations of superior judgment, conflating all modes of double reference with irony may lead to begging major questions about the ways of living and building in our multiple world. If by definition we must be either simpleminded or ironic, the choice is obvious, but not very helpful. Are there other forms of irony which are not caught in the blunt opposition between premodern enclosure and modern distance?

Romantic Irony

Muecke (1985) distinguishes two types of irony, closed and open. Closed irony comes about when the ironist stands within one set of beliefs and pretends ironically to hold a rival set. For example, members of one religions or political party might make ironic use of the beliefs of another. The politician may also state his own beliefs ironically, but this is done on the basis of still other, perhaps more general, beliefs that are not ironized. In contrast, what Muecke calls open irony occurs when the ironist has no particular beliefs at all to share, but wishes to be ironical about simple believers of any stripe. This irony attacks not so much the content as the act of believing. Does it still presuppose a superior position?

Renan called irony "the act of the master by which the human spirit establishes its superiority over the world."[8] That superiority can be established in many ways, and there has been a steady growth in the abstractness of the platform from which irony can be exercised. Consider Voltaire, who in *Candide* and elsewhere used irony as a weapon. He had fairly straightforward beliefs of his own, but there was something about his beliefs that made them particularly apt for ironic moves. The Enlightenment critical intellect could look down on religious and political fundamentalisms from a position of relative universality; his allegiance to reason did not involve any particular substantive commitments to tradition except those demanded by the law of nature. This gave him room to maneuver in ironic ways, pillorying the simple faith of those dogmatists who had not attained his more universal point of view.

In the next century the same maneuver would be performed on Voltaire's own beliefs, first by Kant's refinement of the Enlightenment that reduced natural law to the formal demands of practical reason, and then by a series of modern ironists who saw the Enlightenment (and also Kant) as involving simpleminded commitments that could be ironically transcended by developing even more refined and formal theories of the self and its relation to the world.

The usual authority cited for this more general irony is Friedrich Schlegel. His is often called "romantic irony," but Schlegel never used that term except in personal notes. He sought for an ironic attitude embodied in an art that expressed the contradictions of our situation. A commitment to reason is only one aspect that needs to be put in ironic contrast with its opposite, the boundless energy of the universe.

> It is equally fatal for the mind to have a system and to have none. It will simply have to decide to combine the two.

> Everything should be playful and serious, guilelessly open and deeply hidden . . . perfectly instinctive and perfectly conscious. . . . [Art should] contain and arouse a feeling of indissoluble antagonism between the absolute and the relative, between the impossibility and the necessity of complete communication.[9]

It is not true that this kind of irony avoids basing itself on a particular set of beliefs. Schlegel's work involves an explicit metaphysics and epistemology drawn from the philosophy of his day. According to this view we are finite beings faced with an infinite universe where nature is overflowing with forms in an infinite process of creation and destruction. Our concepts try to fix the flow because we cannot live without creating fixed objects, but we are never completely successful. We cannot reconcile subject and object, feeling and form, art and life. So Schlegel relies on a non-ironic metaphysical description of the world and of the process of having beliefs.

Hegel pointed out that romantic irony takes its stand on self-consciousness as a process that is aware of its own form and of its movement beyond all definite content. Such irony affirms the value (or at least the inevitability) of this formally described movement of transcending whatever is given in experience. Hegel finds many problems with this view, not least with its immediate separation of form and con-

136 tent. But what is important for our purposes is his point that the romantic ironist does have a place to stand, a place described by straightforward philosophy of nature and subjectivity.[10]

DECONSTRUCTIVE IRONY

In our century we go the romantics one better by finding an ironic stance from which the romantic theories of nature and knowledge can themselves be seen as simple beliefs subject to ironic qualification. Romantic irony depended on oppositions between the boundlessness of feeling and the restrictive necessity of form, between the ideal of communication and its inevitable frustration, and so on. Twentieth-century irony has tried to add another dimension: the ideals of perfection and communication implicit at the positive poles of those oppositions must themselves be held ironically. It is not merely their frustration that we must live with, but an inherent rot at the core of the ideals themselves. We move here into deconstructive attacks on the elements constitutive of the theory of romantic irony.

This latest ironic mode does not depend on a theory about the world or about the relation between subject and object. But does this irony manage to avoid having a platform from which to judge? In many cases this is provided by a theory of the relations of signifier and signified, or of the conditions for identity and meaning.

The problem faced by deconstructive thinkers who emphasize irony is that they attack distinctions that seem constitutive of the notion of irony. We have already seen how dependent everyday irony is on the notion of intended meaning, which is a frequent target of the newest criticism. Similarly, that irony enacts some version of the distinction between appearance and reality. One thing appears to be meant, another is really meant. Romantic irony also depends on this distinction. The beliefs that seem so firm to the simple consciousness reveal their real status to the ironist.

This suggests that if we take seriously deconstructive doubts about the distinction between appearance and reality, or about the notion of intended meaning, or about the possibility of complete self-reflection or of literal meaning, we should be careful if we use "irony" to name the result, especially if that result is declared to be universal, since irony in the ordinary sense only exists by contrast with non-ironic communication.

There is a way to make the platform from which deconstructive irony is performed *almost* disappear, but doing so demands a complex strategy. If we are to be ironic about all simple beliefs and all straightforward identities, without ourselves professing some simple meta-beliefs, we must give up metaphysical and psychological platforms. Even semiotics must go. If there are universal claims that allow our irony, they must be quasi-transcendental ones. They cease to be particular beliefs, if they can be shown to be conditions for the possibility of any belief whatsoever. Inescapable and necessary, they would provide a universally applicable but formally defined place to stand. But these are not to be the formal and synthesizing conditions one might find in Kant. They will be Derrida's *différance* and its cousins. Because of their peculiar character these conditions cannot really be taken as forming a unified position. They qualify their own enunciation. They involve and enact difference, deferring, the lack of center or whole. Taken in themselves they make no whole, they form no immediate or mediated totality; as the conditions for grasping anything as unified and for relying on anything as a place to stand, they cannot be so grasped or used as a foundation. They provide no first or last word, but they do still provide something the ironist knows and the ordinary mortal does not.[11]

The effect is a position that affirms and denies itself as a "position." Through doubling and deferred self-reference this comes close to what Muecke calls open irony, though it still depends on some universal gambits, qualified and undercut as these may be.

However, some writing labeled deconstructive also promotes immersion in the flux of life beyond stable identities and fixed oppositions; this brings back a metaphysics similar to that of the romantic ironists. Such writing is caught in the same tension as was Nietzsche, between the critique of knowledge and the desire to give us knowledge about a life that escapes concepts and critique. And, as in Nietzsche, the solution can only be in indirect communication. But is all indirect communication to be called irony?

Still, even if so far successful, deconstructive irony runs up against a problem that also infected romantic irony. As theories these do not do justice to the *location* of the ironic move. All sets of contrasts that produce meaning have the slipperiness and self-undermining that deconstruction can show. It makes no difference where we start. Hegel pointed out that the theory of romantic irony treats our finitude in general but does not look at our finite location in particular. Since all particular and determined forms of belief or life express the same ironic impossibility of their achieving the fixity and definitiveness they claim, any belief or way of life can be treated as ironic. But this can be turned around: no account can be provided for the appropriateness of the

138 choice of certain beliefs or ways of life over others. Insofar as the irony
relies upon general claims about the nature of language and truth, its
point can be made from anywhere.

Thus the ironic move risks becoming a gesture that neutralizes itself
by its very ubiquitousness. All texts and all forms have the same irony.
Demonstrations of this self-transgressing quality of all texts, using any
present text as an example, can become as repetitious as appeals to original sin, and as unhelpful in dealing with particular cases in their
particularity.

There is one more step to take. Can irony be freed from notions such
as intended meaning and the distinction between appearance and reality? To do so would be to arrive at irony as indeterminancy and
undecidability. "The old definition of irony—saying one thing and
meaning another—is superseded; irony is saying something in a way
that activates not one but an endless series of subversive interpretations" (Muecke 1985, 100).[12]

I am skeptical of extreme claims about undecidability, because our
social practices do fix accepted meanings. We stop at the red light, understand the directions for the microwave oven, recognize the entrance
to the building, comprehend the general point of the classical columns
on the courthouse, and so on. What our practices cannot do is *limit*
meaning to these accepted contours, either now or in the future. We
can live with the awareness of this lack of security. Such life can be conveyed only by indirect communication (or in the act of metaphoric
innovation). If we call this indirect communication irony, it can indeed
be quite different from judgmental irony.

The deconstructive thought that emphasizes undecidability finds
irony not in the contrast of two fixed meanings, but in the contrast between the attempt to fix meaning and the impossibility of that attempt.
But even this irony can be haughty or humble. It can preen itself on a
platform from which it looks down on those who do not understand or
who fear the openness of all systems of meaning. Or it can acknowledge
that we are all in it together, in a spaciousness which, while it is no longer dominated by the old unities, does not set itself up against them.

What often gets lost is the quiet spaciousness involved in belonging
somewhere. There is a way of not taking our beliefs and location too
simply that is not itself the result of another level of meta-theory
providing yet one more place to stand. I am not speaking of a doctrine
but of an awareness of how we inhabit doctrines, a wry acknowledgment of our fragilities that affirms togetherness rather than superiority.
This comes from that motion and spacing which is a condition of our

inhabiting any system of meaning or practice. In philosophical and critical discourse this keeps getting twisted into something else, something that embodies hierarchy and superiority.

This is not an exercise of cognitive or valuation mastery. It offers no solid critique, except to surround any claims to solidity. Perhaps it ought not be called by the name of irony, for it is a species of compassion. But if we will use the term, perhaps we should qualify it as humble irony. The accomplishment here is one Nietzsche demanded but seldom achieved: to purge ourselves of resentment. Can we purge irony of resentment and the desire for a higher point of view than the naive simple believer? What would irony be like if it were more play than judgment?[13]

ARCHITECTURAL IRONY

Postmodern architecture does not usually succeed at these refined forms of irony considered in the last section. But then, buildings have not usually been thought of as ironic at all. Even now we do not find much irony in the earnest buildings of masters like Frank Lloyd Wright or Mies van der Rohe. Ironic distance or play is the last thing Wright has in mind; he wants to convert us. Much of the history of architecture is about public buildings, and buildings meant to celebrate community values are seldom intentionally ironic; think, for example, of courthouses, and the ubiquitous memorials to the American Civil War dead.

Architecture may seem less equipped for irony than the other arts.[14] It is probably true that architecture has the greatest proportion of masterpieces that contain little or no irony. But this overlooks that there are many kinds of doubling that are not ironical. Buildings can avoid single-mindedness in their presentation and still be non-ironic in the sense that they do not stand detached from their world and announce self-consciously "we are not wholly involved in this game we play." A pyramid may be simple, but Chartres is not, even though neither is outstandingly ironic. Chartres takes up and extends current conceptions and values in the direction valued by the Chartres school of medieval theology; the building does not simply ratify what is already current.

What is important is not the immediacy of architectural form but the relation of the building to its world. That relation does not have to be the straight affirmation typical of American Civil War monuments. Think about some recent Vietnam War memorials; they are not ironic, but neither are they simply affirmative.

140   Blatant incongruity and parody are alive in postmodern architecture. And they are fragile; parody and self-parody have little staying power. As the context changes, buildings outlive the irony they were meant to have. A building may be carefully designed with ironic references, perhaps in a way that subtly undercuts the authority that ordered the building for its own glory. As time passes the building gathers its own immediate identity. Parody depends on shared reference to the style or action being parodied. With its intended contrast forgotten or ignored, today's intentional parody can be tomorrow's dull design, or, worse, it may end up as an example of that which it parodies. Parody and irony can be as frail as architectural citations, which are often not lived as such by the ordinary users of the building.

It is also possible for a text or a building to become ironic even if it was not "intended" that way. Such ironical rereading still demands a double level with reference to context. We cannot deal with the classical orders as if they stood only in the set of contrasts described by Vitruvius. In the case of this rereading no signal may be given by the work itself, but something happens in a changed context that allows irony. No text or building possesses its form all to itself; as context changes, the form of the work changes; the possibility of irony cannot be blocked any more than can the possibility of new metaphors and multiple readings. In this sense irony is a permanent possibility, but it is not permanently available, since it depends on contrasts which can never be completely held within the work itself. To imagine that irony is always waiting to be revealed is to fall into modernist illusions about the completeness and independence of the aesthetic object (cf. Harries 1980).

As they proclaim an irony of play and ambiguity, most postmodern architects stand on non-ironic theories about the nature of architectural communication and meaning. Jencks speaks of our strong eclecticism as based on a knowledge of semiotics. Moore and Graves discourse on the way architecture means. In so doing they rejoin the modern movement, which also claimed to work from universal theories about architectural meaning. Except in some recent deconstructive projects, we do not see in architecture much of the self-undermining irony to be found in recent literature and criticism.

The postmoderns stand with the moderns against the presumed simple inhabitation of our ancestors. What moderns and postmoderns share is a distance due to self-awareness. We are told that our eyes have been opened and it is impossible to live within one style or vocabulary. When we use a style we need to signal this awareness by an ironic move.

Vitruvius certainly was aware of the rules for classical architecture, and he could contrast it with other modes of building used, say, in Egypt. What he did not do was refer to it as a *style*. Styles come in the plural; the notion indicates that there are many styles available compared to the one we choose or are given. Theories of appropriate and natural styles are designed to overcome the distance created by the very use of the notion of style (cf. Crook 1987).

People have always known that others built differently, but we are told that they did not always see these different ways as a palette of styles from which they might choose. They just built the way people did in their community. We tell ourselves that from the Renaissance on builders developed a more open attitude that led to a swifter pace of change, culminating in the eclecticism of the nineteenth century, which seems to have returned today. This story neglects the mutual influences and metaphoric combinations that have gone on at a slow pace throughout history. But whether or not it is a new phenomenon, the distance implicit in the notion of style is not the same as irony.

One way to make irony out of that distance is to add some platform from which the ironist can pass judgments. Another way is what I have called humble irony. Humble irony qualifies the inhabitation of particular places. It is not an affirmation of a universal theory, though we recognize in it a universal condition. We can enact our inhabitation in ways that convey our awareness of its fragility. For example, if we create or find new meanings and let them work *as* new, the sidelong awareness of contingency and fragility is signaled by the act of changing or blending the vocabulary. This is not done from some distanced survey but on the spot, extending the field as we walk over the old borders. That act is enough to remind us of our finitude; we do not need signs with Day-Glo colors (see the Capistrano library photo).[15]

In architecture, traditional vocabularies might be used and metaphorically changed in ways that affirm a solidarity that is not that of shared immediate belief, a solidarity that remains comfortable with future reinterpretation. There is room for buildings that are neither naive celebrations nor elitist games. Often, though, ironic use of traditional motifs becomes a doubly coded way of indicating how much more the architect knows. Postmodern buildings may avoid the modern movement's antagonism for the past, but they have a harder time avoiding the avant-garde's resentment for the bourgeoisie.

PARODY, IRONY, AND POLITICS

Irony has often been used as a weapon, because of its overtones of judgment and its reference to a presumably wider scheme of belief. What I

142   am calling humble irony puts no directed pressure on beliefs or practices. A wry acknowledgment of the contingency and fragility of our
world does not challenge it in any particular way. It does, however,
make easier those impertinent moves which extend and change our language and practices.

Linda Hutcheon argues that in postmodernism, irony is part of a
larger parodic gesture with political intent. Her aim is to defend the
postmodern use of history as more than nostalgia; postmodern works
are "resolutely historical and inescapably political precisely because
they are parodic" (Hutcheon 1986; see also Hutcheon 1985). Fredric
Jameson had argued that postmodernism degenerates into pastiche because of the loss of norms against which parody could play (Jameson
1983). In response, Hutcheon argues that postmodern art forms "use
and abuse, install and then subvert convention in parodic ways, self-
consciously pointing both to their own inherent paradoxes and provi-
sionally asserting ironic difference" (Hutcheon 1986, 180). Her aim is
to show that postmodernism provides a public discourse that avoids
the hermeticism associated with aesthetic modernism.

Hutcheon claims that in postmodern works "the past as referent is
not bracketed or effaced, as Jameson would like to believe; it is incorporated and modified, given new and different life and meaning" (182).
Postmodern architecture can offer "both a homage and a kind of ironic
thumbed nose" to the past (194, the phrase is from John Fowles). She
cites examples from the work of Portoghesi, Moore, and others, where
the parodic use of past themes is supposed to provide a way for the
community to be involved in a process of signification that the pure
forms of modernism had closed off. However, it is one thing to overcome modernist hermeticism, another to activate political discourse in
the sense Jameson seeks, and I am not persuaded that Hutcheon's examples succeed in this latter task, which remains more a goal than a
reality for postmodern architecture.

Nonetheless she usefully distinguishes parody as "ridiculing imitation" from the more complex gesture she finds in postmodern art. This
distinction parallels to some extent that between haughty and humble
irony which I have been developing. The differences lie in the fact that
as a feature of human inhabitation of any scheme of meaning, humble
irony is possible at any time and is not a specifically postmodern gesture. So it does not further any particular political agenda. Only if one
thinks that our essential danger is complete immersion in a hegemonic
discourse will one think that any distance is automatically political. If
we always have spaciousness about us as part of our inhabitation any-

where, then although the potential for contestation is always present, more than a distancing act is needed to mobilize it.[16]

Parody too can be haughty or humble, distancing or connecting, Johnny Carson or Garrison Keillor. Parody, however, does have a community potential which irony lacks. Haughty irony depends on distance and breaks solidarity. A parodic gesture might reaffirm solidarity while it teases us about some feature of our lives. We can stand together enjoying the parodic distance within our community rather than standing at opposite ends of an ironic relation from outside.[17]

Such parodic gestures are not distinctively postmodern; traditional societies are filled with them; earlier I mentioned a medieval example in the Carmina Burana. At its best postmodern architecture can accomplish the kind of generous parody that affirms our solidarity while refusing any simple definition of our community. But parody in this sense is not the contestatory gesture Hutcheon demands; it can reinforce the status quo. Nor is parody the only tool we might have; many kinds of doubling could allow us "to speak *to* a discourse from *within* it, but without being totally recuperated by it" (Hutcheon 1986, 206).

At the other extreme from Hutcheon, who argues that irony and parody are automatically political, Richard Rorty argues that ironic gestures are politically useless and fit only for private self-creation. Rorty speaks of irony as a sense of the contingency of the particular "final vocabulary" that happens to shape one's world; this sense can include painful doubts as well.

> I shall define an "ironist" as someone who fulfills three conditions: (1) She has radical and continuing doubts about the final vocabulary she currently uses, because she has been impressed by other vocabularies . . . (2) she realizes that argument phrased in her present vocabulary can neither underwrite nor dissolve these doubts; (3) . . . she does not think that her vocabulary is closer to reality than others. . . . I call people of this sort "ironists" because their realization that anything can be made to look good or bad by being redescribed, and their renunciation of the attempt to formulate criteria of choice between rival vocabularies, puts them . . . never quite able to take themselves seriously because always aware that the terms in which they describe themselves are subject to change, always aware of the contingency and fragility of their final vocabularies, and thus of their selves. (Rorty 1989, 73–74).[18]

Rorty sees the sense of contingency as motivating us in two ways. In public, it helps us accept (but does not ground) a liberal tolerance which sees cruelty to others as the worst thing we can do. In private the

144   public liberal is Harold Bloom's "strong poet" who overcomes contingency and the fear of death by reworking his cultural parents and creating himself anew. The ironic recognition of the contingency of our world combines with the Nietzschean ideal of overcoming the past by redescribing the influences that have made us what we are, so that we become our own self-authored story.[19]

Rorty has few disagreements with Habermas about practical political issues, but he argues against the latter's attempt to put liberal democracy on a philosophical foundation. Rather than see unconstrained dialogue as a self-critical method for arriving at truth, Rorty is content to call true whatever results within our dialogue, and to deny that there can be criteria for decisions among "final vocabularies." Rorty's problem is how to defend Kierkegaard's aesthetic life without also defending the Marquis de Sade. Rorty's liberalism has less public drive toward self-criticism. I indicated earlier my distrust of the idea of a unified self-critical project such as Habermas urges, but Rorty's divorce of private irony from public tolerance could deny opportunities for internal and dialogic criticism that might exist even without a unified critical project.

Although Rorty's is not a haughty irony of distance and judgment, it hinges on the modern distinction between those who are simply bound into tradition, and those whose self-awareness puts them above all tradition. Rorty's innovation is to argue that ironic awareness need not inhibit commitment and human feeling. He seems to me entirely correct in this, though his discussion of contingency in terms of "doubt" remains too much within the vocabulary of grounds and certainty that he is attacking. However, the rhetorical strategy Rorty uses in all his recent writings drives the positions he discusses into two extreme camps between which we are told to choose. Middle grounds get lost, and all positions are defined by one or two leading oppositions. Thus, while his characterization of irony is close to what I have been calling humble irony, the balance ends up very different. Rorty's strategy still involves the modernist opposition between total self-immersion and total self-creation. The Nietzschean ideal of becoming one's own cause, of transforming the past into a "thus I willed it," is yet another modern refusal of history. Rorty admits that our self-creation will always be "parasitical" on established practices and languages, but for him this is an unfortunate limitation rather than a hopeful opportunity.

Humble irony does not refer to any particular double level, and it cannot by itself produce new structures for life. It may, however, unite us in the feeling that we are all in this together, in our confusion and fragility and mortality, and make us more ready to experiment. Kenneth Frampton speaks of the "semiotic cynicism" of some recent works. Opposed to that might be what the architect Steven Moore calls "generous references" to context and traditional vocabularies that allow us to participate in a local code while extending and criticizing it. Such generosity comes when we are aware of our shared poverty, not when we possess a rich theory that allows ironic manipulations.

SELF-IDENTITY AND PLACE

How, especially in a world that names itself homeless, are we to create places for ourselves? Should we even try?

Buildings are not neutral containers; they shape the way we stand and move, the way we feel, the way time and space come to us. The dense reality of a building can affect us on more levels than our analyses provide. Often the building only repeats, or narrows, the forms and possibilities we already live. But architecture can offer us new ways to hold ourselves, to move and to be, and so criticize our current life by helping us feel how we might be differently.

The modern movement saw in this a chance for its buildings to focus the energy of a new age. Their masterworks still amaze us with the power they impart. Yet, caught in its own restrictions and in the homogeneity of the modern economy, the modern movement could not keep its promise. More and more, it reproduced everywhere one diminished set of possibilities. Postmodernism wanted to build freer places, but what has often resulted is an affirmation of one ironic meta-place.

In current discussions *place* does not mean merely a location with some functionally convenient structures. Place is where we feel at home in an articulated, legible pattern of locations and buildings that sustain and shape us by opening possibilities, supporting our forms of life, embodying priorities, and perhaps by expressing social ideals or cosmological patterns.

Discussions about place understandably tend to pit modernity against tradition. We imagine the past as filled with intensely local places each with its own unique character: European villages, regional American small towns. Modernism decreed that architecture would signify the uniform utopian life of the new age, and it continued industrial society's march toward rationalized homogeneity. Mass consumption and the dominance of exchange-value over use-value render it more efficient to make locations similar to one another, reducing their differences to surface decoration.

To reclaim a more human dwelling, perhaps here and there amid the landscape of consumption and efficiency there should be spots for centering and renewal that will keep us in touch with a history that goes beyond functionalism.[1] A traditional home might furnish a refuge

146

from the anonymous world, or a public building might embody communal aspirations and rekindle our idealism (cf. Moore, Allen, Lyndon 1974). Such a prescription stays within the modern project: people have a functional need for some special places, so planning should provide them. This is Weber's strategy of retreat: a rich domestic architecture provides a haven but cannot challenge the anonymous world outside.

DIFFERENTIATED PLACES

Habermas notes that everyone in the current debates over place recognizes the problems we face.

> [Modernist and postmodernist] agree in the critique of soulless "container" architecture, of the absence of a relationship with the environment and the solitary arrogance of the unarticulated office block, of the monstrous department stores, monumental universities and congress centers, of the lack of urbanity and the misanthropy of the satellite towns, of the heaps of speculative building . . . the mass production of pitch-roofed doghouses, the destruction of cities in the name of the automobile. (1985b, 318)

The postmodernist sees these "atrocities" as consequences of modernism's basic stance; the modernist sees them as betrayals of the avant-garde spirit. Habermas counts himself among those who want to continue with the unfinished projects of modern architecture.

He diagnoses the problem using the notions of system and lifeworld that I described in an earlier chapter. The lifeworld is that background of beliefs, values, and practices that provides a horizon of meaning for our actions. It is a cultural construct that must be renewed and handed along to provide community identity. Buildings embody and help form the distinctive practices and values of a community, and so they are one way of transmitting the lifeworld. But in our day the reproduction of the lifeworld has been dominated by imperatives stemming from the workings of the economic system. Lifeworld meanings are being thinned out, and so places become thinner as well.

In the ideal situation the reproduction of the lifeworld and the workings of the economic system would be distinct but would constrain each other. Community practices and values would put limits on the instrumental considerations of the system, and systematic restrictions would keep community practices truly practical. But in our world the influence has become one-way. The common lifeworld is

148   ever more subject to considerations of instrumental efficiency, while
the system is unconstrained by communal values and mutual decision
procedures. More and more the act of building becomes determined
only by systemic considerations of profit and efficiency.

There is, for Habermas, no architectural or design solution to this
problem. It requires new institutions for community decisionmaking,
and a form of democratic social control of the economy that keeps the
system from overwhelming the lifeworld. But even if we imagine such
sweeping changes to have been accomplished, there would still be
something different about modern places that would keep them from
being equivalent to those old villages and towns.

Recall Habermas's emphasis on the differentiation of modern
culture into independent spheres where art, law, and science develop
free of outside influences. He believes that we must preserve the expert
status of art. Architecture "is subject, as is art in general, to the
[modern] compulsion of attaining radical autonomy" (1985b, 323).
At its best, the modern movement's ideal of functionalism was the co-
incidence of a shape that developed from the "inner logic" of pure form
and a solution that met the building's program.

So, any cure for the problems of place today must preserve autonomy on several levels. We need to overcome the dominance of systemic
forces on the lifeworld, so that the autonomy of community values and
practices will be preserved, and places can reproduce a richer lifeworld.
But we should avoid anti-modernists who ask for "a de-differentiation
of the architectural culture" (1985b, 318). We must allow the artist to
have the autonomy to generate forms according to the independent
logic of the art. (How this will result in connection with lifeworld values and practices Habermas does not say; here as elsewhere he is
unclear about the way the expert spheres connect to everyday life.)

We also must safeguard the autonomy of the community in evaluat-
ing and changing its values and practices. This means that no place
should impose a past upon us. Tradition cannot simply dictate how we
build. Habermas has no use for nostalgic programs that prescribe cov-
ert returns to unliberated modes of life.

Habermas poses the problem as a choice between undoing differentiation (and so moving back from modernity into a traditional
culture) or accepting differentiation and working within it to complete
the modern project. One reason it is crucial to maintain the independence of the expert spheres is that they provide a haven from which
criticism can be launched against the systemic homogenization of life.
But is it necessary to provide the spheres with their own independent

inner logics for this to be possible? Especially in architecture it seems that many languages and games cross and intersect, and there is no process working under its own radically autonomous logic.

Earlier I argued that Habermas's notion of the lifeworld, which is meant to put us back into history, fails to do so because of the way the lifeworld is related to the universal project of self-criticism in his Socratic three-world story. Our inhabitation of our history is more spacious than his picture of traditional society, and we can criticize from within rather than invoke universal formal goals. But does this avoid the nostalgia he rightly criticizes?

Heidegger's Deep Places

Many thinkers influenced by Heidegger think of place not as an occasional refreshing center amid the wider world, but as itself a world.[2] Heidegger pictures a net of places that support forms of life; these places "open a domain in gathering things which here belong together" (cf. Risser 1987). These are "things" (in Heidegger's special sense of that word) that call us to activities and open up modes of relating within a world or meaningful context of significance. He writes of the wine jug that in its use brings together a whole way of life with its practices, its past, its ideals, and its projects. He speaks of the place gathered by the bridge over the river that supports and calls together a differentiated world of town and country ways of living. He writes of the Greek temple that centers the life of the people while also allowing the natural environment to appear within that context as something that transcends our human worlds. The jug, the bridge, and the temple are not neutral facts onto which meanings are projected. Rather they are encountered as gathering together a life that has no distanced standpoint outside the world called forth.

Rejecting the modern subject/object picture of meaning and activity, Heidegger argues that we should not conceive of the self as the source of some activity that reaches out to a world of neutral objects. Rather the self always finds itself already out amid a world of meaningful things, already in motion with goals amid a network of relations to other goals. There is no center from which a pure projection of meaning and value (or self-criticism) could issue.[3]

This includes purposes as well as meanings. In rejecting the subject/object picture Heidegger also rejects the fact/value distinction. We do not encounter bland objects to which the self then attaches a value. There is no self except in the encounter with a world that already

150   contains paths we are in the process of treading and tasks we are in the midst of doing.[4] We can never find ourselves within some purely individual project of meaning and purpose whose determination is totally the work of the self. Nor can we get behind all projects to pure neutral events set loose from all involvement in the network of meanings and purposes (Heidegger 1962, 284). The space (*Spielraum*) within which we move already has its own harmonies and structures.[5] There is no moment of original constitution, no state of nature free of meaning and purpose, in which the naked individual or society chooses how to limit its original possibilities down to those of one culture or language.

Heidegger used the term "project" (*Entwurf*) in an attempt to describe the situation of the self as always flung out among things. The term is ambiguous because it could also signify that we fling out onto the world our subjective nets of meaning and values; this is just the opposite of what Heidegger intended. To emphasize that our projects are not completely our own he speaks of us as "thrown projects" (*geworfene Entwürfe*).[6] We can never get behind this "thrownness" to some pure construction of meaning and purpose which is totally the work of the individual self or society.

This notion of a thrown project clarifies Heidegger's claim that a real *place* would gather the world as a network of meanings and goals within which we find ourselves. It also helps us understand that when Heidegger speaks about "authenticity" he does not propose a return to a mythical state of subjective naked choice, but rather a resolute taking up for ourselves of the finite meanings and paths we find ourselves among.

Heidegger does not see the limitation inherent in authentic place as frustrating some drive toward unlimited possibilities. That would be to repeat the modern mistake. He speaks rather of the power of the rooted life that "thrives in the fertile ground of a homeland and mounts into the ether, into the far reaches of the heavens and the spirit"; and he worries that everything will now "fall into the clutches of planning and calculation, of organization and automation" (1966, 49) as the ruthless efficiency of modern technological society levels all regions to a bland availability and devours their traditions.

We could not build just a few locations that would meet Heidegger's definition of a true place; we would have to change our whole life. But Heidegger thinks we cannot make that change. The overall meaning of our world is not something we can plan or manipulate, even though our modern world's meaning itself centers around the revelation of all things as available for planning and manipulation. Indeed, this is what has destroyed real places, but it is more our destiny than it is some error we can correct.

Heidegger dearly loved the rural culture of his region. Though he proposes no romantic escape from our technological world, he imagines that things might be different. In the past there were local places and gathered ways of life. In the future, when the technological world has run its course and new ways of life have been granted to us, real place may once again be possible. In dreaming of such a world Heidegger suggests that there would be little travel and no tourism there, because people would be at home in a sense no one can achieve today (Heidegger 1977b, 127). Modern life's travel and media level all places out to a mute availability that makes everywhere equally distant while destroying real nearness. In true places our explorations would be in deep, not wide, travel. Such assertions come in part from Heidegger's provincial suspicion of the cosmopolitan world of the more established German intellectuals. But they also stem from Heidegger's claim that all possibilities are intrinsically limited.

The places Heidegger describes are intensely local; his examples are all contained within mountain valleys that provide natural limits and centers. Yet they encompass the whole life of their inhabitants. They are not domestic enclaves but whole, though qualitatively distinct, worlds.

Heidegger misses a crucial aspect of the modern problem of place and roots. It is wrong to contrast the rooted life with modern anonymity as if our options were either finding a single unified world in an Alpine valley or else losing all true place in a featureless spread of calculated locations. Ours is a world of many places that interpenetrate and shift and influence one another. We who talk about these things will never find a quiet deep-rooted valley with strong enough walls to make us forget that the world is wide. There may be people in actual valleys who do not think much about that wider world, but if we are partaking in the present conversation then we no longer live in such valleys. Too often today we encounter the ersatz valleys of narrow belief walled in by anger. The key to our escaping the non-place Heidegger fears is not a retreat to lovely valleys but a pluralism without resentment.

The issue is multiplicity, even within single places, and what it would mean to make places in a multiple world. Meditation, not dialogue, marks the way of Heidegger's thinking. He always distrusted those who spoke too easily and broadly; for him dialogue was a sign of shallow thought. It was best to meditate silently, then pronounce authori-

152 tatively. Heidegger did not understand the need for travel and dialogue across places because his philosophical commitments forced him to evaluate the contemporary multiplicity of discourses as a degenerative rather than a creative condition. It could only mean that real places and things had been reduced to the status of objects to be manipulated. If we had things and places in his strong senses of those words, we would have a tradition and a world. Other things and other traditions there would be, and we would relate to them in various ways, but our own identity would remain firm. Heidegger's move is always to explore our roots in depth rather than encounter the Other.

It may sound strange to speak of Heidegger as defending "firm" identity. He is, after all, one of the originators of deconstruction, and for him there is no calm center to the self. We are never totally "in" any world or identity. But the disruption Heidegger finds within any identity lies in the way that identity is revealed; the "content" of the identity can still be quite unified. Heidegger felt quite able to make remarks about the deep identity and destiny of the Germans, or the national character and fate of the Americans or French.

According to the early Heidegger, to become authentic we must face up to our mortality and limits. When we become authentically resolved we take up our *whole* thrownness (our *ganz Geworfenheit* [Heidegger 1962, 382]). But this presupposes that our thrownness has enough unity to be taken up as a whole.

The simplest way of interpreting what Heidegger means would be to say that in becoming authentic we take up and ratify the whole *formal* structure of our thrownness. That is, we admit and resolutely accept the groundless historicity of our projects, whatever content they may have. Resolute authenticity would in this interpretation refer to *how* our thrown projects exist, not to their content.

But for Heidegger our thrownness includes something that is not purely formal, a particular understanding of being (Heidegger 1962, 221). Heidegger emphasizes the content of our projects. What we take up, says Heidegger, comes to us as a "heritage" (*Erbe*). Our past comes to us as a path for the future. Heidegger speaks of the world of meaning and projects already in motion as our "fate" (*Schicksal*). And it is clear that this heritage or fate has some unity. Indeed, he says it is only an aspect of the larger "destiny" (*Geschick*) of our time and generation; there is some task for our generation to do (cf. the reference to Dilthey in Heidegger 1962, 385, and the remarks in Heidegger 1971 about inheritance and task).

This is not a simple historical determinism, for in authentic resolve we take up that destiny in a way that finds new meaning in its depths. That is the activity Heidegger calls "retrieve" (*Wiederholung*), whereby our thrown possibilities are taken up *as* possibilities for creative renewal.

Still, with such talk Heidegger moves very far from modern notions of free subjectivity. The problem has been highlighted by (but is not limited to) Heidegger's Nazi activities in the 1930's, which have been continuously controversial to the present day.[7] Does Heidegger's idea of destiny mean that the individual is fated to take up the cause of his *Volk*? Is the emphasis on the thrownness of our projects an affirmation of blood and soil? It certainly sounds that way in some of Heidegger's pronouncements in the 1930's, where he describes the task of his generation and of the German people in terms resonant with National Socialist ideology. And in his silence afterward he seems to suggest that there is no way to judge that destiny. And Heidegger talked about the technological world as a fate that surrounds and directs all our projects.

To my mind Heidegger's notion of "thrown projects" is an important contribution to the overcoming of modern illusions. Heidegger's difficulties stem not from the notion itself but from the fact that he mistakes the unity appropriate to our projects. Talk of our *Volk* and our generation suggests a whole unified world already enfolding us. But need the world be so unified?

Heidegger would argue that our thrownness must be in some way a totality. He is willing to grant that our reflective conceptual account of the world does not need to be unified into some systematic whole such as philosophers have sought. But he demands that our pre-reflective active world have the unity of a single meaning of being. Any such understanding must be of "beings in totality" or "beings as a whole."[8] But even granting that a project includes an understanding of the being of the entities that it lets stand revealed to us, why must we presume that those entities must include beings in totality?

Heidegger is making the Kantian presumption that all local languages and practices must have an inner skeleton of fully general categories and principles. But need this be the case? Perhaps language and practice are, as Wittgenstein would claim, a motley assemblage of local activities without any deep unity or general reach. Could not our pre-reflective world be an interpenetration of many different understandings and projects, and in the way that our ordinary language is a jumble of local theories and ontologies and projects? Nor need this multiplicity be gathered together in the background. To demand that it

154 be so encountered is to demand too much unity from the self. Any presentation of the multiplicity *as a whole* would be in a subsequent act of reflection.

We can relate this to an earlier point. It is tempting to think of modern individuals as exemplifying a process that has its own built-in goals independent of all contingent content. Thus we might define individuals as preference or interest maximizers. The interests are the contingent material, while the process of maximizing is defined in a formal way that does not include any particular content. But there is a hidden substantive commitment even here. Why maximizing? Why not minimizing our interests? Or satisficing? Or spurning them for creativity? Maximizing is chosen because it is presumed that the organism has needs and desires it wants to fulfill, not frustrate. This seemingly innocent biologic or psychological presupposition hides the real issue. For wants and desires come already coded, and maximizing is just one operator within the codes. By the time we are sufficiently developed to be individuals, to be able to say our desires or choose our projects, we are already strung on language and culture. There are no naked desires; it is always too late for that. But that does not mean there is one deep language that structures all our desires.

If there is no final language before or behind the multiplicity, then we should not be seeking with Heidegger for some unified secret sense of our age, or for nostalgic places where we can finally be at home. Our task is, as Nietzsche says, to "give style" to our character and to our places, style that does not come from some necessary deep unity so much as from openness and a willingness to take up the possibilities we are thrown among in a way more multiple than Heidegger would approve.

This would mean toning down the seductive "history of being" in Heidegger's later thought. The descriptions of the various epochs of that history become at most heuristic guides to tangled situations. In particular we should mistrust Heidegger's analysis of technology and *Gestell* as "the essence" of modernity.[9]

EMPIRICAL PLACES

Thinkers influenced by Marx share Heidegger's distrust of contemporary culture, but diagnose the problem in a much more empirical way. They argue that the postmodern world has a material base that Heidegger and his followers need to take more seriously (cf. Foster 1983 and Jameson 1983 and 1985). Place is not being destroyed by a destiny of

being, nor by the metaphysical search for security and selfhood, but by
the socioeconomic facts of life. The international flow of capital, the
loss of control over national and regional markets, the commoditiza-
tion of architectural use-value, these are what doom any attempt to
stabilize places today.

At its most pessimistic, with Manfredo Tafuri (1976 and 1987), this
line of thought leads to the conclusion that the architect can do nothing to influence the overall system. While Le Corbusier could offer
architecture as a way to accomplish the goals of revolution, for Tafuri
there will be no architecture until after the revolution. A slightly less
pessimistic Fredric Jameson and Kenneth Frampton see the possibility
for architects to keep alive the ideal of place as a sign of resistance.

Lyotard deals very differently than Frampton or Jameson with the
problem of local places (1984 and 1986b). He certainly opposes the
rule of flowing capital that turns all our language games into strategies
of exchange. But the postmodern condition is not just due to the flow
of capital erasing local places. It is a semiotic condition, a universal circulation of signifiers released from the myth of a direct relation to the
signified. Chains of signifiers float and interpenetrate; firm identities
are myths; neither the self nor society has enough consistency to build a
stable place. Any attempt to hold on to a rigid system of signification
can be a form of terrorism.

For Lyotard the flow of capital actually restricts postmodern flexibility. Capital introduces its own terror as it reduces the flow of signs to
the simple exchange of performance and profit. The cure is not to further restrict the flow by making solid local places, but to widen it with
new language games that challenge what has been established, and present new forms and phrases that cannot be translated into the common
coin of information exchange, at least for a time. In doing so we rein-
vent ourselves. This is similar to and follows the same stages as the
metaphorical transformation of language that I described earlier,
though Lyotard stresses discontinuity and independence where I stress
affiliation and intersection.

I argued above that Heidegger burdens his discussion of place with
undue emphasis on unity and totality. There is a similar danger when
critics speak about our being dominated by the system and flow of late
capitalism. This can sound like modernism's universal force of rationalization that was to have overwhelmed all historical styles. We are
no longer so convinced that modernism made history vanish; perhaps
we should be slow to believe that capital is already universally dominant. Is this the only way we are to describe our situation? Must we

156 characterize everything in terms of its subservience or resistance to that flow? Why should we assume that the deepest description of our lives is that of the financial or cognitive masters? Why not assume that the natives might be in touch with their own situation? Certainly, we cannot deny the pressure on local places. That capitalism completely dominates may be a fantasy of totality, a fantasy which has been strengthened by the modernist concepts we tend to use to describe our situation.

Horkheimer and Adorno's apocalyptic despair has become popular again today, but Habermas seems to me correct in his conclusion that our problems stem from a pressure upon the lifeworld rather than a complete victory of the impersonal imperatives of system flow and efficiency. I criticized Habermas for the purely formal goals contained in his three-world story and tried to suggest ways in which his attempt to broaden the notion of rationality could be widened even further; but his overall picture of system and lifeworld seems more useful than the dramatic totalizations in much postmodern thought. I take up these issues again in the section on consumer culture in the final chapter.

DECONSTRUCTED PLACES

If we are not imperial rationalists, nor Heidegger's rooted peasants, nor easy ironists, what kind of place can we make for ourselves? Neither the moderns nor most postmoderns challenge the goal of making places that express our identity. But should we even try to be "at home"?

For Derrida and others the desire to be at home in a place is an attempt to close the gap between us and some centering values and ways of life, as if we could overcome the distantiations and divergencies that make it possible for us to have a way of life at all. There is no way to embody the center, which is always deferred; the indwelling center has always no longer been where it was supposed to be. The unity of dwelling always escapes us; like any structure of thought or language, a built place contains the movement of its own deconstruction. Architecture should make this manifest by using the local language to show how it never fully comes together (see the Eisenman drawing).

We should, in this view, give up the picture of buildings as something in which an individual or a community can represent itself to itself. Our attempts to be at home are made possible, and ultimately frustrated, by the labile non-presence of the building "in itself." Peter Eisenman attempted to design a house that showed this. His House X dealt with the problems of centering and multiple readings as he deconstructed the purist language of his own earlier plans. The line between this and the ironic postmodern mode can be hard to find; but House X, which is full of complex inner relations and references that frustrate one another as they allow multiple readings and pit standard unities against one another without achieving totality, is not an exercise in ironic historicism.

Eisenman's task was made simpler because the purist language he chose to deconstruct already contained explicit centering principles that made wonderful targets. It is less clear how the deconstructive gesture would be accomplished with a fuller and more ambiguous historical vocabulary, but there is no reason to think it could not be done.

But such buildings would lose their point if there were very many of them. They need contrast with an accepted language; if a deconstructive mode itself became the accepted language, the buildings would lose their inner tension. Turned into architectural vernaculars that could fill the fabric of our cities, such buildings would no longer work as they were intended(!) to do. Deconstruction does not allow us to make places but only to dance on the borders of the almost-places we have. All places have borders even in their centers, and the deconstructive task is to find those borders and the ways in which our constructions cross them while denying that they do.

If all unified places maintain their limits because in marginal ways they enact their own decentering and self-transgression, this is a permanent condition of all places. But it does not mean that we cannot have effective places to the extent that they are possible. And for the play of deconstruction to work, they have to be possible. Marginality demands pages. If there were no text to deconstruct then either deconstructive architecture would become a kind of sarcasm, or it would collapse into a new orthodoxy. In either case there would be a new metaphysical text and the deconstructive task would begin anew.

But if they remain deliberately marginal and play against the mass of others, deconstructive buildings could have a crucial role. Instead of extending architectural vocabularies, as I have urged for ordinary buildings, deconstructive architecture could demonstrate the limits of any vocabulary and the ways our vocabularies are implicated in wider codes and systems. There is a sense in which every building does this, but the city would be helped if some did it explicitly.

There is a tendency to run together deconstructive criticism with the critique of late capitalist society. This is useful but dangerous, for it can

158   turn the delicacy of deconstructive operations into a blunt instrument of totality. Homelessness, transgression, decenteredness, and the like become reified as tools with which to oppose current trends. Deconstruction is not a theory which reveals some hidden level of forces waiting to be enlisted on our behalf. It can free us for more creative gestures and resistances, but it does not by itself take a stand on the issues of the day. To think it does is to change it into haughty irony and hidden totality.

Too much discussion about place presumes a single identity for each self or community. That identity is to be expressed in a place or to be overwhelmed by some universal flow. But if our identities are not single-ply, if tradition is not a simple immediate given, then a livable place may not be a matter of dogged resistance. Frampton is right when he says that our universal civilization and our local cultures must qualify each other (1983). But how are we to find in the local culture projects and forms of life that can help define places? The next chapter discusses what we might find in ourselves and our communities to guide our building.

] 13 [

MAKING PLACES FOR OURSELVES

If we are to build places for ourselves, we need to know who we are, but there are no magic mirrors. Nor would we receive a single reflection. There is no unique home corresponding to some neatly single self or form of life defining us. And even if we were more unified, we could not make a place that would fully enclose us. Architecture cannot do away with the differences and tensions that make it possible to be in places at all. We will always be inside and outside, complicitous and critical.

But still there remain the ordinary questions. It is good to criticize the search for centered perfect dwelling, but where will the septic system go? Which rooms will face the street? How will the building relate to those next door? Doors must be placed, the roof shaped. The design process is not an infinitely open Socratic discussion. Nor, even if the end result is meant to have many inner tensions and be open to future reinterpretations, can the design itself avoid being definite. Lines must be drawn.

Even today too many buildings succeed too well in making vital places; we cannot deny the possibility that we might draw those lines well. We do not have to embrace the ideal of perfect unity in order to build places that shelter and energize us as they open new possibilities. Our lack of a deep center does not imply that we should not have such places as we can. If we refuse this middle condition, we remain too controlled by the demand for totality and presence.

CRITICISM AND POSSIBILITIES

When it comes to finding out who we are, we tend to list our individual preferences and choices. For instance, Charles Moore remarks that

> Easy travel, books, glossy magazines, films, and television have revealed an almost unlimited array of styles our own houses might embody. . . . Conspicuously absent among most of these images are heartfelt, personal convictions about what a house really should be like. In the absence of dreams all choices are reduced to pseudo-choices, no significant choices at all. (Moore, Allen, Lyndon 1974, 132)

159

160   This is stated in terms of the individual. Given the purpose of Moore's book this makes practical sense; clients need to be in touch with their feelings and aspirations. Still, one's aspirations are not so intensely personal as American ideology makes them out to be. Our dreams are in many ways our least individual feature, as the media know, despite what they tell us.

If we put aside the illusion of being the unique source of our life plans, we see how much we are set in motion by history and language. Finding the constraints that make choice meaningful is not a process of delving into the depth of an individual personality after some unique core. To think of it as an exploration of the secret preferences of the individual still clings to the notion that unlimited possibilities lie before us, to be constrained only by personal whim or natural scarcities. [1]

Earlier I discussed the differences between the modern slimmed down personal identity (as maximizers of utilities) and the thicker identities Habermas and Lyotard urge (as self-critical communicators, or as creators of language games). If we are to have more than purely functional places, we need a thicker identity with some historical memory.

The modern movement planned to remove history from architecture; ironic postmoderns make history their material. Both of these gestures put the designer up in the balloon. I opposed the equal access to history demanded by these approaches. They remove from history the purposes for which they would have us use it. If on the contrary history is not something we consult but something we are, if our projects are both opened and limited by the intersections of the multiplicity that is ourselves, then there is no equal access and no free floating. If we are to be pragmatic it is not because, separated from history, we use it for our material.

If we do not try to rise above history with Gropius or Lyotard, we have the task of retrieving the languages and motions we are thrown among, in ways that reveal and change the shape of our possibilities. The multiplicity in which we live does not reduce to a single rational process or structure, and amid that multiplicity there is more that is relatively constant than claims like Lyotard's allow. The aim is not to widen our possibilities toward some impossible maximum but to change them locally. In this process, what I have called metaphor is necessary and irony is not enough.

This means coming to understand ourselves, but self-understanding does not equal assembling a list of preferences. What we need is allegiance, belonging, building this way because it fits, because we are already in that stream, because we inhabit that world. Such inhabitation does not have to be unreflective; one of my major themes has been that self-consciousness need not destroy belonging. To deny this is to confuse all forms of double reference and reflection with superior irony.[2]

We already speak a language. We are not bodiless wraiths blown about by winds of Sophistic rhetoric; we have measures and identities, and confusing though these may be they are not entirely formless. Consumer society tries to wash out those identities, so that we will purchase endlessly to fill that void. But there is still some *what* to who we are. We have roots, but not foundations. Roots divide and multiply and get thinner as they go lower, but they still can hold even if they grasp no metaphysical rock. Our identities may be themselves plural and excessive, but they have historical shapes that are not infinitely malleable.

Theories (or practices) that try to detach us from history do so by seeking a set of principles (or factors) which can be described (or enacted) in relatively formal terms as a platform from which to view the rest of life. This is not necessary; although we cannot do without some formal descriptions of our situation, they need not be thick enough to form a basis for theoretical or ironic distance.[3] Our task is not to choose from some detached point of view, but to see what is happening and criticize it as we can. That criticism does not need a unique platform from which to study and make recommendations.

If there is no strong and deeply unified set of conditions defining the location of our lives, then there is no unified central set of principles that can unfold into a unified field of possibilities to be surveyed. If our selves and our possibilities are constituted by intersections and collocations, by a multiplicity of factors, the variety of their materials will not support indefinitely large spans of possibility. But with such origins neither will our possibilities make a neat set with a limited shape cut from some larger field.

I am not saying that our possibilities are limited in number; the issue concerns their qualitative limits, and whether they form a set that we can measure with a surveying glance. In the modern conception, whatever the size of our set of possibilities, we are able to survey them because the distanced self floats above it all. Instead, I would maintain that we and our community exist as the intersections of thrown projects and possibilities in multiple ways. While we can say some interesting things about the conditions for being selves and societies that have possibilities, none of that will define a point for a universal language game.

162   Any activity or language game makes distinctions (the three colors for traffic lights, the pieces in chess) and embodies rules; these define appropriate and inappropriate moves (there are many ways I can move chess pieces; some are good, some bad, some illegal by the rules of the game, and others simply have no point in the game). But the distinctions and grammars and possible moves for chess games cannot be added together with those for backgammon and soccer to make a unified super-game. At least, there is no floating point of view that could do so. What would be required would be a metaphoric combination or extension to create a practice that gave a point to the new possibilities. But such an extension would be made down on the field, not up in the balloon.

Further, our practices and possibilities intersect each other. Architectural vocabularies are not pure; their choice and the manner of their use are themselves moves in other games, so they limit and constrain one another. How I build and what I do with the vocabulary of the building are not purely aesthetic questions; they are also political statements, class identifications; they are involved in power relations within the group commissioning the building and within the group designing it, and in tensions within individuals, and so on. These other games crisscross in turn, but they do not form a neat hierarchy within a highest game that calls all the moves.

If our possibilities come from no unified origin, there will always be nooks and crannies, leverages, permanent tensions that are not part of any overall structure. There may be large structures, but there will be no overall structure. There will be historical continuities that can help resist the leveling desired by the bureaucracy or worked by the market. And there will be historical discontinuities that have the same effect.

ARCHETYPAL GUIDANCE

But where do we start? We start from where we are. We are always moving within and from current conventions, already on the move in projects we did not choose, in languages we did not create. We do not have to choose between architecture and revolution. It is always too late to start from scratch; there is always language and meaning ahead and behind. That is the condition the moderns tried to overcome, but the tabula cannot be razed, and the attempt to do so leaves what was to be denied present as resented.

But if we have no centered overview, if we are extending our languages and forms of life as we build, how do we know which moves to make? Only some new combinations and moves suggest themselves. We work in a disciplined way, judging what is appropriate, and neither the discipline nor the judgment are universally rational. We work within history—but how?

Defenders of place often presume that a true home for us will be easily recognized, because of some inner harmony with our true self-identity and our deepest needs. But why should this be so? We have no equal access to our selves; we are not always aware of our needs, nor are our selves and needs so unified they are capable of being harmoniously expressed. And when architectural languages grow, a sensitive response may take some time, especially if the new place invites changes in our forms of life.

If, then, there is a question of community and self-discernment, what guides can we find that will help us discover what we have been thrown among?

In previous chapters I discussed self-discernment in general, and later the particular view of Norberg-Schulz (and related views of Harries) that natural archetypes can guide our building. We are to consult those inevitable constants such as our posture, light and dark, opening and enclosing, gravity and support, and the like. Then we should examine the locale for the language of its natural features, and build in a way which lets us dwell in what is given to us.

There are vital places which seem to have been built in this way; for instance, Norberg-Schulz's presentation of the old quarters of Khartoum is very convincing (1984). But the connection between the design and the environment does not show that only this design could have fitted the locale. I argued earlier that the factors Harries cites do not of themselves provide an architectural language. Because they are almost universal, these factors do not by themselves provide guidance for how one might modulate them appropriately to a given project.

Further, the fact that a successful place can be read in this fashion does not show that this is the only way to create places. It might be that abrupt transgression of the natural scene would give us what is needed. Harries and Norberg-Schulz are too influenced by Heidegger's totalizing description of the modern world. While I agree with them that the alternative to modernity is for us to look for the languages and projects that we are thrown among, I question whether this means we should look for a natural or primal language.

Another recourse to archetypes is to guide our place-making by classic building types. These need not be absolutely universal; it is enough if the types are embedded deeply in our tradition and environment.

164 Thus the colonnade, the domed building, the open market could have an almost universal significance, or at least a natural basis for their conventional significance. Some have elaborated this into a defense of classicism as providing a permanent set of types (Krier 1987, Porphyrios 1984).

But reference to types is not a helpful general solution. As I remarked earlier, any system of building types is inherently fragmentary. Because building types receive their significance from ongoing forms of life, they do not fall into systems except insofar as daily life does. It would be a mistake to presume that we have a clearly articulated system of cultural activities on which we could hang a contemporary or revivalist set of building types. Our building types share the confusion of our social practices.

If we pretended that they formed a unified system, an enforced set of canonical building types might end up replacing the modernist universal pure language with a universal historicist language. Would we be better off? If we avoid this static trap, however, then we countenance metaphorical changes in, among other things, building types. But that process of change is what the appeal to archetypes was supposed to control in the first place.

REGIONAL GUIDANCE

A more promising guide is regionalism. Consider first a simple criterion that dictates adherence to the region's particular shapes (or types or vocabularies). Something seems right about the idea, for it highlights the historical nature of real possibilities for concrete communities. But there are many problems; foremost is the lack of homogeneous regions. While the natural context may be constant in New England or in the Southwest (to name two regions that do maintain some architectural distinctiveness), even there the social and cultural scenes multiply and change. Maine natives and those who moved to Maine "from away" may not agree on the appropriate shape and amount of development, yet each claims a vision of the region. Recently Phoenix, Arizona, held a design competition for a civic center that would express the city's regional essence; there turned out to be no agreement on what that essence was, except for general references to the desert and the area's Spanish heritage (Attoe 1987). Simple regionalism takes its regions too simply.

Our ideal of regionalism comes from Europe, where nations and cities have long histories with distinctive building traditions. But

America lacks such convenient separations. No place today here or anywhere can rest serenely within a unique central tradition. This does not
mean that there are no regions, only that we must not expect tight internal unity.

Kenneth Frampton urges regionalism as a strategy of resistance, because a regional identity is not something that can be exchanged for a
more up-to-date model. Regional identities can hold out at least for a
time against the maximization of profit and efficiency. This resembles
Weber's retreat to humanistic enclaves. However, Frampton's regionalism provides more than refuge.

> Everything will depend on the capacity of rooted culture to recre-
> ate its own tradition while appropriating foreign influences at the
> level of both culture and civilization. . . . Regionalism is a dialec-
> tical expression. It self-consciously seeks to deconstruct universal
> Modernism, in terms of values and images which are quintessen-
> tially rooted, and at the same time to adulterate these basic
> references with paradigms drawn from alien sources. . . . Any at-
> tempt to circumvent this dialectical synthesis through a recourse
> to superficial historicism can only result in consumerist iconogra-
> phy masquerading as culture. (Frampton 1982, 77; cf. Kurokawa
> 1988, 31)

Such regions would not be tight static unities. Frampton does not
want regional identities to block the flow of change and capital, but to
call on local resources that can shape the flow. He seems to me correct
in his claim that "the model of the hegemonic center surrounded by
dependent satellites is an inadequate description of our cultural possibilities." Those who deny that there is any such regional energy to
qualify the universal flow are still too mesmerized by images of totality; they mistake claims about universal dominance for an achieved
total mastery of the local scene. Frampton himself sometimes talks in
this manner and envisions his regions more as hard blocks resisting a
universal solvent. In the next chapter I will have more to say about this
picture. Still, the general point made in the above citation seems right,
that we must find some dialectic that allows historical identities and
larger processes to interact in a way which qualifies both sides. But
those historical identities seldom if ever sort themselves out into neat
regions.

Regionalism as a strategy then becomes the broader task of finding
our native languages and vocabularies in their messiness and intersections. Instead of presuming that there is some core identity to be
preserved, we should rather seek to extend those languages, taking ad-

166 vantage of what we find already in action. A regional tone is partly found, partly created, always changing. But, again, just because it is historical and multiple does not mean that it is totally malleable. Judgments about such identities and their changes call for discerning appropriateness, for which there can be no rules, but which is not arbitrary.

PRECEDENT AND REREADING

We can gain some insight about ways of dealing with our multiple history by considering the process of reaching decisions in the common law, which tries to maintain connections with the past while introducing changes as they seem appropriate. Peter Collins (1971) discusses the role of precedent in law and architecture, arguing that professional competence in architecture is joined with creative innovation in ways akin to what occurs in the law. Collins tries to show that architectural judgment, like legal judgment, "must have a rational basis which can be intelligibly explained" (179). "Rational" here does not mean reliance on universal principles but on precedent and on the details of the problem set by the commission. It is the problem-solving aspect of architecture that distinguishes it, for Collins, from the "fine arts" (whatever the validity of that category, about which Collins has his doubts). Architecture will work best when it keeps continuity with the past in a manner similar to the flexible way precedent functions in the law (see the River Crest and Hillingdon photos).

William Hubbard (1980) analyzes a classic series of eleven common-law liability cases dating from 1816 to 1932. The judges in each case "made their opinions plausible by showing how they submitted to the wisdom of their predecessors, but they made their opinions convincing by showing how they exceeded their predecessors" (121). The judges explained what they took to be essential in the precedents; their explanations go beyond the intent of the earlier cases, as far as that can be determined. The later cases reread the earlier and create a kind of continuity that expands the definition of liability. Continuity is not identity.

For architecture, Hubbard cites the six strategies of "misreading" from Harold Bloom's *The Anxiety of Influence*. Bloom shows how poets redescribe past works to make them fit with new ones, how they emphasize those aspects of the structure of old works that prefigure the new, how they present the new as doing more fully what they say the old was trying to achieve. Such claims need not be made by theoretical pronouncements; they can be enacted in the new work itself.

It would be a mistake to take Bloom's term "misreading" as saying that the poets depart from a strictly historical reading of the past. What they are doing is what a historical reading always does when it is involved in new production.[4] I argued earlier that we could copy the past by duplicating old buildings, but that a copied Notre Dame, like a copied Don Quixote, does not have the same form as the original.

Hubbard avoids the Freudian themes that for Bloom define the poet's situation, and so he bypasses much of what Bloom is trying to say. Still, Hubbard applies Bloom's strategies to architecture in interesting ways. For instance, he compares Jefferson's University of Virginia campus and Moore's Kresge College, using Bloom's rubrics to show the mixture of continuity and criticism by which Moore asserts himself.

It seems right that what Bloom calls "strong misreadings" bring a rewarding sense of continuity and difference. But even with all the nuances Bloom suggests, continuity is only one way of relating to the past. Abrupt contestation or the appearance of a radical break are other ways that have been employed in architecture.

Hubbard, however, has reasons to desire at least the appearance of continuity. He contends that a crucial function of any organized activity (a game, the law, architecture) is to keep at bay our sense of the lack of ultimate grounds for what we do. We hide the void by a screen of conventions that, if we lend them our complicity, keep us finding new reasons to do things their way. A good building rewards our complicity by seeming inevitable; it continually provides new reasons for cooperating with the design, new aspects and meanings, and new relations to the past. A bad building gives us no reasons why it is designed this way rather than another, and so it reveals the dangerous void behind all design.[5]

This presupposes that we will be damaged if we must face frontally our lack of absolute grounds. It is true that when we confront the limitations and mortality that make us what we are, we do not lose the desire for absolute grounds, but that confrontation may make us more, not less, accepting of the historical givens amid which we find ourselves (cf. Krell 1986).

Hubbard's detailed analyses move in what seems to me the right direction: a forceful hermeneutics that questions accepted continuity but does not pretend to ascend above its own history even when changing

168   or opposing it. But historical continuities and reinterpretations are more satisfying than he supposes. Nietzsche wanted us to own up to the death of God; but at least in his less resentful moments Nietzsche did not want us to keep our teeth clenched in disappointment. Hubbard's claim that we have to hide the groundlessness of conventions continues the metaphysical tradition's avoidance of the partial grounds and reasons that we do have. We need appropriateness, not necessity.

In the end Hubbard remains too much a disappointed modernist. That is not to say many postmodern buildings are not empty bombast. But critics who insist that postmodernism has departed from rational (or traditional) fixed principles into a no-man's-land of arbitrary show are themselves still in thrall with the modernist desire for the inevitable design (cp. Kimball 1988). We cannot build places for ourselves if we remain under that severe rule, because that rule defines us as creatures of no place.

THE PRESENCE OF THE PAST

Bloom's strategies bring the past into the present. Once there, it is submitted to our contrasts and meanings even as its rereading helps establish those contrasts. Earlier I pointed out how the architect's original intention, and architectural citations, irony, and parody, all decay when the building comes to be lived without reference to its original context. In such cases the past disappears; in Bloom's strategies the past remains but is overcome. In both cases the present dominates.

Can this process be generalized? Can we say that all our relations to the past are acts of Nietzschean reappropriation that take it into contemporary schemes of contrast and meaning? The past would be causally related to the present, but there would be no depth to its inclusion in the present. It is not clear if Nietzsche himself believes this exactly, given the ambiguities of his notion of genealogy. But modern Nietzscheans do; in Baudrillard (1985) we hear most boisterously the claim that the past has no presence save as a collection of elements reappropriated into a net of signifiers defined by current conditions of interchangeability. The past lingers as a simulacrum of itself inside our networks of exchange, to which it contributes nothing but more tokens. So the past provides no deep roots; there is only the rhizome that crawls along making synchronic connections.

In one sense it is obviously true that the sets of contrasts which provide meaning are all contemporary. The modern horse evolved from the ancient eohippus, but that does not mean that we have to learn about eohippus in order to deal with modern horses. The relation is only causal and does not affect the contemporary networks of meaning and practice in which horses appear. But not all relations to the past are of this type. Modern democratic institutions have evolved from a variety of older practices and theories. In this case, however, that background allows one to find tensions and repressed possibilities in the modern arrangements which may not be noticed by one who takes them as present immediacy. (For instance, the tensions between democracy as the general will, democracy as compromise, and democracy as dialogue.) The past provides an encounter with the otherness and unfulfilled possibilities that have not been totally leveled out within modern practices; they are not tokens in circulation but partial projects under way.

The Nietzschean claim about our relation to the past is quite general, and it does not try to restrict the form our appropriation of the past will take. In current discussions, however, the reduction of the past usually ends up with the claim that all our activities and language games become variants of one game of exchange, whether this is defined in semiotic or in capitalist terms (which I argued earlier are not equivalent). What is it that is supposed to have so reduced the apparent variety of activities we engage in? What has happened to love and cooking and running for office? They are all involved in exchange, but they are not the same. Just because all languages link noun phrases to verb phrases does not make French the same as Japanese.

One could claim that the reduction is due to a universal condition for the possibility of any symbolic system, a condition that we have finally noticed for what it is. This claim can be read two ways. The unobjectionable reading points out that the slide of signifiers, self-transgression, and lack of a center condition and afflict *all* the games we play. This is important and true, and a source of what I have called humble irony. The objectionable reading is that self-transgression and exchange of signifiers is the *only* game we play. This is either trivial or false. It is trivially true in the sense that everything we speak is a language. It is false as a historical claim (and as a claim that invokes two suspect principles, essentialism, and the standard modernist story of final self-discovery).

Second, one could argue with Heidegger that some quasi-transcendental condition of modern existence, something like the essence of technology, reduces all human activities to such flattened play. If this

170   does not reduce to the ambiguous claim in the previous paragraph, it begs the question by postulating as a condition of possibility for today's culture the very unity of culture which is at issue.[6]

Finally, one could claim more empirically that there is something currently active, perhaps the new technology or the media or the systemic imperatives of late capitalism, that has overpowered or undermined historical activities, reducing them to simulacra or commoditized versions of their former selves. While this claim again presupposes the kind of total dominance that is in question, it opens the door for discussion about the actual reach of the influences cited. This returns us to discussing ordinary processes and history, where we should mistrust such totalizing analyses.

We have complex historical identities that do not dissolve into total play. In designing places for ourselves we need to find ways to discern the languages and projects we find ourselves among. There are no infallible guides for such discernment. We need to read the multiple texts of our lives, to reread and write again. This will not lead to an inevitable place where we will be fully at home. Abandoning that metaphysical goal frees us to work from where we are. I have repeated too often that this work does not have to be ironic, though it cannot help being reflective. But can it be self-critical? The last chapter deals with the problems of self-criticism and wholeness in the multiple city.

] 14 [
BUILDING TOGETHER/
BUILDINGS TOGETHER

We have to build together since our products refuse to stand apart. Despite what is said in the critiques of modernity, we need to be mindful of the whole. Unlike the other arts in which totality has been attacked, architecture exists in a finite real space. Buildings stand together in the space of our daily activities, not only in the space created by criticism and artistic reference. Like texts and paintings, buildings may have complex relations one to another, with all the "intertextuality" desired, but buildings also stand immobile, blocking one another's view. One painting does not have to be demolished to make room for another. Places cannot ignore one another completely; too much must be shared by way of services and infrastructure. A city forms a whole no matter what we do, and we live with the results. So even if we are opposed to the notion of a total vision, we have to care for the city as a whole. But what is this care that is not a total vision?

With this question we return to issues raised earlier with the Sophists and the Habermas/Lyotard debate. Can we be self-critical without a universal project? Socrates either never finishes or appears as one more cabal. If his wisdom is unavailable, we might try liberal tolerance, but the city cannot be cared for by the simple principle of respecting one another's projects. There is not enough space and time, and we share too much. Your building may overshadow mine, or strain the transit system, or destroy the scale. When mutual respect gives way to regulation and bargaining, the planning czars become only another voice in the crowd, since there are many kinds of force that can be brought to bear by all the parties concerned. Lyotard's more avantgarde vision of justice also fails in the city context; faced with building together (rather than against) it reduces to a liberalism that does not demand internal self-criticism.

I have urged self-criticism by metaphorical extension and rereading the past. In our world of many languages and forms of life, we need a multiplicity of interactions and a care for the whole, but how do we *build* that?[1]

IS THERE A POSTMODERN WORLD?

One way to unify the whole is to demand that it express some unified spirit of the age. Buildings gather up our world, and if we feel our world is distinctive we may want a distinctive new style. So it was with the nineteenth century's search for a style appropriate to their perception that a new age had dawned (cf. Crook 1987). So it was again with the modern movement's claim that the new technological and democratic world demanded a new purity in design. Celebrating that new world turned out to be difficult, since bureaucracy and power kept slipping into what were supposed to embody progress and democracy.

So it is that postmoderns now claim the world has changed again and needs a new architecture. The self-consciously pluralistic world needs eclectic historical references, twisting and colliding styles, and irony that calls attention to itself. Again there has been a problem with what is being celebrated, the quoted historical traditions or the self-consciousness that does the quoting. Does postmodernism reveal our continuity with traditional worlds, or does it level all traditions into a bland availability for consumption? Can it care for the whole, or only flatten it out?

With these questions we return to the issue Hegel raised in speaking of "the substance of consciousness." The modernists claimed that there was no longer any substantial content inherent in our lives. Self and society were freed from the limitations of tradition, and without any except pragmatic restrictions we faced an indefinitely open field of possibilities. This would find its embodiment in an architecture of pure form.

Postmodern writers reject these claims to purity and universality. I argued, however, that in important ways most postmoderns continue modernism. Both presuppose a version of distanced subjectivity (rational or ironic). Weber's detached manipulative subject returns in the guise of the chameleon architect who seeks to embody the postmodern condition in building forms that treat all history as equally accessible.

Notice that both modernists and postmodernists share the presupposition that there is a unified theme to our world that ought to be expressed in our buildings. While they proclaimed a revolution against nineteenth-century historical styles, the modernist pioneers agreed that it was the business of the architect to express the spirit of the age.

> [Modern architecture] is based on the same Victorian presuppositions about architecture as undergirded the Gothic revival more

than a century ago: it results, that is, from a self-conscious attempt 173
by the architect to invent a style that will express what he presumes
to be the unifying spirit of his age and that will at the same time
(paradoxically enough) propagate and inculcate that spirit in a recalcitrant populace which grievously lacks it. (Smith 1971, 81)

Here are a series of nineteenth-and twentieth-century statements of
that presupposition:

1808: The design of almost every age and country has a peculiar
character . . . [every house] should maintain the character of a
house of the age and country in which it is erected. (Richard
Payne Knight, quoted in Crook 1987, 30)

1860: [We need] an indigenous style of our own for this age of
new creations. (Thomas Harris, quoted in Crook 1987, 138)

1863: [Is] the nineteenth century condemned to end without ever
possessing an architecture of its own? Is it to transmit to pos-
terity nothing but pastiches and hybrids? (Viollet-le-Duc,
quoted in Crook 1987, 85)

1902: Art as the commentator or the recorder of human life, re-
flecting not only its physical aspects but its mental attitude . . .
registers the prevailing sentiments of its period. (Walter Crane,
in the Arts and Crafts Movement, quoted in Smith 1971, 16)

1906: At no time and in no instance has Architecture been other
than an index of the flow of the thought of the people—an ema-
nation from the inmost life of the people. (Louis Sullivan,
quoted in Smith 1971, 16)

1923: The character of an epoch is epitomized in its buildings. . . .
A vital architectural spirit, rooted in the entire life of a people,
represents the interrelation of all phases of creative effort, all
arts, all techniques. (Walter Gropius, quoted from Smith 1971,
21).

1923: A great epoch has begun. There exists a new spirit. . . .
Style is a unity of principle animating all the work of an epoch,
the result of a state of mind which has its own special character.
(Le Corbusier 1931, 3)

1983: The world now emerging is searching freely in memory, because it knows how to find its own "difference" in the removed
repetitions and utilization of the entire past. (Portoghesi 1983,
13)

The delicate question is this: are we now living in a world whose
unified meaning is a new kind of multiplicity and mixture? Or does
that multiplicity mean that we are not living in a world with a unified
meaning at all?

174   What is the difference between saying that we live in a world whose unified theme is multiplicity, and saying that we do not live in a unified world? The difference is that in the second case irony (or any other meta-attitude) is not required as the expression of the true spirit of the age, for there is no spirit of the age to express. There is no special attitude one must have toward one's local practices or vocabulary in order to be fully in accord with the age. There is nothing that must be expressed along with the local language.

The claim that our age has a unified spirit seems obvious until one tries to prove it.[2] Testing all the details of our age would be an endless task. Citing a few typical or metonymic examples does not prove a universal spirit. No social-scientific investigation could establish such a strong claim. The evidence cited by Lyotard, Baudrillard, and others may exist; the question is whether they prove a universal condition. In fact the claim can only be supported by some elaborate philosophical scaffolding, usually Hegelian or Heideggerean, whose soundness is itself deeply suspect. Once that scaffolding is seen for what it is, the most we can claim is that there may be some very large-scale processes and movements, but they exist together with others and have no guaranteed primacy.

This means that there is no modernist or postmodernist platform from which one can survey in principle the limits of local practices and languages without confronting those limits by working in the local languages. It means that vernacular architecture need not be a naive decline from self-consciousness. Nor is "invisible" architecture necessarily a second-rate form. You are not missing some essence of the postmodern world when you use the local vocabulary, with awareness that there are others but without ironic commentary. The limits of the local language become apparent as you speak, and you can try to extend that language.

You can be straightforward. But you will always be in context with other forms of life; there is no escaping the awareness of diversity. But there is no requirement that you signal that awareness in your every act of building.

On the other hand, none of this means that there is a requirement of straightforwardness. Saying that we can be simple does not mean that we should all be fundamentalists. To claim that there is no unified spirit of our age may seem to imply that there are at least some smaller unities. But that does not necessarily follow. I suggested earlier that the many forms of life are not isolated or insulated worlds, or even internally unified. The individual exists as an intersection of many languages and practices; there is no automatic unity on any level, no unity that has only external relations with other unities. If there is no unified spirit of the age, neither is there a single unified spirit of America, or of Chicago, or of a Polish-American neighborhood—which is not to say that these have no characters of their own. We are all strifes and dialogues, but we are not shapeless. This multiplicity is not neat; it does not form a list; it is not made up of items with clean boundaries. Identities overlap and exceed as stories twist.

And that does not mean that the multiple worlds do not have to deal with one another—or measure up to new facts, or to the consequences of their values, or to the intersection of practices, or to what the neighbors think. Or to their own internal diversity. These are issues people have always had to face, and there are good and bad ways of facing them.

We are not simply products nor simply members of anything. What it means to be "in" a language or a community already involves inner spaciousness and openness to what I have called metaphorical change. Our selves are constituted at and as the intersection of multiple language games and practices that are themselves internally multiple, the result of previous extensions and blendings. And if there is no place from which the multiplicity within and among us makes a uniquely ordered whole, that does not mean that the multiplicity is totally indeterminate, or that we see it from nowhere.

We can know that our lives have many contingent forms, without having to constantly advertise that fact as the unified meaning of our lives. But that fact must influence us, nonetheless. What does it mean to live in such a world, if it does not mean we must adopt an ironic stance toward any given language or form of life? If we are not fundamentalists, it means self-criticism. But how do we build that, together?

THE PROBLEM OF JUMBLE

History may not make a whole, and within ourselves and in society there may be no neat order. But when we act, we act together. When we build, we build next to one another. Intellectual and cultural space may have a strange discontinuous topology, but physical space remains stubbornly finite and continuous. Our buildings will stand together whether we do or not.

So the modern movement had some point in decreeing the abolition of historical jumble. What was imperialistic about modernist planning was the message that demands for historical continuity and tradition were part of the past. When a new building seemed disconnected or unintelligible, it was up to us to change. This sounds elitist and it was.

The moderns oscillated between the total plan that rigidly controlled every aspect of the city, and the practice of making each building an isolated monument with no regard for its neighbors. There are, however, more kinds of architectural wholes than these. Colin Rowe's eloquent attack on modernist planning points to other wholes, such as his "collage city" where many intentions and small domains coexist without being neatly integrated (Rowe 1976). Most postmodern architects have embraced some descendant of this picture, although there ought to be some difference between a collage and an arbitrary collection of objects.

We are left with the jumbled cities the moderns were trying to avoid and to which they finally contributed. We cannot solve the problem of jumble by returning to some imagined uniform community and a hierarchical set of building types. Should we then just learn to love what we have?

Around many cities, towers rise here and there, separately and in small clusters, above a carpet of low-rise buildings and tree-shaded streets. The overall outline is reminiscent of Le Corbusier's dream city of neatly separated perfect towers rising above a park. But these are not modernist forms: these buildings are in competition for tenants, so each strives to be different from the rest. At the feet of the towers lies neither Le Corbusier's park nor Jane Jacobs's urban mix, but tract housing, condo developments, and commercial strips.

Is this a satisfactory urban form? People are buying the condos and flocking to the malls; is this what they want? If we are suspicious of the elitism of the modernists, we should be slow to condemn recent developments. One might argue that the new suburban (some have called them "post-suburban") centers are a new community arrangement that we have yet to learn to do well. Why not let the normal forces of markets and popular dynamics take their natural course? Here is a typical defense:

> People forget that Venice was built by hook or by crook. Venice was as mercantilist as Tysons [a suburban center outside Washington]. It was full of land speculators and developers. The merchants' primary concern was about the flow of goods, of traffic. Those who now romanticize Venice collapse 1,000 years of history. Venice is a monument to a dynamic process, not great urban planning. It is hard for us to imagine, but the architectural harmo-

ny of the Piazza San Marco was an accident. It was built over centuries by people who were constantly worried whether they had enough money.[3]

This quote is misleading in the usual American way: it pictures the only options as centralized planning or the free market. Those who produced the buildings around the Piazza San Marco looked at the whole they were making. They did not make context-ignoring monuments or ironic rhapsodies.

The defense of sprawl and jumble continues: people will get the cities they want; if they wanted more they could protest. The architect should speak the people's language, doing it a little better, adding some art, but not assuming the role of Cultural Tutor.

This sounds reasonable, but like all invocations of the invisible hand it ignores the fact of differential access to power. In our age the sources of decision about building are not easily located or influenced when people want to mount a protest. We are not necessarily "the people" who "want" what *we* get. Architecture is reduced to its commercial common denominator, a shapeless mass now resurfaced with historical goodies. We live amid the results by learning not to look, but we owe ourselves an environment that we can respect.

The aesthetic and planning consequences of the laissez-faire position have often been associated with Robert Venturi's slogans that "Main Street is almost all right" and that we should "learn from Las Vegas." In their defense of popular culture Venturi and Scott Brown do oppose the elitism of "European critics" who see "consumer folk culture" as only "the manufactured fantasies of mass taste." In line with American populism and pragmatism they see people's preferences as something to be trusted, especially on the occasions when those preferences can be manifested in a less constrained environment. "Why must architects continue to believe that when 'the masses' are 'educated' they'll want what the architects want? Why do we turn to exotic folk cultures, as interpreted by other architects . . . rather than learning directly from the cultures around us?" (Venturi and Scott Brown 1984, 35).

Venturi's position is more nuanced than appears from the way he is often cited. He does emphasize the need to abandon dreams of formal purity and to learn from the vitality and complexity of the actual urban landscape. He insists that the contemporary city can teach us not to oversimplify. Variety has its price, however; in our world we cannot develop a new building type for every function and every group. Instead Venturi encourages a symbolic architecture of "decorated sheds,"

178   plain forms with applied decoration that advertises history and current use. We should deal with pluralism by allowing symbols, rather than forms, to proliferate. The whole becomes an assemblage of symbols in space.[4]

The symbols need not be clamorous in the Las Vegas manner. Venturi's design for the new wing of the National Gallery in London shows the subtlety of his approach. The building is a simple mass decorated on each facade to match the neighborhood that the side faces. This "serial contextualism" allows the building to avoid competing with the famous monuments in the vicinity, while quietly "calling attention at every turn to its own polite behavior" (Boles 1987).

Yet Venturi's symbolic method could lead to a second-level uniformity, where all buildings displayed themselves in the same manner no matter how different their logos might be. Compared to that strategy, the postmodern attempt to discover new building forms or rework old ones offers more variation of type, but it makes for another kind of clutter. While individual programs and sites might respond to the needs and histories and taste cultures of the clients, the whole city would not cohere. Disneyland does have a greater variety of building forms than Las Vegas, but is it a solution to the problem of jumble?

One might claim that the many different architectural forms in a postmodern city could be unified by their common ironic tone. I argued, however, that the kind of irony associated with most postmodern meta-theories creates only a decorated version of the modernist city, which either lacks coherence or imposes far too much uniformity.

It is possible to build a public space that celebrates and yet remains ironic. Moore's Piazza d'Italia in New Orleans seems to have worked well for the local Italian community. The ironies that it proclaims to the knowledgeable critic do not seem to bother the local inhabitants; this is a successful example of Jencks's double coding. We should worry, however, that such showy postmodern historicism works best in commercial buildings and spaces where what is celebrated is consumption and fantasy. Kenneth Frampton attacked these as "cardboard scenography" and "never-ending fashionable displays" (Frampton 1982, 76).[5] This begins to wear thin as it becomes a standardized language for commercial developments whose claim to historical memory has no more validity than their older cousins' claim to functional rationality.

Leon Krier's acerbic sketches pillory awkward postmodern juxtapositions of one shape after another (cf. Porphyrios 1984). His own

solution offers a classical vocabulary that is capable of wide variations.
It seems doubtful that this would bring the heterogeneity Americans treasure in their cities, but it raises the key questions: what does it mean for a city or a neighborhood or a region to cohere architecturally? Is coherence the only alternative to jumble?

The way artists change their rules makes it impossible to find useful general criteria of coherence for works of art. Even the negative criterion of avoiding contradiction has problems in metaphorical discourse, so it is of little help in art, where contradiction is not precisely defined (and insofar as it is, can be used toward new forms). We are not going to come up with any clear positive or negative criteria for a coherent city. Even functional inconveniences might work well on other levels, as when disruptions in smooth traffic patterns create opportunities for interaction and festivity.

The problem of coherence is finally the same as the problem of appropriate and disciplined judgment, as when we estimate the success of metaphorical changes in a vocabulary. There are no rules, but that is not to say that the judgment is arbitrary, or that one person may not possess more than another.

We saw in the last chapter how strong rereadings of history can extend architectural language. The same strategy can also be applied synchronically to the city. The urban context can be treated much as I suggested that historical precedents be treated. We care how what we build relates to what is around, but we cannot rely on some secret essence or unified spirit of the locality. It could be that we reread the context and our building changes the place by completing a form or function that was not quite there before. Cesar Pelli's buildings at Battery Park City mix modernism, historical fragments, and fantasies of a New York that never was, and they catalyze a new wholeness in their corner of the city (see photo).[6] In a sense the city could become not a collection of monuments but "an immense construction site of traces and residues" always being reworked with a care for our fragile inhabitation.[7] This could resemble a process of planning by incremental rereading, as discussed by Christopher Alexander (1987).

The classical ideal of hierarchical centered unity has a strong hold on our image of the city. The idea of a unified city with its integrated design and culture does not describe our lives anymore, but we yearn for its order. This makes it difficult to envision other kinds of urban wholes. Habermas remarks that "the urban agglomerations have outgrown the old concept of the city that people so cherish" (Habermas

180 1985b, 327). Among newer concepts I mentioned above Rowe's "collage city;" there is also much to be learned from Kisho Kurokawa's notion of an intermediate continuum.[8]

Still, the classical exemplars cannot be simply denied; doing so allows them to continue to dominate us as that which is to be avoided. They need to be opened up; we have to find their limits. Perhaps paradoxically, if we had more buildings built in a deconstructive manner they could enhance the togetherness of the city, although not its coherence in any usual sense. If we had more buildings that were self-consciously marginal, deconstructing, but making visible, the codes that pervade the city, we would be more aware of our common definitions, and their limits, and our common plight. Such buildings would not be a solution to the problem of designing the average building that fills the urban fabric, but they might help us build together without enforcing any one central identity.

REGIONALISM AND THE CONSUMER SOCIETY

I spoke in the previous chapter of a strategy that Kenneth Frampton refers to as "critical regionalism." Unlike a simple regionalism that seeks to maintain unquestioned coherence with given local forms, critical regionalism works with the tension between universal and local culture. As a general strategy I find this appealing because it recognizes that we are not wholly immersed in either a regional or a universal context.

But Frampton's chosen examples do not always fit his strategy; they are timid in their use of regional vocabulary. For instance, if we compare the principles and the examples found in Frampton (1982), we find that while the examples are all of high quality, they remain modernist experiments with function and form. With the exception of Utzon's church, they could be transplanted to other contexts without much difficulty.[9]

That Frampton is basically a modernist is a description that I presume he, like Habermas, would cheerfully accept, since for both of them the alternatives to modernism are regressive tradition (what I called "simple regionalism") or nihilistic play. Neither of these alternatives allows the kind of self-criticism they deem necessary in our world today. But are these the only choices?

Frampton pictures waves of commercial jumble beating against resistant enclaves. He urges us to create "the bounded urban fragment against which the inundation of the place-less, consumerist environ-

ment will find itself momentarily checked" (1982, 82). He sees the
need for "monuments . . . bounded realms and large-scale representative forms . . . within which the memory and practice of a liberative
culture can still be nurtured and sustained" (26). Instead of the dialectic of local and universal Frampton described in the statement quoted
in the last chapter, these statements conceptualize the city as a war between two factors, straightforward regional identities and undifferentiated consumerism. We recognize again the problematic dichotomy
between simple inhabitation and placeless distance.

Frampton's monuments and bounded realms are supposed to have a
solid meaning. To those inside the region, that meaning acts as a support, and to the consumerist culture outside it acts as a brake, because
that identity cannot be exchanged away. Frampton overemphasizes the
immediacy of regional culture, but the "critical" side of his regionalism
can correct that emphasis. The real problem is the idea of one undifferentiated consumer culture. This is a common enough idea today,
and it is one more version of the modern attempt to separate form from
content.

No one can deny the contemporary tendency to homogenize the environment. But is this equivalent to a way of life and culture defined
purely in terms of maximizing consumption without any substantive
content? The notion of a consumer culture is the backside of the modern ideal of triumphant rationality. If we have questioned the adequacy
of the modern picture of a purely rational society whose projects are
defined in purely formal ways, we should also question the adequacy of
the notion of consumer culture.

Consumer culture does not exist as a total way of life made up only of
maximizing consumption and the flow of goods. What does exist is a
consumerist way of living local cultures. Only if it could have its own
character independent of that multiplicity from which it arises could
we say consumer culture had its own universal identity. But while the
architecture and the products may be the same, they make different
moves in different local games.

Cultural patterns and goals have their meaning by contrast. We can
find the same fast-food emporia in New York and Tokyo, but they are
inserted into different local networks. Everyone may use VCRs and eat
burgers, but this does not mean that the motivation for buying is the
same, nor that their use is the same, nor that their uses stand in the
same contrasts.

The massive influence of American products and ways of behavior all
over the world should not be taken as proof that some abstractly de-

182 fined consumer culture is conquering all. Insofar as there is influence of one culture upon another, what is spreading is a local American culture with its own substantive content of ideals, virtues and vices—listen to the lyrics. This form of life amounts to more than sheer consumerism. It is true that this culture can be debased, but that does not render it purely abstract. It is also true that as it spreads it can weaken traditional cultures, but we should not be too quick to claim that those weakened versions become indistinguishable from one another.

We fear that the acid might eat away all the local culture, leaving only consumerist maximization. This is another version of Plato's fear. History would have made a change that abolished itself by wiping out its own genesis and internal relations. This is the modernist illusion. Our era is seen as the final expression of a universal human condition; once history has accomplished the liberation of some unchanging basic process, history becomes irrelevant. This depends on being able to separate form from content and so constitute a process with its own ahistorical goals. It is against this that I have urged variations of Heidegger's notion of a "thrown project," though with more pluralism than Heidegger would allow.[10]

It is misleading to think of our community values and practices as a matter of simple immediate inhabitation. It is also misleading to think of some pure force arrayed against this resistant core. Habermas's distinction between lifeworld and system is useful here. Instead of thinking about consumerism as a unified culture, think about systemic pressures on the lifeworld. These pressures are not a set of contrasts that produce meaning. They are a network of mechanisms aimed at maximizing flow and return, mechanisms which treat cultural values and roles as impediments.

What makes the system seem to be a modern incarnation of the power of the Sophist is its protean maneuverability. The system "itself" cannot be represented. It operates through endless substitutions and strategies. But we can find it in our wounded places. We experience it in the weakening of identities. Also, we experience it because architecture and city planning deal not only with the infinity of exchange and spectacle but also with particular limits: where does the sunlight fall, and will the building overload the sewers? These reveal systemic effects and constraints.

In talking about the inscription of the system on our social body I am in danger of romanticizing some virginal social unit. Foucault attacks an analogous illusion in his discussion of sexuality when he argues that we have no unified sexuality waiting to be uncovered, but only scattered economies of desire and pleasure to be let free in their multiplicity (Foucault 1980). Actually, though, his point supports mine. I agree that there is no unified social body to be recovered. But systemic imperatives work at simplifying our social inhabitation into a commodified simulacrum of itself, all surface and show and peak experience. The loss of multiplicity and interpretative potential reveals the systemic pressures.

While we can experience its effects, it seems impossible to picture the operation of the system as a whole.[11] Is this because it is a pure power, above history and capable of infinite flexibility? Among other reasons, the operations of the current economic and productive arrangements are hard to describe because, unlike earlier arrangements, they separate their imperatives from political and religious projects. Because it has no intentions, the system is not an agent with an agenda. As a complex of impersonal mechanisms it cannot be treated as a unified actor (although insofar as the system appears in the actions of this or that corporate or governmental agent it can be dealt with as we do any "crude" power or persuasion). But for all this, the current systemic arrangements do have a definite shape, in the sense that they can be distinguished from other past or possible economic and productive arrangements.

We can't be or embody the system. To imagine that we could live the systemic imperatives in their naked state is the same mistake as to imagine that the operative form of a building could be nakedly expressed in its perceived form without entering into any new contrasts and meanings. Insofar as the systemic imperatives appear as something lived, they are already within other contexts and cultural networks. Those contexts are inhabited with the spaciousness that is a condition for any inhabitation. This means that there are always discontinuities (and continuities and intersections and contrasts and differences) that provide room for metaphor and self-criticism.

SELF-CRITICISM TOGETHER

I argued earlier that we have no single unified project of self-criticism that might be blocked or subverted. Because the occasions and projects of criticism arise in multiple and indirect ways, they cannot be systematically suppressed. We should not presume that the only way to liberate ourselves is to have a theory of the structure of the whole, so that we can oppose some total vision to current fragmentation or to oppressive totalities. There can be a liberation resulting from the ten-

184 sions and crossings we find ourselves within. We can care for the whole without a map of the whole.

My effort has been to discourage absolute claims, including those made in postmodernist attacks on modernist absolutism. There is a difference between being above and being amid it all. We are building together in the shifting discourse and the shifting life. There is no guaranteed overview, but nothing is in principle hidden. We must be careful not to conceptualize this as a conflict of solid inhabitation and placeless forces.

Do we then follow Habermas's pattern, which is the old Socratic story? Yes and no. What we have is endless critique without any definitive distinction of persuasion from rational argument; this makes for discourse guided by intellectual virtues rather than transparent principles. We need dialogue, but I am suggesting a shifting that has less structural unity and yet is more tied to historical roots than Habermas (or Lyotard) would allow. But we cannot deny the role of local reflection and argument in freeing us from restrictive contexts and making it possible to build together in new ways.

In building together we cannot each go our separate ways. We should accept Habermas's goal of open discussion and community participation, with no one barred from the circles of decision about building. That is far enough from the reality of today to be worth fighting for.[12] Habermas is right that we need to encourage self-examination and reflection on our own vulnerabilities and limitations. But rational agreement is only one kind of appropriate, disciplined judgment, and being argued into changing our beliefs is only one way of altering the language we speak.

I recall the Apollo astronauts' photo of the earth rising in the distance above the moon's horizon. That picture appeared so many times in magazines and on posters. It spoke to an awareness of our situation in a fragile whole, but the photo did not argue for any of the rival claims to total vision. Often that image has been presented in appeals for nuclear and ecological good sense, in the hope that concern for all life's flourishing might help us avoid catastrophe. But such awareness and concern is not only for the grand scale; we need it in the city, too. There also we should take account of one another with an eye to the fragility of the whole.

NOTES

Introduction

1. The quoted paragraph is from the unsigned "Comment" introducing the volume of *Center* 3 (1987) devoted to "new regionalism."

2. This present book grew out of ideas developed in the last two chapters of Kolb 1987, especially the closing paragraphs of chapter twelve.

3. I will have little to say about the wide currents of postmodernism in the other arts. In literature both modernism and postmodernism are much more difficult to define; also, modern literature never blocked out the past as did modern architecture. The only break in painting comparable to the reentry of history into architecture was the turn away from abstract expressionism toward pop art and other movements. The revolt against abstraction in literature and painting has many parallels to the changes in architecture, and painters such as Rauschenberg and Warhol share the tactics of ironic historicism and quotation. Cf. Jencks 1987b for a discussion of these issues, although his selection of painters is idiosyncratic.

4. The debate over modernity in this book is not the same as the "quarrel of the ancients and the moderns" renewed in Straussian and conservative circles. That quarrel stays too much within the original Platonic parameters. For a recent discussion of that debate, cf. Rosen 1987 and 1989. Rosen sees postmodernism as a continuation of modern and Enlightenment quarrels with the ancients over the understanding of nature, and over whether theory and politics remain forever at war. To my mind he is on the right track in naming pure spontaneity as the culprit in modernism. This is related to the distanced subjectivity I will be describing, and the separation of a pure process from its content. But Rosen fails to see the ways in which this spontaneity is questioned by postmodern and deconstructive thought. Cf., for instance, his strange reading of Derrida's *différance* as pure spontaneity (1987, 7).

5. For *modern* and its relatives cf. Calinescu 1977 enlarged as Calinescu 1987. The discussion of *postmodern* in Calinescu 1987 (265–312) is very useful. A comparison with his earlier treatment (1977, 6, 77, 132ff.) is very instructive about the rapid expansion of the term. For some information on its penetration into different disciplines, see the results of the survey reported in Megill (forthcoming), and compare Jencks 1977 with Jencks 1987b.

6. "Literary modernism [is] modern in its commitment to innovation, in its rejection of the authority of tradition, in its experimentalism; antimodern in its dismissal of the dogma of progress, in its critique of rationality, in its sense that modern civilization has brought about the loss of something precious" (Calinescu 1987, 266).

7. Manfredo Tafuri claims that "the most ruthless critique of modernism is contained in the culture wedged into the fracture of modernism itself" (quoted in Frampton 1982, 58). Habermas argues that aesthetic modernism represents a protest by the true modern spirit against the perversion of modern autonomous reason by instrumental and systemic forces. But he disagrees that postmodernism continues these impulses. He argues that since it lacks the proper critical tools, postmodernism betrays

185

186   the impulses behind aesthetic modernism (1983). He seems, however, to make exceptions for some types of postmodern architecture (cf. Habermas 1985b).

8. Deconstructive projects such as Eisenman's House X and House El Even Odd, Tschumi's proposal for la Villette, or the work of Hiromi Fujii, exceed the "postmodern classicism" Jencks (1987b) discusses. Jencks's postmodernism is a synthesis of tradition and modernity in a conscious attempt to reappropriate the social and cosmic whole. This is foreign to the more radical experiments in architecture and the other arts, experiments Jencks would call "late modern." His label seems correct for some of his examples, but others do go beyond the presuppositions of any modernism, early or late.

9. The word was used in a different sense by a Spanish critic, Frederico de Onis, in the 1930s. While Toynbee meant the word to refer to the era after about 1880, those who picked the word up tended to use it to refer to the time after World War II. Calinescu points out that as the word slipped into the literary critical vocabulary—with Irving Howe, Harry Levin, then Ihab Hassan, who was the first to use the word to name a unified trend in criticism and society—the connotations of the prefix "post" varied from negative to positive. It settled down into a generally laudatory meaning during the sixties when "post" was being used as a prefix for many other words as well (1977, 132–40). Robert Venturi reports that Jean Labatut at Princeton was using the word about architecture as early as the 1950s (Venturi 1984, 113). It became popular in architectural discussions due the efforts of Charles Jencks and Robert Stern (cf. Jencks 1977 and Stern 1977).

10. Andrew Benjamin describes the attitude of deconstructive thought towards modernity in an elegant sentence: "that which dominated is housed within what emerges as the consequences of its no longer being able to dominate" (Benjamin 1988, 50; cf. Norris 1988, 29).

11. A typically modern philosophical investigation seeks a guaranteed method for certifying some cognitive (or moral or aesthetic) possibilities as "correct." This presupposes that we have an indefinitely open set of possibilities to begin with. If we are somehow restricted to a limited initial set, our best criteria may not give us correct judgments. For the modern vision the only options are that our choices be correct, or that they be arbitrary, or that they be forced upon us.

12. For a start, such dichotomies as: language versus desire, theory versus practice, facts versus values, energy versus pattern, texts versus power, action versus reflection, and the nature of self-criticism.

13. We cannot simply negate the Socratic search for unity; a single-minded devotion to chaos would merely invert the old story. We need to locate Socrates rather than remove him; to find Socrates in his limited place is already to deny his total claims.

14. While I do presuppose some formal descriptions of our situation, these are not such as to provide a platform from which practical maxims can be pronounced. There has been much talk lately about the ethics of virtue as opposed to the ethics of rule. Virtue ethics, as exemplified in Aristotle, talks of developing character traits that help us meet situations, rather than giving us rules about what to do. There is an intellectual analogue to the ethics of virtue, and it should be encouraged.

Chapter One

1. Much of the confusion surrounding recent discussions of the "end of philosophy" have to do with uncertainty about what story such discussions should belong to.

Chapter Three

1. Kant makes this point in the "Canon of Pure Reason" in the first *Critique,* and Hegel makes a similar point in the preface to the *Phenomenology of Spirit.*

2. Plato seems to reserve the term "dialectic" for the entire ensemble of the wandering way to principles and the structured way back down to the particular issues in question.

3. It may seem that the we are faced with only two choices: either there is a distinction of degree or one of kind between persuasion and rationality. A continuum or a sharp division. But these are not the only kinds of distinctions available. It would be interesting to work out a distinction between persuasion and rationality along the lines of the medieval distinction between two aspects that can be distinguished but never exist separately.

4. It may seem I am making Plato too much of a Manichaean who imagines the love of truth and the desire for persuasion at war for our souls. According to Plato's metaphysics there is only one such power, the desire for order and truth. Sophistry is possible because of the disorder in the world and in the human soul. That disorder is inherent in the realm of change; our task is to bring our inner world to order and stability. Sophism has no unitary origin, only the chaos of impulses that makes us manipulable. But Plato writes more wisely than his metaphysics allows. Just as Plato has trouble accounting for the possibility of willful evil, so he needs more than the turmoil of desires to account for the Sophist. The master Sophist is not just a desiring man flailing about, but a calculating person of skillful means. Plato's official psychology is based on the contrast between order and disorder. If your life is not polarized by the love of truth and reality, you have no unified personality. He means to portray Callicles in the *Gorgias* as less a unified person than a collection of stray desires. But the portrait takes on a life of its own and the Sophist comes to us with his own principle of unity, a counter-personality for which there is no real room in Plato's theory. Instead of being within the movement from disorder to order, we are caught between rival sources of order.

5. One might object that I should not compare the Sophist, whose persuasive efforts are directed by a will toward a goal, with the more impersonal influences implied in modern theories of culture, language, and ideology. But fear of these more diffuse influences should be reduced by the same gestures. If the influence on us of language or history or culture is in no way traceable but only to be feared, without that fear ever being in any way capable of being substantiated and worked against, then that influence has become a power so subtle that it makes no discernible difference.

It is tempting to locate the ultimate deceiver in our own unconscious. We have all experienced the shock of discovering that our own motives were not what we had thought. But of all the sources, our unconscious is least like a focused power. Evasive and eternally ambivalent it may be, and protean in its always being elsewhere, but these very same qualities prevent it from being a modern embodiment of the concentrated power of the Sophists. It makes our inhabitation of the world uneasy and ambivalent, but just for that reason it does not create a seamless web of deception.

Later I will discuss what might appear to be yet another version of the Sophist's power, the distorting effects of the "system" on the "lifeworld" that Habermas discusses.

Chapter Four

1. Whatever the truth of Lyotard's Lévinasian points about obligation, the historical claim about the Sophists is not convincing, since the arguments for the necessity of law (for instance in the Anonymous Iamblichi) involve a kind of cost-benefit analysis that Lyotard elsewhere rejects.

2. Lyotard would also like to have something like Kant's negative moral judgments, a way of saying that this or that particular claim or language game cannot be reconciled with the Idea. He realizes the difficulties of this and of his position generally, since it implies that he, at least, is taking the stance of one who prescribes for all language games. To prescribe noninterference is still to prescribe. On this see Lyotard's remarks in *Just Gaming* about his own descriptions (51) and his laughter when the objection is brought against his prescriptions (100), and the perceptive deconstruction of Lyotard's text in Weber 1985. In a later essay, "Judicieux dans le différend," Lyotard tries to describe this Kantian attitude in more detail, without reference to the Sophists (Lyotard 1985, 195–236).

3. There is a serious problem with Lyotard's demand for the creation of new language games as it is stated in *Le Différend*. His notion of a language game encompasses several different levels: (a) the standard Austinian examples such as describing, promising, prescribing (what he calls *régimes de phrases*), (b) more extended speaking that involves linking many kinds of sentences towards some chosen goal (what he calls *genres de discours*), (c) concrete institutional examples such as getting married, (d) very complex activities, such as present-day capitalism, that seem to be built up out of the other levels. It is not clear what constant innovation would mean on the first level, nor whether the others are sufficiently alike for his injunctions to apply on all levels.

4. "The work of the artist or scientist consists precisely in seeking operators capable of producing phrases that have never been heard before and are thus by definition—at least at first—noncommunicable." "The important thing in art is the production of works which bring into question the rules constituting a work as such." (Lyotard 1986b, 212, 214)

5. In his discussion of terrorism Lyotard emphasizes the need to deal directly with another party and not manipulate through threats to a third person. Direct assassination attempts are more acceptable than holding hostages. Might there be a textual or dialogical analogue to this distinction?

6. I am not sure Habermas would or should agree to the description of communicative action as a language game, particularly given Lyotard's broad use of that term, but the disagreement concerns how much or how little is needed to characterize speakers or language users in general.

7. So far as modern thought attempts to devise universal formal systems of representation on a different level than the content they unify, neither Habermas nor Lyotard are modern. Habermas argues that his analyses of discourse must be submitted to the structures of discourse they reveal (Habermas 1979). Lyotard claims that his analyses of language remain submitted to all the operations and forms they describe; there is no independent metalanguage; the synthesis of the series is also an element in the series (Lyotard 1983, no. 97).

Chapter Five

1. Could we know in general that our activities were influenced by factors such as unconscious motives without knowing in particular what specific influences were working on us? This depends on the strength of the claim that we could not know the details. The claims that we as a matter of fact may not know what is influencing us at the moment can be accepted with the proviso that new methods and ways of talking may alter our abilities. A stronger claim would be that it is always impossible to know in detail what is influencing us in our current acts; this, however, depends either on the suspect Greek connection mentioned above, or on a definition of "current acts" that is too restrictive.

2. In Habermas's ideal scenario, discussants seek a consensus based on mutually accepted principles and shared descriptions of the situation. In such discussion the parties to a dispute come to agree about what counts as rational argument and what counts as irrational persuasion. However, in another kind of agreement the parties agree only on some very general principles about interaction, and they forswear the use of crude power on one another. There may not be any very full description of the problem at hand on which they can agree. (Consider the differing views of what constitutes the "problem" in the case of abortion.) This pragmatic agreement can come in several styles. The most obvious is Hobbsean, but another is liberal, where the agreement to avoid coercion does not include substantive agreement on some shared concept of the human good. The parties are not required to justify their positions to one another, *or even to themselves.* This kind of discussion does not demand a precisely located distinction between rational argument and persuasive rhetoric, and in practice the parties usually accept some degree of manipulative discourse on each side since they do not completely agree on what counts as unfair rhetoric. The issue for Habermas is whether anything more is required of the performer of a speech act aimed at coordinating action than the willingness to be open and avoid crude power, and to offer a degree of sincerity and tolerance. Must the space of public discussion be structured by agreed-upon reasons and criteria, and surveyed by a totalizing discourse? Must the openness of public discussion be the openness of a process with its own unifying form?

3. For a discussion of notions of truth and knowledge that broadens these out in a direction parallel to my suggestion here, cf. the final chapter of Goodman and Elgin 1988.

4. Although I am not treating Foucault explicitly in this book, my contentions later about the multiplicity of our lives will challenge that part of his analysis that gets interpreted into a uniform picture of modern society after the fashion of Heidegger's *Gestell.* But this is not necessarily what he was trying to say (cf. Foucault 1977).

5. In his book *Excesses* (1983) Alphonso Lingis paints portraits of actions and interrelations that are neither rational nor irrational in the classic sense and that illustrate how one might mutually perceive and relate in ways that do not fit the usual economy of talk about rationality, beliefs, and desires. What is important to personhood may lie in the interstices, in that which gets lost when one translates a person's world into sets of beliefs and desires.

6. Habermas does not demand that the poets be thrown out of the city, but he does cordon them off into a sphere of autonomous aesthetic culture. Neither the philosophers nor the citizens can make judgments for the poets, who alone are competent to

190   evaluate the appropriateness of productions within their specialized field. Habermas also contends, however, that there is a moment when artistic productions are reintegrated into the common lifeworld and function to stimulate thought and criticism there. So far, though, it is not clear how this is to operate, nor the degree to which rational argument or judgments of appropriateness are involved in such integration (cf. the discussions in Jay 1985 and Ingram 1987). The question is whether such discussion would have to converge on any ideal meta-agreement.

7. I am most familiar with this kind of dialogue in the Asian context. Examples of this dialogue, which encourages self-criticism without being part of a project of universal agreement, can be found, for instance, in the journals published by the Nanzan Center for the Study of Religion and Culture, in Nagoya, Japan.

8. It is tempting to think that before modernization the crafts and spiritual traditions were not so self-critical as they later became, when subject to modern differentiation. This, however, underestimates the degree of movement and self-criticism in the premodern traditions, and it begs the question by assuming that all self-criticism stems from nascent processes of rationalization.

9. Saying this does not endorse Lyotard's opposite claim that some situations are unresolvable in principle because of the different forms of life involved. The appeal to principle, this time in the negative, still misleads.

CHAPTER SIX

1. As in many myths, the three-world story murders the parents. Its picture of traditional society presumes too much unity and too little self-consciousness. I discuss some aspects of this problem in the next chapter.

2. Habermas accepts the general lines of Robin Horton's discussion of the difference between traditional and modern inquiry. Horton argues that modernity brings encouragement rather than repression of large-scale theoretical alternatives to received views and practices. But his analyses need to be qualified. Even in a traditional society with taboos on considerations of any but the received views there can be nothing that eliminates the possibility of self-reflection and criticism. There is no doubt that institutionalized theoretical reflection is a special development that vastly increases the amount of talk about the presuppositions of people's lives. But it is not the only locus of social self-knowledge. Social practices get discussed, roles complained about, views wondered at. To see how a traditional society talks about itself one should not go to the guardians of orthodoxy whom Horton examines, but to the traders and travelers and other practical people who have to deal with social patterns and presuppositions in their everyday life.

3. "From the moment when the past, which traditionally prescribed a plan of action to both individuals and groups, was outdistanced by the historical sciences, an objective world was established, open to critical scientific investigation. Modern man gains the freedom of an open future which, alone, can make him capable of transforming, according to scientific conceptions, the natural and the social environment. The lack of historicity of modern society, demonstrated through natural and social procedures, has then, the scientification of the past as an assumed premise." (Habermas, quoted in Portoghesi 1983).

4. This is quite similar to Hegel's argument that civil society cannot do without the spirit of the nation to give it content and help make the transition to the rational state. Except that for Hegel the content provided by the historical traditions is already inher-

ently rational. This rationality needs to be made evident; it does not need to be constituted by critical discussion. Hegel does not believe that modern citizens can or should actively constitute their values by reworking contingent history; the values must be already guaranteed by their logical place in the process of spirit's development.

5. The lifeworld has a unity more like a collection than a system. There is no one theme or understanding or set of meanings which somehow protects the lifeworld from changes that might threaten some core identity. The lifeworld functions to make possible our explicit beliefs and actions, but it does not do so as a transcendental, but only as a necessary, condition.

6. In Hegelian terms, what Habermas has done is to allow the difference between universal and particular to be posited as such, but not their unity. This is just Hegel's diagnosis of the problems of civil society. Hegel wanted to find a rational content for life that helped form the conditions for consensus rather than being judged by consensus. He claimed that the universal process of spirit's development involved definite historical contents that were more than purely formal and yet were guaranteed independently of any particular community decisions.

7. In a sense there is a common difficulty with both Habermas's communicative rationality and Lyotard's shared language games. They have no historical depth that requires discernment. This is most obvious in Lyotard; as in Nietzsche, everything is remade by the present desire and history is subdued by the will to power that revalues its elements *now*. No interpretation is required, only forceful reinterpretation. The same problem results from the fact that the lifeworld in Habermas is composed of heaped-up beliefs, rather than intersecting practices, and its consequent total availability to reworking.

8. In Hegelian terms, we need to understand that the distinction of form from content may be made concerning our activities and creative efforts, but that it cannot be posited as such within them.

CHAPTER SEVEN

1. What I say in this chapter does not directly address changes in meaning that proceed not through extension but through wholesale replacement of one language by another which is incommensurable with the first and not defined by any relation of filiation or opposition to it. Do such changes exist? To settle that dispute would take a good deal of argument in the history and philosophy of science, and the objections raised by Donald Davidson and others would have to be addressed. Whatever the result for questions of language and knowledge, the parallel question for art and architecture would remain.

2. "It would be enough / If we were ever, just once, at the middle, fixed / In This Beautiful World of Ours and not as now, / Helplessly at the edge, enough to be / Complete, because at the middle, if only in sense, / And in that enormous sense, merely enjoy" (Wallace Stevens, "The Ultimate Poem is Abstract." *Collected Poems* (New York: Knopf, 1964), pp. 429–30).

CHAPTER EIGHT

1. Tafuri and Dal Co's careful but unorthodox survey of this century's architecture shows that there were many different movements and levels of movements, not all going in the same direction, and while all had to respond to this century's develop-

192   ments in technology, politics, and the real estate market, they did not all share a common set of responses to these conditions. Cf. Tafuri and Dal Co 1986, and the contrasting stages of modernism discussed in Klotz 1988.

2. Habermas is only half right when he says that the modern movement in architecture "originate[d] from the avant-garde spirit; it is the equivalent to the avant-garde painting, music, and literature of our century" (1985b, 319). The modern movement did seek, with the avant-garde, the death of the old and the birth of something purely new. But it also sought "the rationalization of human life . . . the integration of each and every human habit, pattern of behavior, desire, or way of thinking into human life as a consistent, non-contradictory whole. The carnevalesque as a realm completely lacking in restraint, as the other that remained non-other, becomes impossible" (Schulte-Sasse, 1986a, 35–36).

3. All the quotations are from Gropius's description of the Bauhaus educational program (reprinted in Gropius 1965). Habermas (1985b, 325) points out that Gropius is here at one with William Morris in the desire to remove the split between system and lifeworld, but his functionalism remains suspended uneasily between the user's and the economic system's desired functions. Brolin (1976) and Portoghesi (1983) offer criticisms of the breach with history, and Herdeg (1983) discusses its effects on the students Gropius taught at Harvard. Le Corbusier wrote similarly to Gropius, but for him, "architecture has another meaning and other ends to pursue than showing construction and responding to needs (and by needs I mean utility, comfort, and practical arrangement). Architecture is the art above all others which achieves a state of platonic grandeur, mathematical order, speculation, the perception of the harmony which lies in emotional relationships" (Le Corbusier 1986, 110). But this too leads away from history.

4. Attempting to gather the variety together into some kind of unity, Klotz (1988, 421) suggests ten defining characteristics of postmodernism: regionalism (instead of internationalism); fictional representation (instead of geometric abstraction); emphasis on building an illusion (instead of functionalism); multiplicity of meanings (instead of the single machine metaphor); poetry (instead of utopianism); improvisation, spontaneity, and incompleteness (instead of finished perfection); memory and irony (instead of banishing history); historical and regional relativity (instead of autonomously valid form); variation of vocabulary and style (instead of one dominant style); aesthetic distance (instead of identifying architecture with life). In a similar attempt, Jencks (1987b, 330–50) describes what he takes as the emergent rules of postmodern classicism: disharmonious harmony and the difficult whole; pluralism and radical eclecticism; a concern for the urban fabric; anthropomorphic forms; the use of suggested recollections ("the reversible historical continuum"); a return from abstraction to content; double coding and irony ("the most prevalent aspect of Post-Modernism"); multivalence; the reinterpretation of tradition that displaces former conventions; new rhetorical figures; and a signified return to an absent center. Notice that the closer these lists are examined the less unified they become.

5. It is this process of rational justification that makes Hegel's way of uniting form and content different from the more Kantian way Habermas unites the process of self-criticism with contingent historical content. I have quietly passed over the complexities introduced by Hegel's doctrine of necessary yet contingent historical content, just as I passed over his intricate relations between the logical and the historical sequences in his system.

6. For Hegel there is a stage beyond this subjective art. That final stage he calls "objective humor," which does not show off the subjective facility of the author so much as the play inherent in the subject matter. Speaking of Goethe's *West-östliche Divan*, Hegel says: "Here love is transferred wholly into the imagination, its movement, happiness, and bliss. In general, in similar productions of this kind we have before us no subjective longing, no being in love, no desire, but a pure delight in the topics, an inexhaustible self-yielding of imagination, a harmless play, a freedom in toying alike with rhyme and ingenious meters—and with all this a depth of feeling and cheerfulness of the inwardly self-moving heart which through the serenity of the outward shape lift the soul high above all painful entanglements in the restrictions of the real world" (Hegel 1975, 610–11).

7. Hegel opposes such affirmative interest to the ironical mode he finds in that romanticism which is "a variety which does not come into a unity, so that every character destroys itself as a character. By irony this is regarded as the real height of art, on the assumption that the spectator must not be gripped by an inherently affirmative interest, but has to stand above it, as irony itself is away above everything" (Hegel 1975, 243). In a later chapter I examine varieties of modern and postmodern irony.

8. As I stated earlier, deconstruction seems to me sufficiently different that despite current usage it should not be classed with those movements which proclaim a new age.

9. No version of postmodern thought gives comfort to those who want to continue the modern quest for pure significant form. E. M. Farrelly, whose call for a "new spirit" in architecture combines modernist and romantic demands for totality, castigates the standard postmodern architects as "pasticheurs . . . toytown tarter-uppers . . . an aesthetic of least resistance" (1986, 79).

10. Jencks has broadened his notion of double coding in his latest treatment of postmodernity, where it is no longer restricted to the popular/professional doublet, but has expanded to embrace almost any method that leads to multiple reference. Cf. Jencks 1987b, 279, 282, 340.

11. Expressing his modernism more directly, Jencks now worries that we lack a substantive cosmological vision to give unity to our historical borrowings. Cf. Jencks 1987b, 291, 300, 315, 352.

12. It does no good to say that the architect is always hampered by background and recalcitrant circumstances from reaching an ideal openness and flexibility. This, too, stays within the modern picture which postulates a pure freedom restricted by contingent limitations.

Chapter Nine

1. Cf. Donougho 1987 for a helpful study of the various ways in which architecture might be said to involve a language.

2. Roger Scruton makes this the key to his argument that all talk about architectural languages and vocabularies should be scrapped in favor of talk about conventions and styles (cf. Scruton 1979, and, in reply, Donougho 1987, Rustin 1985).

3. There is no strict separation in architecture between what in sentences might be distinguished as "ungrammaticality" and "semantic impertinence," both of which might be used in metaphorical moves in Ricoeur's sense of the term.

Chapter Ten

1. The spatial image of a "field" of possibilities misleads us by suggesting some indefinite extent, perhaps divided here and there by walls that we can see over. It suggests

194 that possibilities lie spread out before the distanced eye, to be organized or classified as we see fit.

2. This use of the term *metaphor* also differs from that which has become customary in structuralist and Lacanian circles. Their association of metaphor with substitution is closer in spirit to the Aristotelian tradition. My use also differs from discussions of buildings that resemble another object, such as Saarinen's "Yale Whale" skating rink. For the general theory of interactive metaphor, cf. Black 1962, Goodman 1976, Ricoeur 1977. Goodman and Elgin (1988, chap. 2) extend Goodman's theories about artistic meaning to architecture. This theory does not demand that there exist ultimate basic elements at the root of all vocabularies, elements that would be the first uncombined elements in some basic language. But it does demand that there be relatively settled expectations that can be violated.

3. Miriam Gusevich (1987) refers to these operations as paradigmatic and syntagmatic transgressions, and she illustrates them in the work of Le Corbusier.

4. Vattimo (1988, 87–88) argues that it is typical of postmodern thought not to make distinctions between the central identity of a work of art and added decorative touches. This seems right, especially for postmodern literature, but it is also true that throughout the sequence of metaphorical changes and traces that make up the tradition such identities are less stable than they seem.

5. Cf. McCumber (1989) for an extended discussion of the becoming of meaning as seen in Heidegger, and how this relates to social context and interaction as seen in Habermas.

6. A more apt criticism of the previous section would be that while it conceives of meaning as differential, it does not think sufficiently about meaning as deferral, and so stays within the orbit of repetition and an architecture still policed by the traditional *telos* (cf. Benjamin 1988). To this charge I would plead half–guilty, since I am not convinced that deconstructive theories and experiments are useful for the body of architecture that must fill the fabric of our cities. In the final three chapters I argue that deconstructive monuments must remain exceptional and marginal if they are to avoid collapsing into a new metaphysical discourse.

7. However, cf. Harries's discussion of self-representation (1984a and 1988b).

8. Harries argues that because of these universal human experiences, we encounter space and basic architectural forms differently than is reported by the Cartesian subject facing an indifferent extension, or by the aesthetic subject contemplating a unified aesthetic object.

9. A building's operative form is subject to so many natural constraints that while aleatory decoration would be possible, an aleatory plan or elevation could only be a randomized choice within a narrow range of parameters, where defining those parameters already did most of the work.

10. Cf. also Kurokawa's analysis of Japanese space in terms of streets rather than plazas (1988, chap. 2).

CHAPTER ELEVEN

1. For earlier uses of the word, cf. Knox 1989.

2. *Random House Dictionary of the English Language,* Unabridged ed. (New York: Random House, 1967), s.v. "irony."

3. *Roget's Thesaurus in Dictionary Form,* edited by Norman Lewis (New York: Berkeley, 1966), s.v. "irony."

4. Cf., for instance, Booth 1974, Wilde 1981, and Muecke 1969 and 1985.

5. Booth (1974) discusses such signals in literature; analogies to many of his categories could be found in architecture. Could there be noncommunicable irony, something that one can't convey but only feel? With relation to a particular audience there might be irony that they could not detect, but this would make no sense in relation to all audiences. Like a private language, if the attitude could not be shared, there is a question whether it would be an attitude at all.

6. Such a structure might, I suppose, become a piece of performance art. Cf., however, the discussion of how architecture ought to relate to its traditional *telos* (Norris 1988 and Benjamin 1988). The new spaciousness they describe is not a case of irony.

7. There is a further question whether all parody makes reference to some fixed community ideals and standards. It is the failure of postmodern parody to do so which leads Fredric Jameson to label it pastiche rather than parody (1983). Linda Hutcheon replies to this charge in the article discussed below (1986).

8. Quoted in the *Larousse Universelle,* s.v. "ironie."

9. Friedrich Schlegel, Fragments 108, 24, quoted in Muecke 1985. Cf. Schlegel 1968.

10. Useful examples of Hegel's scattered remarks on irony can be found at the end of the "Conscience" section of the *Philosophy of Right* (1967), in the treatment of romantic art in his *Aesthetics* (1975), and in his essay "Über Solger's nachgelassene Schriften" (1968, 202–52).

11. Cf. the discussion of Derrida by Rodolphe Gasché (1988) and Christopher Norris (1988). Richard Rorty argues that Gasché's interpretation, while it may apply to the earlier writings of Derrida, fails when applied to the later writings. In these Derrida gives up lingering transcendental ambitions and works his irony by stylistic innovations and private associations that provide no general theory at all (Rorty 1989, chapter 6). The later Derrida seems to me to show many kinds of doubling and spaciousness for which the word "irony" is not a very helpful description.

12. I am inclined to agree with Muecke that this undecidability should not be labeled irony, but the word is already so stretched that more will do little harm. Muecke continues, "[This] rules out irony as I have defined it. . . . Of writing that is designed to prevent interpretation in terms of intent one could use the word 'irony' only, it seems, as a synonym for 'uncertainty,' that is, as a word without any additional content and therefore redundant." (1985, 100–101).

13. Alan Wilde (1981) finds something like this humble irony present in some postmodern literature. He works at describing what he calls an ironical perception or tone of experience, rather than an ironical act or expression. In Wilde's typology, the early modernists perceive the world as split and fragmented, and react by seeking unity through penetrating down to a truth unavailable to those who stay on the surface of life. Late moderns give up depth and attempt to find the truth by perceiving the surface aright. Not superficiality but a kind of dyslexia hides the truth from us. The postmoderns, in contrast, give up the search for truth, deny any final or privileged meaning either in the depth or on the surface, accept our inevitable distances, accept contingency and chaos, and, most importantly, view all this from within rather than above. Postmodern irony can involve an acceptance of contingency and multiple interpretations, without nostalgia for the one deep or total truth. While this too can be haughty or humble, it allows more room for our native spaciousness than the fixed distances of modernity could ever permit.

196

14. Muecke, for instance, takes a dim view of the possibilities of irony in the non-representational arts (1985, 2–6).

15. For some of the ideas in this section I am indebted to conversations with Eugene Gendlin.

16. Hutcheon's concern about total domination by hegemonic discourse is the modern version of the fear of the Sophist's rhetoric. As I indicated earlier, I am skeptical of this fear, and of the existence of singular weapons to ward it off.

17. In making this point I am indebted to the remarks of an anonymous reader from the University of Chicago Press.

18. "The ironist—the person who has doubts about his own final vocabulary, his own moral identity, and perhaps his own sanity—desperately needs to talk to other people, needs this with the same urgency as people need to make love. He needs to do so because only conversation enables him to handle these doubts, to keep himself together, to keep his web of beliefs and desires coherent enough to enable him to act. He has these doubts and these needs because, for one reason or another, socialization did not entirely take" (Rorty 1989, 186).

19. As does Lyotard, Rorty seems to run together different levels of language and practice. Under his general rubric of a "final vocabulary" we can find scientific theories, terms used in literary criticism, metaphysical and epistemological principles, hierarchies of values, social roles and self-images, language games such as promising and arguing, and the stories that might result from psychoanalysis or autobiography. These are not systems of meaning in the same sense, nor are they all contingent and changeable in the same way. Some are much more easily changed by reflection and retelling, others demand the kind of habituation Aristotle speaks of, and still others would require unforeseeable social changes.

CHAPTER TWELVE

1. Cf. the bibliography in Seamon 1987.

2. Although much of the current talk about place stems from Heidegger, it is questionable whether his word *Raum* is adequately translated by *place*. Cf. Frampton 1982, 49.

3. In this postwar "Letter on Humanism," Heidegger claims that if we think of projects as posited by the individual subject (as a *vorstellendes Setzen*), we miss the point that it is being itself which "throws" our existence. ("Das Werfende im Entwerfen ist nicht der Mensch, sondern das Sein selbst, das den Menschen in die Ek-sistenz des Daseins als sein Wesen Schickt. Dieses Geschick ereignet sich als die Lichtung des Seins, als welche es ist" [Heidegger 1946, 17, 25]). This precludes any Sartrean freedom in giving meaning to the world. But it also precludes the kind of self-active critical process described by Habermas. Heidegger acknowledges that it also affects his own critical project, and he makes complex maneuvers around this point, which prefigure the attempts of deconstructive writers to be both critical of and complicitous with the tradition. Cf. Vattimo (1988) for a development of Heidegger's idea of *Verwindung* as a mode of critical relationship.

4. Heidegger says that our projection of goals is neither prior nor subsequent to the projection of the world as a meaningful whole; these two are equally original (*ebenso gleichursprünglich,* Heidegger 1962, 141).

5. On this point Heidegger plays with the distinction between *bestimmen* and *gestimmen*. Our projects are given a determinate shape (*bestimmt*) as they are harmonized

(*gestimmt*) with our world and with the meaning of being that provides the underlying theme of that world.

6. "Any project—and therefore also any 'creative' action of a human being—is *thrown*, that is, determined by a un-controllable delivering of *Dasein* over to what already is as a whole" ("Aller Entwurf—und demzufolge auch alles "schöpferische" Handeln des Menschen—ist *geworfener*, d. h. durch die ihrer selbst nicht mächtige Angewiesenheit des Daseins auf das schon Seiende im ganzen bestimmt" [Heidegger 1962, 212]).

7. Among recent publications, cf. Victor Farias, *Heidegger et le nazisme* (Paris: Verdier, 1987); and the more definitive examination by Hugo Ott, *Martin Heidegger: Unterwegs zur seiner Biographie* (Frankfurt: Campus, 1988). Cf. also the suite of articles assembled in *Critical Inquiry* 15, no. 2 (Winter 1989), and the discussion by Thomas Sheehan, "Heidegger and the Nazis," *New York Review of Books* 25, no. 10, 16 June 1988, 38–48.

8. He would claim that as an understanding of the being of beings as a whole, our thrown project must affect all beings it discloses, and it must be unified, since a disclosed plurality of understandings of being would be contradictory; in which sense of being would they "be" a totality, or "be" at all?

9. The question about modernity's universal perspective becomes the question whether we can have a formal and universal language that can embody a set of pure goals above any historical project. Originally this pure language was proposed to house metaphysical systems; lately it has been proposed (especially by Habermas) for self-criticism. Critiques of the ideal of a pure language abound today; I will not repeat them here. What I want to stress is that the consequence of these critiques is that all our projects, even our projects for self-criticism, are "thrown projects" rather than pure self-activity.

CHAPTER THIRTEEN

1. I have argued throughout that we should conceive choice as already involved in qualitatively limited projects and possibilities. What I have spoken of as metaphoric transformation of vocabularies is related to Heidegger's notion of retrieving our possibilities.

2. Karsten Harries has written movingly about the problems caused by modern self-reflection. It seems to me, however, that he keeps the notion of simple inhabitation—and so overstates the power of reflection—when he says "reflective man is as such displaced" and "just as modern man has fallen out of nature, so he has fallen out of history. . . . Time has been reduced to a coordinate on which we move back and forth with equal facility" (1975, 14). This gives too much credence to Heidegger's unitary *Gestell*.

3. In Hegelian language, the formal conditions need not be capable of being posited as such and able to make a structural difference for our activity.

4. I am bypassing the question whether critical commentary, as opposed to artistic production, can "get at" the historical precedent and preserve a notion of totally objective scholarship. Ultimately, I agree that it cannot do so, but commentary needs to be analyzed differently than artistic production. Not that these form two utterly distinct genres, but there are different stances toward time and unity.

5. Hubbard states that a problem for the architect is "how to create a configuration of forms that has such appeal, that feels so right, that an audience wouldn't want it to be

any other way" (1980, 12). Whereas, "looking at postmodern buildings, we become so aware of how easily the arrangement could have been otherwise that we feel imposed upon; the arrangement feels capricious and we are dissatisfied" (7), "the best modernist buildings have at least the appeal of a quasi-inevitability" (8).

6. Heidegger inserts a level of determination more pervasive than this or that philosophical school or scientific theory, but still determinate vis-a-vis other epochs in the history of being, *and* this determinate level is to be a condition of the possibility of individual propositions and practices.

Chapter Fourteen

1. Jencks contends that "the truth of city building today is that good architecture and good urbanism are opposed. . . . good architects, like good artists, are primarily concerned with the language of form, while good urbanists must have an equal commitment to the things that erode such a language: compromise, democracy, pluralism, entrepreneurial skill and patience" (1987b, 258–9). No one can deny the difficulty of the problems of building together, but they are not helped by a modernist isolation of the language of form, even if this is the way most architects are trained.

2. I argue elsewhere that the notion that we live in one deeply unified world is a mistake whether it is applied to traditional society, the modern world, or to the postmodern condition (see Kolb 1987, chapters 11–12).

3. Dennis Romano, quoted in the *Washington Post,* 19 June 1988, A16.

4. "If you ignore signs as 'visual pollution,' you are lost. If you look for 'spaces between buildings' in Las Vegas, you are lost. If you see the buildings of urban sprawl as forms making space, they are pathetic—mere pimples in an amorphous landscape. As architecture, urban sprawl is a failure; as space, it is nothing. It is when you see the buildings as symbols in space, not forms in space, that the landscape takes on quality and meaning. And when you see no buildings at all, at night when virtually only the illuminated signs are visible, you see the Strip in its pure state" (Venturi and Scott Brown 1984, 63). This dematerialized cityscape seems to fit well with discussions by Baudrillard and others about our dissolution into simulacra. But buildings have both more solidity and more variability to their being than that talk allows.

5. Frampton is sweeping in his condemnation. He lumps together the populism he attributes to Venturi, the ironic historicism of Moore, the deconstructive experiments of Eisenman, and Gehry's dissections of form. But these move in different directions and respond to different problems. The first two are concerned with manipulating signifieds, the last two with questioning the fixity of the signifiers. It is the Venturi and Moore styles which are most easily cheapened.

6. There is a danger that competing "summaries" of the city could set off a new level of jumble. But no one is on a meta-level with respect to all the rest, and the kind of interlocking divergences that could result would be quite different, and more exciting than today's jumble of competing or isolated monuments.

7. The quoted phrase originally was used to describe the situation of the third world today. It is from Remo Guidieri, reproduced in Vattimo 1988, 158.

8. Kurokawa has written about the different kind of coming together that he finds in the Japanese tradition. He discusses spaces and continua that link disparate elements into "intermediate" states (1988, 64ff.). Japanese culture has taken in and preserved a multiplicity of meanings and forms without reducing them to one core identity or to one organized system. As Kurokawa shows, this is reflected in the design even of single

rooms. He also makes provocative remarks concerning the analogues in city planning to Western surgical intervention and Chinese herbal medicine (88). He does not, however, discuss the hierarchical ingredient in Japanese culture that always tries, announces its success, and fails to overcome the disparateness of spatial and cultural intermediate zones.

9. The examples cited in Frampton (1982) include Gwathmey's Perinton Housing, Ciriani's Noisy I, Kleihues's Vinetaplatz Block, Utzon's Bagsvaerd Church, and Pelli's San Bernardino City Hall. Compare these examples to the BBPR Chase Manhattan Bank in Milan (presented in Klotz 1988); the bank keeps to the modernist vocabulary but manages to make local and contextual references more strongly than do Frampton's examples.

10. My attempt to keep hermeneutical depth in history is not the attempt to find a unified form or process there. Cf. Vattimo 1988.

11. Habermas remarks about Venturi that "the language of this stage-set architecture indulges in a rhetoric that still seeks to express in ciphers systemic relations that can no longer be architecturally formulated" (Habermas 1985b, 328).

12. "Here and now in the face of the postmodern logic of interminable deferment and infinite regress, of floating signifiers and vanishing signifieds, here and now I face an other who demands of me an ethical response. This call of the other to be heard, and to be respected in his/her otherness, is irreducible to the parodic play of empty imitations. It breaks through the surface of mirror images, and, outfacing the void, reintroduces a dimension of depth and height. The face of the other resists assimilation to the dehumanizing processes of commodification" (Kearney 1987, 42).

BIBLIOGRAPHY

This list includes the works cited in the text and notes, as well as a selection of other works pertaining to the issues discussed, although it does not pretend to be a comprehensive bibliography on postmodernism.

Alexander, Christopher, Hajo Neis, Artemis Anninou, and Ingrid King. 1987. *A New Theory of Urban Design*. Oxford: Oxford University Press.

Alleman, Beda. 1970. "Ironie als literarisches prinzip." In *Ironie und Dichtung*, 11–38. Munich: C. H. Beck.

Attoe, Wayne. 1987. "Regionalism and Identity for Phoenix: The Municipal Government Center Competition." *Center* 3:28–41.

Austin, John. 1962. *Sense and Sensibilia*. Oxford: Oxford University Press.

Auzelle, Robert. 1965. *L'architecte*. Paris: Freal.

Balakian, Anna. 1986. *Surrealism: The Road to the Absolute*. Chicago: University of Chicago Press.

Banham, Reyner. 1984. *The Architecture of the Well-tempered Environment*. 2d ed. Chicago: University of Chicago Press.

———. 1986. "The Quality of Modernism." *Architectural Review* 180: 55–56.

Baudrillard, Jean. 1985. *Selected Writings*. Edited by Mark Poster. Stanford: Stanford University Press.

———. 1987. *Forget Foucault*. New York: Semiotext(e).

Bellah, Robert N., et al. 1985. *Habits of the Heart: Individualism and Commitment in American Life*. Berkeley: University of California Press.

Benhabib, Seyla. 1986. *Critique, Norm, and Utopia: A Study of the Foundations of Critical Theory*. New York: Columbia University Press.

Benjamin, Andrew. 1988. "Deconstruction and Art / The Art of Deconstruction." In *What is Deconstruction?*, 33-54. London: Academy Editions.

Bernasconi, Robert, and David Wood, eds. 1985. *Derrida and Differance*. Coventry: University of Warwick Press.

Bernstein, Richard J. 1983. *Beyond Objectivism and Relativism*. Oxford: Blackwell.

———, ed. 1985. *Habermas and Modernity*. Cambridge: M.I.T. Press.

Black, Max. 1962. *Models and Metaphors*. Ithaca: Cornell University Press.

Blake, Peter. 1977. *Form Follows Fiasco: Why Modern Architecture Hasn't Worked*. New York: Atlantic.

———. 1984. "What on Earth is Happening to Our Buildings?" *Pennsylvania Gazette*, February 1984, pp. 32–38.

Bloom, Harold. 1973. *The Anxiety of Influence*. New York: Oxford University Press.

Bloomer, Kent C., and Charles Moore. 1977. *Body, Memory, and Architecture*. New Haven: Yale University Press.

Blumenberg, Hans. 1983. *The Legitimacy of the Modern Age*. Translated by Robert M. Wallace. Cambridge: M.I.T. Press.

202   Boles, Daralice. 1987. "The National Gallery Tries Again." *Progressive Architecture* 68:44–46.

Booth, Wayne. 1974. *A Rhetoric of Irony.* Chicago: University of Chicago Press.

Borras, Maria Lluisa. 1970. *Arquitectura Contemporanea Japonesca.* Barcelona: Poligrafia.

Bousma, O. K. 1969. *Philosophical Essays.* Ithaca: Cornell University Press.

Broadbent, Geoffrey. 1980. "The Deep Structures of Architecture." In *Signs, Symbols, and Architecture,* 119–68. Chichester: Wiley.

Broadbent, Geoffrey, Richard Blunt and Charles Jencks, eds. 1980. *Signs, Symbols, and Architecture.* Chichester: Wiley.

Brolin, Brent C. 1976. *The Failure of Modern Architecture.* New York: Van Nostrand Reinhold.

———. 1980. *Architecture in Context: Fitting New Buildings with Old.* New York: Van Nostrand Reinhold.

———. 1985. *Flight of Fancy.* New York: St. Martin.

Bubner, Rudiger. 1982. "Habermas's Concept of Critical Theory." In *Habermas: Critical Essays,* 42–56. Cambridge: M.I.T. Press.

Bunt, Richard. 1980. "Linguistics into Aesthetics Won't Go." In *Signs, Symbols, and Architecture,* 421–37. Chichester: Wiley.

Bürger, Christa. 1986. "The Disappearance of Art: The Postmodernism Debate in the U.S." *Telos* 68:93–106.

Bürger, Peter. 1986. *Theory of the Avant-Garde.* Translated by Michael Shaw. Minneapolis: University of Minnesota Press.

Calinescu, Matei. 1977. *Faces of Modernity: Modernism, Avant-Garde, Decadence, Kitsch.* London: Methuen.

———. 1987. *Five Faces of Modernity: Modernism, Avant-Garde, Decadence, Kitsch, Postmodernism.* Durham: Duke University Press.

Calvino, Italo. 1980. *Una Pietra Sopra.* Torino: Einaudi.

———. 1981. *If on a Winter's Night a Traveler.* Translated by William Weaver. New York: Harcourt.

Caputo, John. 1987. *Radical Hermeneutics.* Bloomington: Indiana University Press.

Casey, Edward S. 1976. *Imagining: A Phenomenological Study.* Bloomington: University of Indiana Press.

Chesneaux, Jean. 1983. *De la modernité.* Paris: La Découverte/Maspero.

Chow, Rey. 1986. "Rereading Mandarin Ducks and Butterflies: A Response to the Postmodern Condition." *Cultural Critique* 5:69–93.

Collins, Peter. 1971. *Architectural Judgment.* Montreal: McGill University Press.

Connerton, Paul. 1980. *The Tragedy of Enlightenment: An Essay on the Frankfurt School.* Cambridge: Cambridge University Press.

Crook, J. Mordaunt. 1987. *The Dilemma of Style: Architectural Ideas from the Picturesque to the Post-Modern.* Chicago: University of Chicago Press.

Dallmayr, Fred. 1984. *Polis and Praxis: Exercises in Contemporary Political Theory.* Cambridge: M.I.T. Press.

Davidson, Arnold. 1989. "Questions Concerning Heidegger: Opening the Debate." *Critical Inquiry* 15 no.2 (Winter): 407–426. This issue contains a collection of essays on Heidegger and the Nazis.

Davidson, Donald. 1984. "The Very Idea of a Conceptual Scheme." In *Inquiries into Truth and Interpretation,* 183–196. Oxford: Oxford University Press.

Derrida, Jacques. 1976. *Of Grammatology.* Translated by Gayatri Chakravorty Spivak. 203
Baltimore: Johns Hopkins University Press.

———. 1978. *Writing and Difference.* Translated by Alan Bass. Chicago: University of Chicago Press.

———. 1981a. *Disseminations.* Translated by Barbara Johnson. Chicago: University of Chicago Press.

———. 1981b. *Positions.* Translated by Alan Bass. Chicago: University of Chicago Press.

———. 1982. *Margins of Philosophy.* Translated by Alan Bass. Chicago: University of Chicago Press.

———. 1987. *De l'esprit.* Paris: Editions Galilée.

Donougho, Martin. 1987. "The Language of Architecture." *Journal of Aesthetic Education* 21:53–67.

Duberstein, Larry. 1988. "From coast to coast, homogenization is ruining our landscape." *Atlanta Constitution,* 19 June.

Eco, Umberto. 1980a. "A Componential Analysis of the Architectural Sign /Column/." In *Signs, Symbols, and Architecture,* 213–232. Chichester: Wiley.

———. 1980b. "Function and Sign: the Semiotics of Architecture." In *Signs, Symbols, and Architecture,* 11–70. Chichester: Wiley.

———. 1984. *Postscript to "The Name of the Rose."* Translated by William Weaver. New York: Harcourt, Brace, Jovanovich.

Eisenman, Peter. 1982. *House X.* New York: Rizzoli.

———. 1988. "The Authenticity of Difference: Architecture and the Crisis of Reality." *Center* 4:50–57.

Farias, Victor. 1987. *Heidegger et le nazisme.* Paris: Verdier.

Farrelly, E. M. 1986. "The New Spirit." *Architectural Review,* 180:79–81.

Fathy, Hassan. 1973. *Architecture for the Poor.* Chicago: University of Chicago Press.

Fekete, John, ed. 1986. *Life after Postmodernism: Essays on Value and Culture.* New York: St. Martin's Press.

Ferrara, Alessandro. 1985. "A Critique of Habermas' Diskursethik." *Telos* 64:45–76.

Feyerabend, Paul. 1987. *Farewell to Reason.* New York: Verso.

Foster, Hal, ed. 1983. *The Anti-Aesthetic: Essays on Postmodern Culture.* Port Townsend, Wash.: The Bay Press.

Foucault, Michel. 1977. *Discipline and Punish: The Birth of the Prison.* Translated by Alan Sheridan. New York: Vintage.

———. 1978. *The Order of Things.* New York: Vintage.

———. 1980-86. *The History of Sexuality.* 3 vols. Translated by Robert Hurley. New York: Vintage.

Frampton, Kenneth. 1982. *Modern Architecture and the Critical Present.* London: Architectural Design.

———. 1983. "Towards a Critical Regionalism: Six Points for an Architecture of Resistance." In *The Anti-Aesthetic: Essays on Postmodern Culture,* 16–30. Port Townsend, Wash.: The Bay Press.

———. 1987. "Ten Points on an Architecture of Regionalism: A Provisional Polemic." *Center* 3:20–27.

———, ed. 1984. *Tadao Ando: Buildings Projects Writings.* New York: Rizzoli.

Frankel, Boris. 1987. *The Post-Industrial Utopians.* Madison: University of Wisconsin Press.

204   Fraser, Nancy and Linda Nicholson. 1986. "Social Criticism without Philosophy: An Encounter between Feminism and Postmodernism." Paper given at the American Philosophical Association, Boston.

Freeman, Kathleen. 1966. *Ancilla to the Pre-Socratic Philosophers.* Cambridge: Harvard University Press.

Gadamer, Hans-Georg. 1975. *Truth and Method.* Translated by Garrett Barden and John Cumming. New York: Seabury.

———. 1984. *Reason in the Age of Science.* Translated by Frederick G. Lawrence. Cambridge: M.I.T. Press.

Gaines, Joan, et al., eds. 1986. *On Precedent and Invention. The Harvard Architectural Review* 5. New York: Rizzoli International.

Gasché, Rodolphe. 1986. *The Tain of the Mirror: Derrida and the Philosophy of Reflection.* Cambridge: Harvard University Press.

Geuss, Raymond. 1983. *The Ideal of a Critical Theory: Habermas and the Frankfurt School.* Cambridge: Cambridge University Press.

Gillespie, Michael Allen. 1984. *Hegel, Heidegger, and the Ground of History.* Chicago: University of Chicago Press.

Goodman, Nelson. 1976. *Languages of Art.* 2d ed. Indianapolis: Hackett.

Goodman, Nelson, and Catherine Elgin. 1988. "How Buildings Mean." In *Reconceptions in Philosophy and Other Arts and Sciences,* 31–48. Indianapolis: Hackett.

Gropius, Walter. 1965. *The New Architecture and the Bauhaus.* Translated by P. Morton Schand. Cambridge: M.I.T. Press.

Gusevich, Miriam. 1987. "Pastiche and Collage: A Reappraisal." Paper presented at the University of Kansas conference of the IAPL.

Haar, Michel. 1985. *Le chant de la terre.* Paris: L'Herne.

Habermas, Jürgen. 1970. "Technology and Science as 'Ideology'." Translated by Jeremy Shapiro. In *Toward a Rational Society,* 81–122. Boston: Beacon Press.

———. 1979. "What is Universal Pragmatics?" Translated by Thomas McCarthy. In *Communication and the Evolution of Society,* 1–68. Boston: Beacon Press.

———. 1981a. "Modernity versus Postmodernity." *New German Critique* 22:3–14.

———. 1981b. *The Theory of Communicative Action. Vol. 1, Reason and the Rationalization of Society.* Translated by Thomas McCarthy. Boston: Beacon Press.

———. 1982. "A Reply to My Critics." In *Habermas: Critical Essays,* 219–283. Cambridge: M.I.T. Press.

———. 1983. "Modernity—An Incomplete Project." In *The Anti-Aesthetic: Essays on Postmodern Culture,* 3–15. Port Townsend, Wash.: The Bay Press.

———. 1985a. *Der philosophische Diskurs der Moderne: Zwölf Vorlesungen.* Frankfurt am Main: Suhrkamp. Translated by Frederick Lawrence as *The Philosophical Discourse of Modernity: Twelve Lectures.* Cambridge: M.I.T. Press, 1987.

———. 1985b. "Modern and Postmodern Architecture." In *Critical Theory ad Public Life,* 317–329. Cambridge: M.I.T. Press.

———. 1985c. "Questions and Counter-Questions." In *Habermas and Modernity,* 192–216. Oxford: Polity.

———. 1987. *The Theory of Communicative Action. Vol. 2, Lifeworld and System, A Critique of Functionalist Reason.* Translated by Thomas McCarthy. Boston: Beacon Press.

———. 1989. "Work and Weltanschauung: The Heidegger Controversy from a German Perspective." *Critical Inquiry* 15:431—56.

————, ed. 1985. *Observations on "The Spiritual Situation of the Age."* Translated by Andrew Buchwalter. Cambridge: M.I.T. Press.

Hamilton, Edith, ed. 1961. *The Collected Dialogues of Plato.* New York: Pantheon.

Harries, Karsten. 1975. "The Ethical Function of Architecture." *Journal of Architectural Education* 29:14.

————. 1980. "The Dream of the Complete Building." *Perspecta* 17:36–43.

————. 1983. "Thoughts on a Non-Arbitrary Architecture." *Perspecta* 20:9–20.

————. 1984a. "On Truth and Lie in Architecture." *Via* 7:47–57.

————. 1984b. "Space, Place, and Ethos: Reflections on the Ethical Function of Architecture." *Artibus et historiae* 8:159–65.

————. 1985. "Modernity's Bad Conscience." *AA Files* 10:53–60.

————. 1988a. "Representation and Re-Presentation in Architecture." *Via* 9:13–24.

————. 1988b. "The Voices of Space." *Center* 4:34–49.

Hegel, G. W. F. 1967. *Hegel's Philosophy of Right.* Translated by T. M. Knox. Oxford: Oxford University Press.

————. 1968. "Über Solgers nachgelassene Schriften." In *Hegel: Studienausgabe.* Vol. 1, 202–52. Frankfurt am Main: Fischer.

————. 1975. *Hegel's Aesthetics.* Translated by T. M. Knox. Oxford: Oxford University Press.

————. 1977. *Hegel's Phenomenology of Spirit.* Translated by Arnold Miller. Oxford: Oxford University Press.

Heidegger, Martin. 1947. *Über den Humanismus.* Frankfurt am Main: Klostermann.

————. 1962. *Being and Time.* Translated by John Macquarrie and Edward Robinson. New York: Harper and Row.

————. 1966. "Memorial Address." Translated by John Anderson and E. Hans Freund. In *Discourse on Thinking*, 43–57. New York: Harper and Row.

————. 1969. *Identity and Difference.* Translated by Joan Stambaugh. New York: Harper and Row.

————. 1971. "The Origin of the Work of Art." Translated by Albert Hofstadter. In *Poetry, Language, Thought*, 3–14. New York: Harper and Row.

————. 1977a. "The End of Philosophy and the Task of Thinking." In *Basic Writings*, 373–92. New York: Harper and Row.

————. 1977b. *Vier Seminare.* Frankfurt am Main: Klostermann.

————. 1981. "Only a God Can Save Us." Translated by William Richardson. In *Heidegger: The Man and the Thinker*, 45–72. Chicago: Precedent.

Herdeg, Klaus. 1983. *The Decorated Diagram: Harvard Architecture and the Failure of the Bauhaus Legacy.* Cambridge: M.I.T. Press.

Herf, Jeffrey. 1984. *Reactionary Modernism: Technology, Culture, and Politics in Weimar and the Third Reich.* Cambridge: Cambridge University Press.

Heyer, Paul. 1966. *Architects on Architecture: New Directions in America.* New York: Walker.

Horkheimer, Max, and Theodor Adorno. 1972. *Dialectic of Enlightenment.* Translated by J. Cumming. New York: Herder and Herder.

Hubbard, William. 1980. *Complicity and Conviction: Steps toward an Architecture of Convention.* Cambridge: M.I.T. Press.

Hutcheon, Linda. 1985. *A Theory of Parody: The Teachings of Twentieth-Century Art Forms.* London: Methuen.

206 ———. 1986. "The Politics of Postmodernism: Parody and History." *Cultural Critique* 5:179–207.

Huxtable, Ada Louise. 1986. *Architecture, Anyone?* New York: Random House.

Huyssen, Andreas. 1981. "The Search for Tradition: Avant-Garde and Postmodernism in the 1970's." *New German Critique* 22:23–40.

Ingram, David. 1987. *Habermas and the Dialectic of Reason.* New Haven: Yale University Press.

Jameson, Fredric. 1983. "Postmodernism and Consumer Society." In *The Anti-Aesthetic: Essays on Postmodern Culture,* 111–125. Port Townsend, Wash.: The Bay Press.

———. 1985. "Architecture and the Critique of Ideology." In *Architecture, Criticism, Ideology,* 51–87. Princeton: Princeton Architectural Press.

Jay, Martin. 1973. *The Dialectical Imagination.* Boston: Little, Brown.

———. 1984. *Marxism and Totality: The Adventures of a Concept from Lukács to Habermas.* Berkeley: University of California Press.

———. 1985. "Habermas and Modernism." In *Habermas and Modernity,* 125–139. Oxford: Polity.

Jencks, Charles. 1977. *The Language of Postmodern Architecture.* 4th ed. New York: Rizzoli.

———. 1980. "The Architectural Sign." In *Signs, Symbols, and Architecture,* 77–118. Chichester: Wiley.

———. 1987a. "Post-Modernism and Discontinuity." In *Architectural Design Profile 65: Post-Modernism and Discontinuity,* 5–8. London: Architectural Design.

———. 1987b. *Post-Modernism: The New Classicism in Art and Architecture.* New York: Rizzoli.

Kant, Immanuel. 1965. *The Critique of Pure Reason.* New York: St. Martin's Press.

Karnoouh, Claude. 1986. "The Lost Paradise of Regionalism: The Crisis of Post-Modernity in France." *Telos* 67:11–26.

Kato, Shuichi. 1981. *Form, Style, Tradition: Reflections on Japanese Art and Society.* Translated by John Bester. Tokyo: Kodansha.

Kearney, Richard. 1987. "Ethics and the Postmodern Imagination." *Thought* 62:39–58.

———. 1988. *The Wake of Imagination.* London: Hutchinson.

Kerford, G. B. 1981. *The Sophistic Movement.* Cambridge, England: Cambridge University Press.

Kimball, Roger. 1988. "Postmodern Architecture." *The New Criterion* 6:21–31.

Klotz, Heinrich. 1988. *The History of Postmodern Architecture.* Translated by Radka Donnell. Cambridge: M.I.T. Press.

Knox, Dilwyn. 1989. *Ironia: Medieval and Renaissance Ideas on Irony.* Leiden: Brill.

Kolb, David. 1987. *The Critique of Pure Modernity: Hegel, Heidegger, and After.* Chicago: University of Chicago Press.

Krauss, Rosalind E. 1987. *The Originality of the Avant-Garde and Other Modernist Myths.* Cambridge: M.I.T. Press.

Krell, David Farrell. 1986. *Postponements: Woman, Sensuality, and Death in Nietzsche.* Bloomington: University of Indiana Press.

Krier, Leon. 1987. "Extract from the SOMAI Statement." In *Post-Modernism and Discontinuity,* 38–43. London: Architectural Design.

Kruger, Dreyer, ed. 1985. *The Changing Reality of Modern Man: Essays in Honour of J. H. Van den Berg.* Pittsburgh: Duquesne University Press.

Krukowski, Lucian. 1986. "Hegel, 'Progress,' and the Avant-Garde." *Journal of Aesthetics and Art Criticism* 44:279–90.

Kurokawa, Kisho. 1988. *Rediscovering Japanese Space.* Tokyo: Weatherhill.

Le Corbusier. 1986. *Towards a New Architecture.* Translated by Frederick Etchells. New York: Dover. The translation was first published in 1931 from the thirteenth French edition.

Lévinas, Emmanuel. 1987. *Collected Philosophical Papers.* Translated by Alphonso Lingis. Dordrecht: Nijhoff.

Lingis, Alphonso. 1983. *Excesses: Eros and Culture.* Albany: SUNY Press.

Lyotard, Jean-François. 1983. *Le Différend.* Paris: Editions de Minuit. Translated (by George Van Den Abeele) as *The Différend: Phrases in Dispute.* Minneapolis: University of Minnesota Press, 1988.

———. 1984. *The Postmodern Condition.* Translated by Geoff Bennington and Brian Massomi. Minneapolis: University of Minnesota Press. Includes the essay "Answering the Question: What is Postmodernism?"

———. 1985. "Judicieux dans le différend." In *La Faculté de Juger,* 195–236. Paris: Editions de Minuit.

———. 1986a. "On Terror and the Sublime." *Telos* 67:196–98.

———. 1986b. "Rules and Paradoxes and Svelte Appendix." *Cultural Critique* 5:209–19.

Lyotard, Jean-François, and Jean-Loup Thébaud. 1985. *Just Gaming.* Translated by Wlad Godzich and Brian Massomi. Minneapolis: University of Minnesota Press.

McCarthy, Thomas. 1982. "Rationality and Relativism: Habermas's 'Overcoming' of Hermeneutics." In *Habermas: Critical Essays,* 57–78. Cambridge: M.I.T. Press.

———. 1985. "Reflections on Rationalization in the *Theory of Communicative Action.*" In *Habermas and Modernity,* 177–191. Oxford: Polity.

McCormick, Peter. 1988. *Fictions, Philosophies, and the Problems of Poetics.* Ithaca: Cornell University Press.

McCumber, John. 1989. *Poetic Interaction: Language, Freedom, Reason.* Chicago: University of Chicago Press.

MacIntyre, Alasdair. 1981. *After Virtue.* Notre Dame, Indiana: University of Notre Dame Press.

———. 1988. *Whose Justice? Which Rationality?* Notre Dame: Notre Dame University Press.

McKeon, Richard, ed. 1941. *Aristotle: Basic Works.* New York: Random House.

Macrae-Gibson, Gavin. 1985. *The Secret Life of Buildings: An American Mythology for Modern Architecture.* Cambridge: M.I.T. Press.

Marder, Tod A. 1985. *The Critical Edge: Controversy in Recent American Architecture.* Cambridge: M.I.T. Press.

Megill, Alan. 1985. *Prophets of Extremity: Nietzsche, Heidegger, Foucault, Derrida.* Berkeley: University of California Press.

———. N.d. "What Does the Term 'Postmodern' Mean?" *Annals of Scholarship.* Forthcoming.

208   Melville, Stephen W. 1986. *Philosophy Beside Itself: On Deconstruction and Modernism.* Minneapolis: University of Minnesota Press.

Moldenschardt, H. Heinrich. 1981. "Der Postmodernismus in der Architectur oder: Die Gegenwart der Vergangenheit." *Tendenzen* 134:15–27.

Moore, Charles, Gerald Allen and Donlyn Lyndon. 1974. *The Place of Houses.* New York: Holt.

Moore, Steven. 1983. "New Architecture/Maine Traditions." In *New Architecture/Maine Traditions*, 6–12. Portland, Maine: Payson Gallery of Art.

Muecke, C. D. 1969. *The Compass of Irony.* London: Methuen.

———. 1985. *Irony and the Ironical.* 2d rev. ed. London: Methuen.

Mugerauer, Robert. 1988. "Derrida and Beyond." *Center* 4:66–76.

Nietzsche, Friedrich. 1968. *The Twilight of the Idols* and *The Anti-Christ.* New York: Penguin.

Norberg-Schulz, Christian. 1965. *Intentions in Architecture.* Cambridge: M.I.T. Press.

———. 1980. *Genius Loci.* New York: Rizzoli International.

———. 1985. *The Concept of Dwelling.* New York: Electra/Rizzoli.

Norris, Christopher. 1983. "Philosophy as a Kind of Narrative: Rorty on Postmodern Liberal Culture." *Enclitic* 7:144–59.

———. 1988. "Deconstruction, Post-modernism, and the Visual Arts." In *What is Deconstruction?*, 7–32. London: Academy Editions.

Novitz, David. 1985. "Metaphor, Derrida, and Davidson." *Journal of Aesthetics and Art Criticism,* 44:101–14.

Ockman, Joan, ed. 1985. *Architecture, Criticism, Ideology.* Princeton: Princeton Architectural Press.

Ogilvy, James. 1977. *Many Dimensional Man.* Oxford: Oxford University Press.

Ott, Hugo. 1988. *Martin Heidegger: Unterwegs zur seiner Biographie.* Frankfurt: Campus.

Owens, Craig. 1983. "The Discourse of Others: Feminists and Postmodernism." In *The Anti-Aesthetic: Essays on Postmodern Culture,* 57–82. Port Townsend, Wash.: The Bay Press.

Papadakis, Andreas, ed. 1987. *Post-Modernism and Discontinuity.* London: Architectural Design.

Paz, Octavio. 1973. *Alternating Current.* Translated by Helen Lane. New York: Viking Press.

———. 1974. *Conjunctions and Disjunctions.* Translated by Helen Lane. New York: Viking Press.

———. 1985. *One Earth, Four or Five Worlds.* Translated by Helen Lane. New York: Harcourt.

Peirce, Charles S. 1955. *Philosophical Writings of Peirce.* Edited by Justus Buchler. New York: Dover.

Pevsner, Nikolaus. 1968. *The Sources of Modern Architecture and Design.* New York: Praeger.

Popham, Peter. 1985. *Tokyo: The City at the End of the World.* Tokyo: Kodansha.

Porphyrios, Demetri. 1984. *Leon Krier: Houses, Palaces, Cities.* London: Architectural Design.

Portoghesi, Paolo. 1982. *After Modern Architecture.* Translated by Meg Shore. New York: Rizzoli.

———. 1983. *Postmodern: The Architecture of the Postindustrial Society*. Translated by Ellen Shapiro. New York: Rizzoli.

Putnam, Hilary. 1983. *Realism and Reason*. Cambridge: Cambridge University Press.

Quantrill, Malcolm. 1987. *The Environmental Memory: Man and Architecture in the Landscape of Ideas*. New York: Schocken Books.

Quine, W. V. O. 1960. *Word and Object*. Cambridge: M.I.T. Press.

———. 1969. *Ontological Relativity and Other Essays*. New York: Columbia University Press.

Rajchman, John, and Cornel West. 1985. *Post-Analytic Philosophy*. New York: Columbia University Press.

Rapp, Carl. 1987. "Coming Out into the Corridor: Postmodern Fantasies of Pluralism." *Georgia Review* 41:533–52.

Rasmussen, Steen Eiler. 1959. *Experiencing Architecture*. Cambridge: M.I.T. Press.

Richardson, John Adkins. 1984. "Assault of the Petulant: Postmodernism and Other Fancies." *Journal of Aesthetic Education* 18:93–107.

Ricoeur, Paul. 1977. *The Rule of Metaphor*. Toronto: University of Toronto Press.

———. 1984—88. *Time and Narrative*. 3 vols. Translated by David Pellauer and others. Chicago: University of Chicago Press.

———. 1986. *Lectures on Ideology and Utopia*. Edited by George Taylor. New York: Columbia University Press.

Risebero, Bill. 1982. *Modern Architecture and Design, An Alternative History*. Cambridge: M.I.T. Press.

Risser, James. 1987. "The Space of Place." Paper presented at the University of Kansas conference of the IAPL.

Robertson, Jacquelin, ed. 1985. *The Charlottesville Tapes*. New York: Rizzoli.

Rorty, Richard. 1982. *Consequences of Pragmatism*. Minneapolis: University of Minnesota Press.

———. 1985. "Habermas and Lyotard on Postmodernity." In *Habermas and Modernity*, 161–176. Oxford: Polity.

———. 1989. *Contingency, Irony, and Solidarity*. Cambridge: Cambridge University Press.

Rosen, Stanley. 1969. *Nihilism: A Philosophical Essay*. New Haven: Yale University Press.

———. 1987. *Hermeneutics as Politics*. Oxford: Oxford University Press.

———. 1989. *The Ancients and the Moderns: Rethinking Modernity*. New Haven: Yale University Press.

Rossi, Aldo. 1982. *The Architecture of the City*. Cambridge: M.I.T. Press.

Rowe, Colin, and Fred Koetter. 1976. *Collage City*. Cambridge: M.I.T. Press.

Rubczynski, Witold. 1986. *Home: A Short History of an Idea*. New York: Viking.

Rustin, Michael. 1985. "English Conservatism and the Aesthetics of Architecture." *Radical Philosophy* 40:20–28.

Sallis, John. 1986. *Delimitations: Phenomenology and the End of Metaphysics*. Bloomington: University of Indiana Press.

Schildt, Göran. 1986. *Alvar Aalto: The Decisive Years*. Translated by Timothy Binham. New York: Rizzoli.

Schlegel, Friedrich. 1968. *Dialogue on Poetry and Literary Aphorisms*. Translated by

210　　Ernst Behler and Roman Struc. University Park: Pennsylvania State University
Press.

Schmid, Michael. 1982. "Habermas's Theory of Social Evolution.' In *Habermas: Critical Essays,* 162–180. Cambridge: M.I.T. Press.

Schulte-Sasse, Jochen. 1986a. "Imagination and Modernity: Or the Taming of the Human Mind." *Cultural Critique* 5:23–48.

————. 1986b. "Modernity and Modernism, Postmodernity and Postmodernism: Framing the Issue." *Cultural Critique* 5:5–22.

Schulze, Franz. 1986. *Mies van der Rohe: A Critical Biography.* Chicago: University of Chicago Press.

Schürmann, Reiner. 1978. "Political Thinking in Heidegger." *Social Research* 45:191–221.

————. 1987. *Heidegger on Being and Acting: From Principles to Anarchy.* Bloomington: Indiana University Press.

Scott, Charles E. 1987. *The Language of Difference.* Atlantic Highlands, N.J.: Humanities Press.

Scruton, Roger. 1979. *The Aesthetics of Architecture.* Princeton: Princeton University Press.

Scully, Vincent. 1988. *American Architecture and Urbanism.* New rev. ed. New York: Holt.

Seamon, David. 1987. "Phenomenology and Environment—Behavior Research." In *Advances in Environment, Behavior, and Design,* 3–27. New York: Plenum. Contains a bibliography on "place."

Shales, Tom. 1988. "The Re-Decade." *Center* 4:18–23.

Shaw, Daniel. 1986. "A Kuhnian Metatheory for Aesthetics." *Journal of Aesthetics and Art Criticism* 45:27–40.

Sheehan, Thomas. 1988. "Heidegger and the Nazis." *New York Review of Books* 25, no. 10, 16 June.

Silverman, Hugh, and Donn Welton, eds. 1988. *Postmodern and Continental Philosophy.* Albany: SUNY Press.

Skinner, Quentin, ed. 1985. *The Return of Grand Theory in the Human Sciences.* Cambridge: Cambridge University Press.

Smith, Norris Kelly. 1971. *On Art and Architecture in the Modern World.* Victoria: University of British Columbia.

Sobol, Judith, ed. 1983. *New Architecture, Maine Traditions.* Portland, Maine: Payson Gallery.

Soltan, Margaret Rapp. 1987. "Architecture and Morality." Paper presented at the University of Kansas conference of the IAPL.

Speck, Lawrence W. 1987. "Regionalism and Invention." *Center* 3:8–19.

Stern, Robert A. M. 1977. "The Doubles of the Post-Modern." *Architectural Design* 4:73–87.

————. 1987. "Regionalism and the Continuity of Tradition." *Center* 3:58–63.

Tafuri, Manfredo. 1976. *Architecture and Utopia: Design and Capitalist Development.* Translated by Barbara Luigia La Penta. Cambridge: M.I.T. Press.

————. 1987. *The Sphere and the Labyrinth: Avant-Gardes and Architecture from Piranesi to the 1970's.* Translated by Pellegrino d'Acierno and Robert Connolly. Cambridge: M.I.T. Press.

Tafuri, Manfredo, and Francesco Dal Co. 1986. *Modern Architecture*. 2 vols. Translated by Robert Erich Wolf. New York: Rizzoli International.

Taminiaux, Jacques. 1985. *Dialectic and Difference: Finitude in Modern Thought*. Translated by Robert Crease and James Decker. Atlantic Highlands, N.J.: Humanities Press.

Tange, Kenzo, and Yasuhiro Ishimoto. 1972. *Katsura: Tradition and Creation in Japanese Architecture*. Translated by Charles Terry. New Haven: Yale University Press.

Taylor, Charles. 1985. *Philosophical Papers 2: Philosophy and the Human Sciences*. Cambridge: Cambridge University Press.

Taylor, Mark. 1986. *Deconstruction in Context*. Chicago: University of Chicago Press.

———. 1987. *Altarity*. Chicago: University of Chicago Press.

Thompson, Deborah, ed. 1976. *Maine Forms of American Architecture*. Camden: Downeast.

Thompson, John B. 1982. "Universal Pragmatics." In *Habermas: Critical Essays*, 116–23. Cambridge: M.I.T. Press.

Thompson, John, and David Held. 1982. *Habermas: Critical Essays*. Cambridge: M.I.T. Press.

Tigerman, Stanley, ed. 1987. *The Chicago Tapes*. New York: Rizzoli.

Trilling, Julia. 1985. "A Future that Looks like the Past." *Atlantic Monthly* 256, July.

Tschumi, Bernard. 1989. *Cinégramme Folie: Le Parc de la Villette*. Princeton: Princeton University Press.

Upton, Dell, and John Michael Vlach. 1986. *Common Places: Readings in American Vernacular Architecture*. Athens, Georgia: The University of Georgia Press.

Vattimo, Gianni. 1988. *The End of Modernity*. Translated by Jon Snyder. Cambridge, Massachusetts: Polity.

Venturi, Robert. 1966. *Complexity and Contradiction in Architecture*. New York: Museum of Modern Art.

Venturi, Robert, and Denise Scott Brown. 1984. *A View from the Campidoglio: Selected Essays 1953–1984*. New York: Harper.

Viollet-le-Duc, Eugene Emmanuel. 1959. *Discourses on Architecture*. Translated by Benjamin Bucknall. 2 vols. New York: Grove Press. The first edition was published in 1889.

Vitruvius, Pollio. 1934. *On Architecture*. Translated by Frank Granger. Cambridge: Harvard University Press.

Walser, Martin. 1981. *Selbstbewusstsein und Ironie*. Frankfurt am Main: Suhrkamp.

Walzer, Michael. 1983. *Spheres of Justice: A Defense of Pluralism and Equality*. New York: Basic Books.

Watson, Stephen. 1984. "Jürgen Habermas and Jean-François Lyotard: Post-modernism and the Crisis of Rationality." *Philosophy and Social Criticism* 10:1–23.

———. 1985. "Criticism and the Closure of 'Modernism'." *SubStance* 42:15–30.

Weber, Samuel. 1985. "Afterword: Literature—Just Making It." In *Just Gaming*, 101–120. Minneapolis: University of Minnesota Press.

Wellmer, Albrecht. 1985. "Reason, Utopia, and the *Dialectic of Enlightenment*." In *Habermas and Modernity*, 35–66. Oxford: Polity.

Wheeler, Karen Vogel, Peter Arnell, and Ted Bickford. 1982. *Michael Graves: Buildings and Projects, 1966–1981*. New York: Rizzoli International.

212   Wilde, Alan. 1981. *Horizons of Assent*. Baltimore: Johns Hopkins University Press.

Wittgenstein, Ludwig. 1963. *Philosophical Investigations*. Translated by G. E. M. Anscombe. Oxford: Blackwell.

Wojtowicz, Jerzy, and William Fawcett. 1986. *Architecture: Formal Approach*. London: Academy Editions/St. Martin's Press.

Wolfe, Tom. 1981. *From Bauhaus to Our House*. New York: Farrar, Straus and Giroux.

Wurman, Richard Saul, ed. 1986. *What Will Be Has Always Been: the Words of Louis I. Kahn*. New York: Rizzoli International.

Zukowsky, John, ed. 1986. *Mies Reconsidered: His Career, Legacy, and Disciples*. Chicago: Art Institute of Chicago and Rizzoli International.

INDEX